VISUAL AFFECT RECOGNITION

Frontiers in Artificial Intelligence and Applications

Volume 214

Published in the subseries
Knowledge-Based Intelligent Engineering Systems
Editors: L.C. Jain and R.J. Howlett

Recently published in KBIES:

Vol. 211. J.I. da Silva Filho, G. Lambert-Torres and J.M. Abe, Uncertainty Treatment Using Paraconsistent Logic – Introducing Paraconsistent Artificial Neural Networks

Vol. 204. B. Apolloni, S. Bassis and C.F. Morabito (Eds.), Neural Nets WIRN09 – Proceedings of the 19th Italian Workshop on Neural Nets, Vietri sul Mare, Salerno, Italy, May 28–30 2009

Vol. 203. M. Džbor, Design Problems, Frames and Innovative Solutions

Vol. 196. F. Masulli, A. Micheli and A. Sperduti (Eds.), Computational Intelligence and Bioengineering – Essays in Memory of Antonina Starita

Vol. 193. B. Apolloni, S. Bassis and M. Marinaro (Eds.), New Directions in Neural Networks – 18th Italian Workshop on Neural Networks: WIRN 2008

Vol. 186. G. Lambert-Torres et al. (Eds.), Advances in Technological Applications of Logical and Intelligent Systems – Selected Papers from the Sixth Congress on Logic Applied to Technology

Vol. 180. M. Virvou and T. Nakamura (Eds.), Knowledge-Based Software Engineering – Proceedings of the Eighth Joint Conference on Knowledge-Based Software Engineering

Vol. 170. J.D. Velásquez and V. Palade, Adaptive Web Sites – A Knowledge Extraction from Web Data Approach

Recently published in FAIA:

Vol. 213. L. Obrst, T. Janssen and W. Ceusters (Eds.), Ontologies and Semantic Technologies for Intelligence

Vol. 212. A. Respicio et al. (Eds.), Bridging the Socio-Technical Gap in Decision Support Systems – Challenges for the Next Decade

Vol. 211. J.I. da Silva Filho, G. Lambert-Torres and J.M. Abe, Uncertainty Treatment Using Paraconsistent Logic – Introducing Paraconsistent Artificial Neural Networks

Vol. 210. O. Kutz, J. Hois, J. Bao, B. Cuenca Grau (Eds.), Modular Ontologies – Proceedings of the Fourth International Workshop (WoMO 2010)

ISSN 0922-6389 (print)
ISSN 1879-8314 (online)

Visual Affect Recognition

Ioanna-Ourania Stathopoulou

University of Piraeus, Greece

and

George A. Tsihrintzis

University of Piraeus, Greece

Press

Amsterdam • Berlin • Tokyo • Washington, DC

ISBN 978-1-60750-596-9 (print)
ISBN 978-1-60750-597-6 (online)
Library of Congress Control Number: 2010930894

Publisher
IOS Press BV
Nieuwe Hemweg 6B
1013 BG Amsterdam
Netherlands
fax: +31 20 687 0019
e-mail: order@iospress.nl

Distributor in the USA and Canada
IOS Press, Inc.
4502 Rachael Manor Drive
Fairfax, VA 22032
USA
fax: +1 703 323 3668
e-mail: iosbooks@iospress.com

Visual Affect Recognition
I.-O. Stathopoulou and G.A. Tsihrintzis
IOS Press, 2010

PREFACE

Human faces, as well as human body motion and gestures, provide a wide range of information about a person's identity, race, sex, age, and emotional state. In this monograph, we study the perception of primarily facial expression of emotion and secondarily of motion and gestures. Our aim is to develop a fully automated visual affect recognition system, which could be useful in novel/future modes of human-computer interaction that include user affect recognition. Our studies begin with a survey of the literature on emotion perception from the scientific - psychological and medical - point of view. Based on these studies, we are led to the following conclusions: (1) a number of brain parts play a significant role in emotion perception and expression, (2) there are six 'basic emotions' that arise very commonly, namely: 'anger', 'disgust', 'fear', 'happiness', 'sadness' and 'surprise' and, (3) there is cultural specificity in emotion perception and expression. The latter assumption is further corroborated by two empirical studies that we conducted on humans. In these empirical studies, the participants were shown face images and asked to classify the emotions. The difference in the correct classification rates demonstrates that there is cultural specificity in the ways people express and recognize emotions. Moreover, from our empirical studies, we were able to identify the emotion classes that are present during a typical human-computer interaction session, namely 'happiness', 'sadness', 'surprise', 'anger', 'disgust', 'boredom-sleepiness', as well as the emotionless state that is referred to as 'neutral'. Towards building our visual affect recognition system, we constructed our own face image database. This database consists of two sets of face images, all in both front and side view: (1) low quality images acquired with use of web cameras and (2) high quality face images acquired with use of high resolution digital cameras. On the basis of these empirical studies, we developed our own visual affect recognition system which consists of two modules: (1) a face detection subsystem and (2) a facial expression recognition subsystem. Our face detection subsystem uses neural network-based classifiers. For our facial expression recognition subsystem, we considered neural network-based and other classifiers, but concluded that Support Vector Machine-based Classifiers demonstrated better results. Details of our visual affect recognition system, such as feature extraction, classifier design, are demonstrated and analyzed along with extensive performance evaluations and test results. Current research avenues in the directions of visual affect recognition via analysis of human body motion and gestures are also discussed.

Ioanna-Ourania Stathopoulou and George A. Tsihrintzis

ACKNOWLEDGEMENTS

A great portion of this monograph is based on the doctoral research of the first author, Dr. Ioanna-Ourania Stathopoulou, which was conducted under the supervision and advice of the second author, Prof. George A. Tsihrintzis. During the course of Dr. Stathopoulou's doctoral studies, the authors were supported by research funds of the General Secretariat of Research and Technology of the Greek government, under the auspices of the PENED-2003 basic research program. The authors acknowledge and appreciate this support greatly.

The authors also acknowledge Prof. Maria Virvou's advice on a number of issues and encouragement during the course of authoring this monograph, which have proved crucial.

Dr. Stathopoulou also thanks her fellow labmates in room 212 for various stimulating discussions, help, and encouragement, as well as for all the fun they had during their student years. However, her deepest gratitude goes to her family for their unflagging love and support throughout her life.

Prof. Tsihrintzis dedicates this monograph to his parents, wife and three daughters for their unconditional love and encouragement.

The authors are indebted to Prof. Lakhmi C. Jain of the University of Australia and Dr. Robert J. Howlett of University of Brighton for agreeing to include our monograph as a volume in the *Knowledge-based Intelligent Engineering Systems* subseries of the *Frontiers in Artificial intelligence and Applications* series of IOS Press which they are Editors of.

Finally, the authors are grateful to Mr. Maarten Fröhlich and the editorial staff at IOS Press for their wonderful work.

Ioanna-Ourania Stathopoulou and George A. Tsihrintzis
University of Piraeus, Greece, June 2010

BRIEF BIOGRAPHY OF IOANNA-OURANIA STATHOPOULOU

Ioanna-Ourania Stathopoulou received a B.Sc. in Computer Science and, later on, a Ph.D. degree from the University of Piraeus, Piraeus, Greece. Her doctoral research was sponsored by the General Secretary of Research and Technology of the Greek Ministry of Development, under the auspices of the PENED-2003 basic research program. Since May 2007, she is with the Department of Software Application Development of the National Documentation Centre (EKT) of the Hellenic Research Foundation, where she works as a software engineer participating in the design and implementation of digital repositories and online journals. Her primary research interests are in the areas of affective computing, human-computer interaction, computer vision, and pattern recognition, and their applications in user modelling, information retrieval and intelligent software systems. She won one of the Best Applications Papers Award of the 29th Annual International Conference of the British Computer Society Specialist Group on Artificial Intelligence, Cambridge, UK, December 15-17, 2009, for co-authoring a paper titled: "On Assisting a Visual-Facial Affect Recognition System with Keyboard-Stroke Pattern Information." She can be reached at **iostath@unipi.gr**.

Ioanna-Ourania Stathopoulou and George A. Tsihrintzis

BRIEF BIOGRAPHY OF GEORGE A. TSIHRINTZIS

George A. Tsihrintzis received the Diploma of Electrical Engineer from the National Technical University of Athens, Greece (with honors) and the M.Sc. and Ph.D. degrees in Electrical Engineering from Northeastern University, Boston, Massachusetts, USA. He is currently a Professor in the Department of Informatics, The University of Piraeus, Greece. His current research interests include Pattern Recognition, Decision Theory, and Statistical Signal Processing and their applications in Multimedia Services, User Modeling, Intelligent Software Systems, Human-Computer Interaction and Information Retrieval. He has authored or co-authored over 200 research articles in these areas, which have appeared in international journals, book chapters, and conference proceedings, and has served as the principal investigator or co-investigator in several R&D projects. He is the sole author of a book on *Image Analysis* (in Greek) and co-author of a book on *Principles and Applications of Signals and Systems* (in Greek) and an upcoming book on *Visual Affect Recognition* (IOS Press, 2010). He has served as a member of Program Committees and/or reviewer of International journals and conferences. He was the founding general and program co-chair of the **2008 International Symposium on Intelligent Interactive Multimedia Systems and Services (KES-IIMSS 2008)**, Piraeus, Greece, July 9-11, 2008, organized jointly by the Department of Informatics of the University of Piraeus and KES International. He was the honorary co-chair of the **2009 International Symposium on Intelligent Interactive Multimedia Systems and Services (KES-IIMSS 2009)**, Venice, Italy, July 16-17, 2009. He is the general and program co-chair of the **2010 International Joint Conference on e-Business and Telecommunications (ICETE 2010)**, Piraeus, Greece, July 26-28, 2010. He is the founding general co-chair of the **2010 International Multi-Conference on Innovative Developments in Information Communication Technologies (INNOV 2010)**, Piraeus, Greece, July 29-31, 2010. He is the general and program co-chair of the **2010 International Symposium on Intelligent Interactive Multimedia Systems and Services (KES-IIMSS 2010)**, Baltimore, USA, July 28-30, 2010. He has co-edited the following books: (1) *Multimedia Services in Intelligent Environments - Advanced Tools and Methodologies*, volume 120 in Studies in Computational Intelligence (SCI) Book Series, Springer 2008, (2) *Computational Intelligence Paradigms - Innovative Applications*, volume 137 in Studies in Computational Intelligence (SCI) Book Series, Springer 2008, (3) *New Directions in Intelligent Interactive Multimedia*, volume 142 in Studies in Computational Intelligence (SCI) Book Series, Springer 2008, (4) *Multimedia Services in Intelligent Environments - Software Development Challenges and Solutions*, volume 2 in Smart Innovation, Systems and Technologies (SIST) Book Series, Springer 2010, and (5)

Ioanna-Ourania Stathopoulou and George A. Tsihrintzis

Multimedia Services in Intelligent Environments - Integrated Systems, volume 3 in Smart Innovation, Systems and Technologies (SIST) Book Series, Springer 2010. He was a guest co-editor of the special issue on "Intelligent Modelling and Data Analysis Techniques" of the **International Journal of Intelligent Defence Support Systems** (Inderscience, 2009). He was a guest co-editor of the special issues on "Knowledge-based Modes of Human-Computer Interaction" and "Knowledge-based Environments and Services in Human-Computer Interaction" of the **Intelligent Decision Technologies Journal** (IOS Press, 2010). He won the Best Poster Paper Award of the 5th International Conference on Information Technology: New Generations, Las Vegas, USA, April 7-9, 2008, for co-authoring a paper titled: "Evaluation of a Middleware System for Accessing Digital Music Libraries in Mobile Services." He also won one of the Best Applications Papers Award of the 29th Annual International Conference of the British Computer Society Specialist Group on Artificial Intelligence, Cambridge, UK, December 15-17, 2009, for co-authoring a paper titled: "On Assisting a Visual-Facial Affect Recognition System with Keyboard-Stroke Pattern Information." He can be reached at **geoatsi@unipi.gr**.

Ioanna-Ourania Stathopoulou and George A. Tsihrintzis

Contents

1 Introduction — **1**

  1.1 Motivation — 2

  1.2 Organization of this monograph — 3

2 Psychological Studies on Emotion Perception — **7**

  2.1 Emotion vs affect vs feelings — 8

  2.2 Emotions and culture — 9

    2.2.1 Basic Emotions — 10

    2.2.2 Culturally Specific Expressions of Emotions — 12

    2.2.3 Higher Cognitive Emotions — 13

  2.3 Neurobiology and Emotion Expression — 13

    2.3.1 Cerebral Cortex — 13

    2.3.2 Amygdala — 17

    2.3.3 Superior Temporal Sulcus — 18

    2.3.4 Implicit and Explicit Perception of Emotion — 19

  2.4 Expression of Emotion — 22

    2.4.1 Written Language — 22

    2.4.2 Speech — 23

    2.4.3 Facial Expressions — 24

    2.4.4 Body movements and Hand gestures — 24

  2.5 Facial Expression of Emotion — 25

    2.5.1 Previous Attempts to Facial Emotion Quantification and Classification — 28

    2.5.2 External Factors in Facial Emotion Perception — 28

    2.5.3 Face and Facial Expressions: Their Role — 29

  2.6 The Importance of Understanding Emotions — 32

  2.7 Meeting Emotional Needs with the Help of Advanced Human-Computer Interaction Techniques — 33

    2.7.1 Supporting emotional skill needs — 34

    2.7.2 Supporting experiential needs — 35

3 Studies and Systems on Emotion Recognition — **37**

  3.1 Face Databases — 37

    3.1.1 Specifying Requirements for an Ideal Facial Expression Database — 37

    3.1.2 Previous Facial Expression Databases — 38

    3.1.3 Section Summary - Results — 40

  3.2 Face Detection — 41

    3.2.1 Specifying Requirements for an Ideal Face Detection System — 41

3.2.2	Previous Works on Face Detection	43
3.2.3	Section Summary - Results	44
3.3	Facial Expression Classification System	45
3.3.1	Specifying Requirements for our Facial Expression Classification System	45
3.3.2	Facial Expression Classification Approaches	48
3.3.3	Section Summary - Results	69

4 Face Image Databases   **71**

4.1	The Database of Low Quality Face Images (DBLQFI)	71
4.2	The Database of High Quality Face Images (DBHQFI)	72

5 Empirical Studies on Emotion Recognition   **79**

5.1	Preliminary Questionnaires	79
5.2	Newer (Detailed) Questionnaires	80
5.2.1	The detailed questionnaire structure	81
5.2.2	The observer and subject backgrounds	83
5.3	Results from Statistical Analysis	83
5.3.1	Statistical Analysis per Expression	83
5.3.2	Difficulties of Facial Expression Classification as Outlined by the Participants	92
5.3.3	Statistical Significance of the Results	94
5.3.4	Extraction of Facial Expression Classification Features	96
5.4	Summary - Conclusions	103

6 Visual-Facial Emotion Recognition System   **109**

6.1	Face Detection	111
6.1.1	P. Sinha's Template	111
6.1.2	The Face Detection Algorithm - Image Preprocessing	111
6.1.3	Artificial Neural Network-Based Face Detectors	113
6.1.4	Performance Evaluation	116
6.1.5	Summary and Conclusions	126
6.2	Introduction to our Facial Expression Recognition System	126
6.3	First attempts for facial expression recognition	127
6.3.1	The Facial Expression Classification Algorithm (1st Attempts)	127
6.3.2	Feature Validation (First Attempts)	132
6.3.3	Neural Network Classifiers (First Attempts)	132
6.3.4	Results from neural network classifiers (First Attempts)	134
6.4	Facial expression recognition system	136
6.4.1	Feature Selection	138
6.4.2	Image Preprocessing and Feature Extraction	142

Ioanna-Ourania Stathopoulou and George A. Tsihrintzis

6.4.3   The extraction algorithm for the rest of facial features 146
6.4.4   Combination of all and computation of feature vector 148
6.4.5   Quantification of Feature Discrimination Power 148
6.4.6   Classifiers for Facial Expression Classification 151
6.4.7   Classification Performance Assessment 153
6.4.8   More Sophisticated Classifiers 154
6.4.9   Experimental performance evaluation 159
6.5   Summary - Conclusions 161

7   **Human Motion and Gesture Analysis**   **163**
7.1   Introduction 163
7.2   Human detection and motion tracking 164
7.2.1   Marker-based approaches 165
7.2.2   Markerless approaches 167
7.3   Hand Gesture recognition 179
7.3.1   The meaning of hand gestures 179
7.3.2   Techniques for hand gesture recognition 182
7.4   Emotion Recognition Systems from Body Movements and Gestures . 188

8   **Conclusions and Future Work**   **197**
8.1   Summary and Conclusions 197
8.2   Current and Future Work 200
8.2.1   Towards a multimodal emotion recognition system 200
8.2.2   Towards extending the visual-facial expression recognition . . 202

Ioanna-Ourania Stathopoulou and George A. Tsihrintzis

List of Figures

2.1 The nature of 'emotions', 'affect', 'cognition' and 'feelings' 10

2.2 Anatomy of the brain 14

2.3 Anatomy of Cerebral Cortex 16

2.4 Brain structures and emotion 23

2.5 The multidimensional affect space of James Russell 26

4.1 Three Camera Configuration 72

4.2 Two Camera Configuration 75

5.1 Error rates in recognizing the expressions in our preliminary question-
     naire 81

5.2 The first part of the detailed questionnaire 82

5.3 The second part of the detailed questionnaire 82

5.4 Graph of the percentage to which the participants mistook the 'angry'
     emotion for other emotions 84

5.5 Graph of the percentage to which the 'angry' expression maps the
     equivalent emotion, based on the correct answers of the participants . 85

5.6 Graph of the percentage to which the 'angry' expression maps the
     equivalent emotion, based on the correct answers of the participants 86

5.7 Graph of the percentage to which the participants mistook the 'bored
     - Sleepy' emotion for other emotions 87

5.8 Graph of the percentage to which the 'bored - Sleepy' expression maps
     the equivalent emotion, based on the correct answers of the participants 88

5.9 Graph of the percentage to which the 'bored   Sleepy' expression maps
     the equivalent emotion, based on the correct answers of the participants 89

5.10 Graph of the percentage to which the participants mistook the 'dis-
     gusted' emotion for other emotions 90

5.11 Graph of the percentage to which the 'disgusted' expression maps the
     equivalent emotion, based on the correct answers of the participants . 91

5.12 Graph of the percentage to which the 'disgusted' expression maps the
     equivalent emotion, based on the correct answers of the participants 92

5.13 Graph of the percentage to which the participants mistook the 'happy'
     emotion for other emotions 93

5.14 Graph of the percentage to which the 'happy' expression maps the
     equivalent emotion, based on the correct answers of the participants . 94

5.15 Graph of the percentage to which the 'happy' expression maps the
     equivalent emotion, based on the correct answers of the participants 95

5.16 Graph of the percentage to which the participants mistook the 'neutral' emotion for other emotions 96

5.17 Graph of the percentage to which the 'neutral' expression maps the equivalent emotion, based on the correct answers of the participants . 97

5.18 Graph of the percentage to which the 'neutral' expression maps the equivalent emotion, based on the correct answers of the participants 98

5.19 Graph of the percentage to which the participants mistook the 'sad' emotion for other emotions 99

5.20 Graph of the percentage to which the 'sad' expression maps the equivalent emotion, based on the correct answers of the participants 100

5.21 Graph of the percentage to which the 'sad' expression maps the equivalent emotion, based on the correct answers of the participants . . . 101

5.22 Graph of the percentage to which the participants mistook the 'surprised' emotion for other emotions 102

5.23 Graph of the percentage to which the 'surprised' expression maps the equivalent emotion, based on the correct answers of the participants . 103

5.24 Graph of the percentage to which the 'surprised' expression maps the equivalent emotion, based on the correct answers of the participants 104

5.25 The participants' answers regarding the level of difficulty of the facial expression recognition task 105

5.26 The participants' answers regarding the most difficult emotion to recognize 105

5.27 The participants' answers regarding the most difficult emotion to recognize 106

5.28 Error rates in recognizing the expressions in our detailed questionnaire 106

6.1 The P. Sinha Template 112

6.2 The eigenfaces of a face image 113

6.3 Sample images of our Face Detection training set 115

6.4 Three Hidden Layer Network (Simple Demonstration) 115

6.5 Three Hidden Layer Network 116

6.6 Four Hidden Layer Network (Simple demonstration) 117

6.7 Four Hidden Layer Network 118

6.8 The face detection neural networks responses 119

6.9 Face Detection results for the first set of images 121

6.10 Face Detection results for the first set of images 122

6.11 Face Detection results for the second set of images 122

6.12 Face Detection results for the second set of images - 2 123

6.13 Face Detection results for the second set of images - 3 123

6.14 The extracted features (orange points) and the calculated distances . 128

6.15 Typical results from our feature extraction algorithm 130
6.16 Facial Dimension Ratio Distribution 133
6.17 Mouth Dimension Ratio Distribution 133
6.18 Results from our 2-class system 135
6.19 Results from our 3-class system with the Cohn-Kanade Database . . 136
6.20 Results from our 3-class system with the Cohn-Kanade Database for training and our low quality database for testing 137
6.21 Results from our 3-class system with the Cohn-Kanade Database for training and our low quality, side view images for testing 137
6.22 The most important facial points which will help us in the extraction of the feature vector for the facial expression recognition task 138
6.23 The extracted features 142
6.24 Eye Extraction with Skin Extraction and K-means Clustering 145
6.25 Morphological Operations 146
6.26 Extracted Eye Features 147
6.27 Some results of the eye extraction algorithm 147
6.28 Probability Density of the 'Face Size Ratio' 149
6.29 Probability Density of the 'Mouth Size Ratio' 150
6.30 Probability Density of the 'Left Eye Size Ratio' 150
6.31 Probability Density of the 'Right Eye Size Ratio' 151
6.32 Probability Density of the 'Texture of the Region of the Chin' 151
6.33 Probability Density of the 'Texture of the Region of the Forehead' . . 152
6.34 Probability Density of the 'Texture of the Region Between the Brows' 152
6.35 The Facial Expression Neural Network Classifier 153

7.1 Classification in the techniques for human motion tracking and human detection 166
7.2 Object representations. (a) Centroid, (b) multiple points, (c) rectangular patch, (d) elliptical patch, (e) part-based multiple patches, (f) object skeleton, (g) complete object contour, (h) control points on object contour, (i) object silhouette, (j) cardboard model, (k) 3-D model. [1] 172
7.3 Gesture taxonomy for Human-Computer Interaction [2] 181
7.4 Skeletal hand model: (a) Hand anatomy, (b) the kinematic model. [3] 185

8.1 The architecture of our multimodal emotion recognition system . . . 202
8.2 Some results from combining the three modalities 203

Ioanna-Ourania Stathopoulou and George A. Tsihrintzis

List of Tables

2.1 Brain areas and emotions (Adapted from [4]) 22
2.2 Summary of emotional effects in speech (Adapted from [5]) 24

3.1 Requirements for an ideal facial expression database 39
3.2 Review of the facial expression databases 40
3.3 Requirements for an ideal face detection system 42
3.4 Review of the face detection approaches - 1 (Before 2000) 45
3.5 Review of the face detection approaches - 2 (2000-2004) 46
3.6 Review of the face detection approaches - 3 (2005 to present) 47
3.7 Requirements for an ideal facial expression classification system (Adapted
from [6]) 49
3.8 Review of the facial expression approaches (Early Years) (Adapted from [6]) 50
3.9 Categorization of the approaches based on the techniques and the input
media 51
3.10 Review of the facial expression approaches (Middle Years) (Adapted
from [6]) 60
3.11 Review of the facial expression approaches (Recent Years) 67
3.12 Performance evaluation and generalization of recent systems - 1 . . . 68
3.13 Performance evaluation and generalization of recent systems - 2 . . . 68

4.1 Low quality Database 73
4.2 Sample images of our low quality facial expression database 74
4.3 Low quality Database 76
4.4 Sample images of our facial expression database 77

5.1 Typical face image subsets in our questionnaire 80
5.2 Percentage to which a facial expression represents an emotion 95
5.3 Error rate comparison between the two parts of the questionnaire . . 97
5.4 Important features for each facial expression 98
5.5 Mapping 99
5.6 Identification of the most and least important features for each expression 107
5.7 Differences between the First and the Second Questionnaire 107

6.1 The computed three clusters 114
6.2 Description of the two neural network classifiers 117
6.3 Results of the Face Detection System for the three datasets 120
6.4 Sample images of our facial expression database 124
6.5 Sample images of the fourth test set - non human faces 125
6.6 Demonstration of the preprocessing algorithm for low quality images 131

6.7 Deformations of the other six expression, compared to 'neutral' . . . 139
6.8 Facial action and resulting Facial Features 140
6.9 Facial action and resulting Facial Features - 2 140
6.10 Facial action and resulting Facial Features - 3 141
6.11 Results of the Facial Expression Classification System Compared to
     Human Classifiers 154
6.12 Sample images of our facial expression database 155
6.13 Sample images of our facial expression database 156
6.14 Human versus computer classifiers 159
6.15 Classification rates for each expression 160
6.16 Confusion matrix for the SVM classifier 160
6.17 Confusion matrix for the RBF classifier 161
6.18 Confusion matrix for the KNN classifier 161
6.19 Confusion matrix for the MLP classifier 161

7.1 Applications of "Looking at People" [7] 164
7.2 Requirements/Test for the emotion recognition systems from body
    movements and gestures 192
7.3 Review of the emotion recognition systems from body movements and
    gestures, based on the requirements in Table 7.2 192

Ioanna-Ourania Stathopoulou and George A. Tsihrintzis

Visual Affect Recognition
I.-O. Stathopoulou and G.A. Tsihrintzis
IOS Press, 2010
© *2010 The authors and IOS Press. All rights reserved.*
doi:10.3233/978-1-60750-597-6-1

Introduction

Η αρχή είναι το ήμισυ του παντός. (The beginning is the most important part of the work.)

—*Plato (428 BC–348 BC)*

FACIAL expressions play a significant communicative role in human-to-human interaction and interpersonal relations, because they can reveal information about the affective state, cognitive activity, personality, intention and psychological state of a person and, in fact, this information may be difficult to mask. The human ability to analyze another person's facial expressions is one of the subjects of study of the scientific areas of pattern recognition and computer vision and the results of this study are applied to the design of interactive systems that support more efficient and friendlier human-computer interfaces, multimedia services, security control systems, criminology etc.

When attempting to mimic human-to-human communication, human-computer interaction systems must determine the psychological state of a person, so that the computer can react accordingly [8]. This may be exploited in the design of advanced human-computer interfaces, which attempt to take into consideration the variations of the emotions of human users during the interaction and make the computer react accordingly. Indeed, facial expressions corresponding to the 'neutral', 'happy', 'sad', 'surprised', 'angry', 'disgusted' and 'bored-sleepy' psychological states arise very commonly during a typical human-computer interaction session [9, 10, 11, 12]. Thus, vision-based human-computer interactive systems with the ability to process computer user face images and extract information about the user's identity, state and intent would prove very effective and friendly. Similar information can also be used in multimedia interactive services, security control systems or in criminology to uncover possible criminals.

Most works in automatic facial expression analysis assume that the conditions under which a facial image or an image sequence is acquired are known and controlled. Usually, the image shows the face in front view and the background is fairly uniform.

In the majority of previous works, the location and the extent of the face is assumed known or easily computed. However, in real environments, this is not the case. Determining the exact location of the face in a digitized facial image is a more complex problem. First, the scale and the orientation of the face can vary from image to image. Also, even if the photos are taken from a fixed camera, there is no way to know a priori the size and the angle of the face. Thus, in order to fully automate the procedure of facial expression recognition, a task is required that consists of two steps, namely: (1) a face detection step in which the system determines whether or not there are any faces in an image and, if so, returns the location and extent of each face and, (2) a facial expression classification step, in which the system attempts to recognize the expression formed on a detected face.

The development of such fully automated face image analysis systems, capable of detecting a face and classifying a person's facial expression with low error probabilities, is quite challenging. Some of the challenges that have to be addressed in developing such a system arise from the facts that faces are non-rigid and have a high degree of variability in size, shape, color and texture. Furthermore, variations in pose, image orientation and conditions add to the level of difficulty of the problem. Moreover, the variability in the ways people express themselves, depending on their culture, psychological state and habits, make it even more difficult to determine someone's psychological condition through his/her face image. These facts can make the analysis of the facial expressions of another person difficult and often ambiguous.

Towards building an automated facial expression classification system, we conducted a series of studies that would help us to understand how emotion perception works and set the requirements for our own facial expression classification system.

1.1 Motivation

It seems to be the case, that computer vision researchers, are still working in isolation to develop ever more sophisticated algorithms to recognize and interpret facial information without necessarily being interested in applications of their work to solve the vision problem. On the other hand, researchers in human-computer interaction are not necessarily aware of recent progress in computer vision, which may have brought the possibility of using facial information in computer interfaces closer than ever. The question of what to do with facial information when it becomes available may actually motivate and foster ongoing research in human-computer interaction, artificial intelligence and cognitive science.

The purpose of this monograph is to identify the emotions during a typical human computer interaction process and to explore the potential of building computer interfaces which understand and respond to the richness of the information conveyed

Ioanna-Ourania Stathopoulou and George A. Tsihrintzis

by the human face. Until recently, information has been conveyed from the computer to the user mainly via the visual channel, whereas input from the user to the computer is given through the keyboard and pointing devices. The recent emergence of multimodal interfaces might restore a better balance between our physiology and sensory/motor skills, and impact (for the better we hope), the richness of activities we find ourselves involved in. Given recent progress in user-interface primitives composed of gesture, speech, context and affect, it seems feasible to design environments which do not impose themselves as computer environments, but have a much more natural feeling associated with them.

1.2 Organization of this monograph

IN this monograph we try to justify the emotion perception from the scientific and human point of view. This is complete work in terms of analyzing the requirements, justifying and developing a facial expression recognition system to be used for the development of advanced human-computer interaction techniques. During the development of this monograph, a extensive research in the scientific areas of psychology and medicine was made. In addition with the empirical studies that we conducted on human observers, we were able to set the requirements for our facial expression recognition system and identify the facial features that are important for the expression classification task. This work is also innovate, because, besides the 'neutral', 'happiness', 'sadness', 'surprise', 'anger', and 'disgust' emotion classes, which are common in the literature regarding the development of facial expression recognition systems, we also added the 'boredom-sleepiness' emotion class, which is very common during a typical human-computer interaction session. Moreover, based on our studies, there is cultural specificity in emotion perception and expression, so we developed our own face database by photo shooting Greek people forming the expressions. Finally, based on the performance evaluation of our facial expression classification system the success rates are quite significant.

This monograph is organized as follows:

In Chapter 2 we study the emotion perception from the scientific - psychological and medical - point of view. This helps us to identify those brain parts that play a significant role in emotion perception and expression. Moreover, it helps us to identify the most important emotions, based on studies made by psychologists, that we need our system to recognize. Specifically, there are some 'basic emotions' that are considered to be similar independently of a person's culture. Namely, these are the 'anger', 'disgust', 'fear', 'happiness', 'sadness' and 'surprise' emotion classes. At the same time, other studies show that there is a cultural specificity in emotion perception and expression.

3

Ioanna-Ourania Stathopoulou and George A. Tsihrintzis

In Chapter 3, we study previous attempts towards the development of: (1) a facial expression database, (2) a face detection system and (3) a facial expression recognition system. This, helps us to understand how to proceed in our own work in order to achieve our goal. In this chapter, we set the requirements on the performance of an ideal system. Specifically, the majority of existing methods usually succeed in several of these requirements, but there is no existing work that could match all the requirements at the same time.

Our review on previous works on facial expression databases showed that these databases were unsuitable for developing our system up to a fully operational form. This was because either the number and/or the classes of different facial expressions or the number of representative samples in existing databases were found insufficient for our purposes. This led us to the creation of two different databases, described in Chapter 4, namely: (1) A database of low quality images: this database consists of many subjects, depicting many expressions, but the image quality is very low as we used web cameras to acquire the data and, (2) A database of high quality images: this database consists of many subjects, depicting the expressions recognized by our system, and the image quality is quite high as we we used digital cameras to acquire the data.

Also, in our study we tried to understand the emotion perception from the human point of view. Our findings are summarized in Chapter 5, in which we present two empirical studies that we conducted on the process of facial expression classification by humans. These studies form the basis of the facial expression classification module of our system. Specifically, we identify classification features, analyze algorithms for their extraction, and quantify their discrimination power. Moreover, we identify the emotions that are present during a typical human-computer interaction, so facial expressions corresponding to the 'neutral', 'happy', 'sad', 'surprised', 'angry', 'disgusted' and 'bored-sleepy' psychological states. Finally, the results of the two empirical studies indicate that cultural exposure increases the chances of correct recognition of facial expressions.

In Chapter 6, we present our system, which consists of two modules: (1) a face detection subsystem and, (2) a facial expression recognition subsystem. Our face detection subsystem is based on neural network-based classifiers. For our facial expression recognition subsystem, we considered neural network-based and other classifiers, but we concluded that Support Vector Machine-based Classifiers demonstrated better results. Performance evaluations and test results are included in this chapter for both subsystems.

In Chapter 7, we discuss previous works in human motion and gesture analysis. Human motion analysis has long been studied in computer vision and it is consider a classic fundamental problem. In the areas of medicine, sports, and video surveillance, human motion analysis has become an investigative and diagnostic tool. Human motion analysis can be divided into three categories: human activity recognition, human motion tracking, and analysis of body and body part movement.Human activity recognition is most commonly used for video surveillance, specifically automatic motion monitoring for security purposes. Human motion tracking can be performed in two or three dimensions. Finally, motion analysis of body parts may also incorporate the gesture analysis process. Motion analysis of body parts is crucial in the medical and sports field, whereas gesture analysis is commonly used in the development of advanced human-machine interaction systems which can be controlled by the user's hands. There has been a tremendous effort in research towards these tasks and we try to cover the majority of the approaches in this chapter, but there is a lack of works in human motion and gesture analysis for emotion recognition, which are also presented in the final section of this chapter.

Finally, we summarize, draw conclusions and point to future work in Chapter 8, where we also discuss the possibility of using other modalities towards emotion perception, such as keyboard stroke patterns and audio-lingual information.

2

Psychological Studies on Emotion Perception

A man should not strive to eliminate his complexes but to get into accord with them: they are legitimately what directs his conduct in the world.

—Sigmund Freud (1856–1939)

IN order to develop ways that effectively allow emotions on computers and aid our interactions with them, we need to understand first what emotions are and what exactly constitutes emotional intelligence. This section starts by providing an overview of what is currently known about emotions, including what causes them, how humans express them, and their influence on the way we feel and behave. An important part in this section is devoted to how people express their emotions using their face and how psychologists interpret and understand these emotions. Some of the topics discussed in this section can be summarized in the following questions:

- What constitutes an emotion?

- Is there a difference between emotion, feelings and affect?

- How do people feel an emotion? Is there a proven scientific approach?

- Is there a similarity on the way people express themselves, regardless of their culture?

- Are there some 'basic emotions' that are similar regardless of a person's culture?

- Can we identify these emotions?

The answers to some of these previous questions still remain under debate among the psychologists. Their believes on these matters will be discussed and further analyzed in this section.

2.1 Emotion vs affect vs feelings

FACIAL expressions are considered as a very important means of conveying information about a person's affective or emotional state. Before considering facial expression of emotion, the nature of emotion itself must be examined first. There is a distinction between affect and emotion, based on the studies of the American Psychiatric Association [13] and between affect, emotion and feeling [14].

Affect is defined as *'a pattern of observable behaviors that is the expression of a subjectively experienced feeling state or emotion'* [13]. The first studies about affect were done by Spinoza, in his book, which is called "The Ethics" and which is written in Latin, one finds two words *"affectio"* and *"affectus"*. Although those two terms are usually mistranslated as *"affection"* the correct translation corresponds to "affection" for *"affectio"* and *"affect"* for *"affectus"*, respectively [15]. Affect is an ability to affect and be affected, it is a pre-personal intensity corresponding to the passage from one experiential state of the body to another and implying an augmentation or diminution in that body"s capacity to act [14]. *Affection* is each such state considered as an encounter between the affected body and a second, affecting, body [16]. Of the three central terms in this section – feeling, emotion, and affect – affect is the most abstract because affect cannot be fully realized in language, and because affect is always prior to and/or outside of consciousness [16]. Affect is the body"s way of preparing itself for action in a given circumstance by adding a quantitative dimension of intensity to the quality of an experience [16].

Feeling is a sensation that has been checked against previous experiences and labeled. Feelings are learnt during a person's life, they are personal and biographical because every person has a distinct set of previous sensations from which to draw when interpreting and labeling their feelings [17]. Based on the studies of Iverson, Kupfermann and Kandel [18], there is a distinction between emotions and feelings. Emotion *'refers to the bodily state of a person'* and feeling *'refers to the conscious experience of the bodily state'*. William James proposed that *'the bodily changes follow directly the perception of the exciting fact, and that our feeling of the same changes as they occur is the emotion'* [19]. Thus, in what has come to be known as the James-Lange theory of emotion, *'cognition is secondary to the physiological expression of emotion'*.

Emotions are considered to be *the projection/display of a feeling and, generally, cognitive responses to information from the periphery*. Unlike feelings, the display of emotion can be either genuine or feigned. This was demonstrated by Paul Ekman [20]. In his experiment, he videotaped American and Japanese people whilst watching some video clips. In these clips, there were demonstrated scenes that would provoke the corresponding emotion, so there were neutral or pleasant events (such as a canoe trip) or less pleasant events (for example, nasal surgery). There were two showings of the video clips: one where subjects watched the clips on their own and another where subjects watched the clips with an interviewer present. When subjects watched the clips in private, similar expressions were noted in both American and Japanese subjects. However, when they watched the same clips in groups, the expressions were different, as each individual's emotions were displayed to the rest of the group.

In a critique of the James-Lange theory, Cannon [21] proposed that bodily changes follow from cognitive processes. His assertion was based on the following observations: (a) removal of the cerebral cortex in laboratory animals does not impair emotional behavior, (b) the same visceral changes occur in different emotional states, (c) the viscera are relatively insensitive, (d) visceral changes are typically too slow to generate emotions and (e) induction of the physical changes typical of strong emotions does not result in the experience of the simulated emotion. However, these observations and conclusions have recently been drawn into question [22]. Current opinion represents a synthesis of the two theories in which emotions *are viewed as the outcome of a dynamic, ongoing interaction of peripheral and central factors* [18].

The nature of the four notions: 'emotions', 'affect', 'cognition' and 'feelings' is summarized in the following Figure 2.1. A major difference lies in the fact that feelings are personal and biographical, emotions are social, and affects are pre-personal. Also, affect is very important in the perception and understanding of feelings and emotions. Without affect feelings do not "feel" because they have no intensity, and without feelings rational decision-making becomes problematic [23]. Affect plays an important role in determining the relationship between our bodies, our environment, and others, and the subjective experience that we feel/think as affect dissolves into experience.

Our knowledge can lead to the following assumptions regarding emotions:

- cmotions are fast

- triggered automatically

- triggered by the environment

- moderated at least partially by cognitive processes

- transitory

2.2 Emotions and culture

EMOTION theorists have debated for centuries about what emotions are and what their primary function in human life is. This debate is far from over and there is currently no universally agreed upon definition of emotions. However, many scholars would at least agree that we experience different types of emotions in our everyday

Ioanna-Ourania Stathopoulou and George A. Tsihrintzis

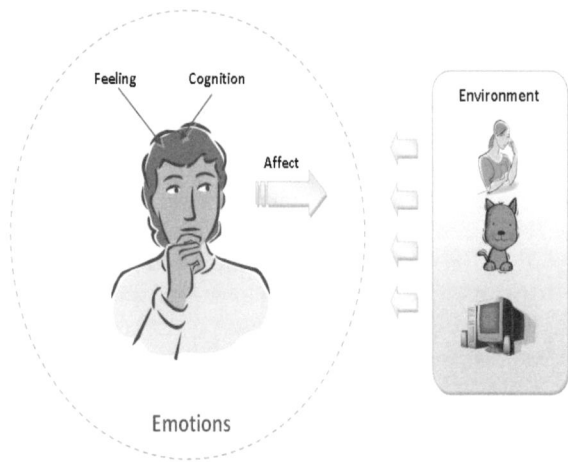

Figure 2.1: The nature of 'emotions', 'affect', 'cognition' and 'feelings'

lives. Most psychologists agree that there is a difference on how people express themselves depending on their culture. On the other hand, the majority agree that there is also a similarity in these expressions because of the theory of evolution that strengthens the connection between all these cultures. First studies on this subject were conducted by Charles Darwin [24, 25] and mostly followed by Paul Ekman [25, 20, 26, 27, 28, 29, 30, 31, 32, 33, 34, 35, 36, 37, 38, 39, 40] and are summarized below.

2.2.1 Basic Emotions

Although efforts were made to understand emotion and some early studies suggest the idea of universal emotions, for much of the previous century, emotion scholars generally subscribed to a cultural theory of emotion, where emotions were believed to be culturally specific learnt behaviors that could only be experienced through observing other people expressing such emotions. As mentioned above, the historical roots of basic emotion theory originate from Charles Darwin, who as a part of his evolutionary theory suggested that the emotional expressions of man were descendants from other animals [24, 25]. Darwin studied not only the behavior of animals but also set to study the question of whether some emotions were universal to all men. Although the idea of universal basic emotions had been mentioned already many centuries before

Ioanna-Ourania Stathopoulou and George A. Tsihrintzis

Darwin in the writings of philosophers such as Descartes, Hobbes and Spinoza [41] and influential facial expression studies had been conducted by other 19th century scientists such as Guillaume Duchenne de Boulogne [42], Darwin was the first to conduct experiments in order to evaluate the recognition of emotions from faces [24, 25]. In his experiments, he tried to identify which emotions were recognized consistently from photographs of representative emotional facial expressions in England and made the first attempts to evaluate the universality of emotions by interviewing his fellow countrymen living abroad on the expression of emotions in other cultures [25]. His methods, in which he asked subjects to judge emotions from certain facial expressions, still remains a part of contemporary research methodology. According to a critical review [43], different basic emotion sets ranging from two to eighteen basic emotions have been proposed by different investigators; however, most of them agree at least on the emotions of *anger, fear, happiness and sadness*.

However, Paul Ekman [25, 20, 26, 27, 28, 29, 30, 31, 32, 33, 34, 35, 36, 37, 38, 39, 40] discovered that some emotions are not necessarily learnt, as previously believed, but are in fact innate and shared across all cultures. In his study, Ekman traveled to a preliterate culture (the Fore, in New Guinea) to ensure that the people there had not been exposed to Western media and had not learned the emotional expressions of the Westerners. The subjects were told a number of stories, then asked to choose from a set of photographs of Americans expressing different emotions, the one which most closely matched the story. When tested, the Fore pointed to the same expressions that Westerners linked to the story. For further clarification, some Fore people were videotaped displaying facial expressions appropriate to each of the stories. After returning home, the experiment was completed in reverse by asking Americans to link the Fore faces to the different stories. The judgements of both the Fore people and the Americans again matched. The studies by Paul Ekman led to the identification of the *'basic emotions'* which are universally common regardless of the culture of the subject. Although researchers often disagree about how many basic emotions there are, the most commonly accepted emotions which can be classified as 'basic emotions' are: *'anger', 'disgust', 'fear', 'happiness', 'sadness' and 'surprise'*.

Later studies by Paul Ekman [31], added *'contempt'* to the 'basic emotions' in addition to the six original ones, and 'contempt' has received some support from a study conducted in ten countries; however, no studies have been made in isolated groups. Furthermore, subjects have failed to recognize contempt from supposedly characteristic facial expressions in more recent studies [44, 45], indicating that contempt *should not be considered a basic emotion*.

Ioanna-Ourania Stathopoulou and George A. Tsihrintzis

2.2.2   Culturally Specific Expressions of Emotions

Besides the 'basic emotions', studies have shown that there are also cultural variations in the way in which humans express emotion. These studies have shown that the emotions can vary: (1) in terms of the expression of emotion, but also (2) in terms of the intensity of the expressed emotion.

The first assumption suggests that some emotions are culturally specific. This difference can be interpreted in many terms:

- some emotions maybe present only in some cultures: This example is demonstrated by J. Ledoux [46]. In his book, he reports about an emotion that is experienced by the Gururumba people of New Guinea that is not believed to be experienced by people of other cultures. This is known as the state of 'being a wild pig' and people who experience this state can become aggressive and often start looting, but rarely is anyone actually hurt or anything of importance stolen. This state is considered as normal among the Gururumba and as a way of relieving stress and maintaining mental health across the community.

- different ways of expression depending on the culture: For example, in many cases, it is stated that Japanese people tend to close their mouth and widen their eyes when they feel 'surprised'. This is contrary to other cultures that tend to open their mouth widely when feeling the same emotion.

The second assumption assumes that although the emotion maybe present, the intense of the expression maybe different, depending on the culture. This, was demonstrated by another experiment conducted by Paul Ekman [20] on American and Japanese people and further discussed by Matsumoto [47]. In this experiment, both American and Japanese men were videotaped whilst watching some video clips. In these clips, there were demonstrated scenes that would provoke the corresponding emotion, so there were neutral or pleasant events (such as a canoe trip) or less pleasant events (for example, nasal surgery). There were two showings of the video clips: one where subjects watched the clips on their own and another where subjects watched the clips with an interviewer present. When subjects watched the clips in private, similar expressions were noted in both American and Japanese subjects. However, when the interviewer was present, Japanese subjects smiled more and showed less disgust than the American subjects. When the videotapes were watched back in slow motion the researchers noticed that when the interviewer was present, Japanese subjects actually started to make the same expressions of disgust as the Americans did, but they were able to mask these expressions very quickly afterwards. Therefore, it appeared that the American and Japanese participants did actually experience the same basic emotions as these were automatic responses hardwired into their brains.

It was only a few hundred milliseconds later, that the Japanese subjects could apply their learnt cultural display rules and override the automatic response.

The cultural specificity of the emotions is further strengthened by studies of Izard [48] and Elfenbein and Ambady [49].

2.2.3 Higher Cognitive Emotions

Besides the 'basic emotions' and the culturally-specific emotions, Paul E. Griffiths [50] believes that, in addition, there are also 'higher cognitive emotions'. There is a similarity between those emotions and the basic emotions. This similarity lies on the fact that they are universal, but there are also variations on the way that they are expressed and experienced by different cultures. Moreover, usually, there is also no single facial expression associated with them. Higher cognitive emotions are considered to take longer than basic emotions to both develop and pass away. As an example, we can consider romantic love. This emotion usually develops gradually in people over a period of weeks and months, while 'surprise' (a basic emotion) is typically a very quick reaction to an event. 'Surprise' can also be recognized by a couple of facial expressions associated with it, while there are no universal facial expression for love. It is suggested that emotions such as *love, jealousy, pride, embarrassment and guilt* should be called *'higher cognitive emotions'*, because these emotions typically require more processing in the cortex of the brain. This essentially means that these emotions can be influenced more by cognitive thought processes, while basic emotions are more reactive and spontaneous in nature.

2.3 Neurobiology and Emotion Expression

ANOTHER fact that can further manifest the statement that there are universally known emotions, is the assumption that a number of brain regions are directly involved in the perception of facial expressions and, generally, emotion understanding and feeling. These include [4]: (1) **the frontal cortex**, (2) **the superior temporal sulcus**, and (3) **the amygdala**.

The anatomy of the brain is demonstrated in Figure 2.2, where we can observe the aforementioned parts of the brain.

2.3.1 Cerebral Cortex

The cerebral cortex is a structure within the brain that plays a key role in memory, attention, perceptual awareness, thought, language, and consciousness. In dead, preserved brains, the outermost layer of the cerebrum has a grey color, hence the name 'grey matter'. Grey matter is formed by neurons and their unmyelinated fibers,

Ioanna-Ourania Stathopoulou and George A. Tsihrintzis

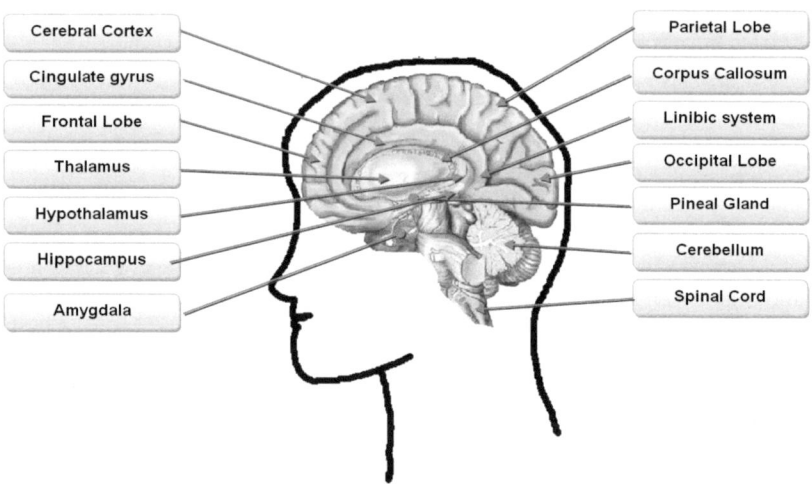

Figure 2.2: Anatomy of the brain

whereas the white matter below the grey matter of the cortex is formed predominantly by myelinated axons interconnecting different regions of the central nervous system. The human cerebral cortex is from 2 to 4 mm thick.

The surface of the cerebral cortex is folded in large mammals, so that more than two-thirds of the cortical surface is buried in the grooves, called 'sulci.' The phylogenetically most recent part of the cerebral cortex, the neocortex, also called isocortex, is differentiated into six horizontal layers; the more ancient part of the cerebral cortex, the hippocampus (also called archicortex), has at most three cellular layers, and is divided into subfields. Relative variations in thickness or cell type (among other parameters) allow us to distinguish between different neocortical architectonic fields. The geometry of at least some of these fields seems to be related to the anatomy of the cortical folds, and, for example, layers in the upper part of the cortical grooves (called gyri) seem to be more clearly differentiated than in its deeper parts

The cerebral cortex is divided into lobes, each of which has a specific function. For example, there are specific areas involved in vision, hearing, touch, movement, and smell. Other areas are critical for thinking and reasoning. Although many functions, such as touch, are found in both the right and left cerebral hemispheres, some functions are found in only one cerebral hemisphere. For example, in most people, language abilities are found in the left hemisphere. The lobes can be summarized as following:

- Parietal Lobe: involved in the reception and processing of sensory information from the body, as well as in the manipulation of objects. Also, plays an important role in the knowledge of numbers and their relations.

- Frontal Lobe: involved in in motor function, decision-making, problem solving, spontaneity, memory, language, initiation, judgement, impulse control, and social and sexual behavior. Also, play an important part in retaining longer term memories which are not task-based. These are often memories associated with emotions derived from input from the brain's limbic system. The frontal lobe modifies those emotions to generally fit socially acceptable norms.

- Occipital Lobe: involved with vision.

- Temporal Lobe: involved the primary organization of sensory input, which plays an important role in emotion, hearing, and language. Also, emporal lobes are highly associated with memory skills, mainly episodic/declarative memory skills [1].

The lobes of the cerebral cortex and their roles are summarized in Figure 2.3.

In summary, the cerebral cortex is responsible for sensing and interpreting input from various sources and maintaining cognitive function. Sensory functions interpreted by the cerebral cortex include hearing, touch, and vision. Cognitive functions include thinking, perceiving, and understanding language. Various studies have showed that cerebral cortex plays a key role in expressing and understanding emotions by the humans. Specifically, Nakamura et al. [51], measured regional cerebral blood flow (rCBF) using positron emission tomography (PET) to determine which brain regions are involved in the assessment of facial emotion. They presented normal subjects with photographs of facial expressions. The right inferior frontal cortex showed significant activation during the assessment of facial emotion in comparison with the other two tests. Based on their assumptions, the right inferior frontal cortex is involved in the processing of both visual and auditory emotional communicative information. Also, this area is involved in metaphor comprehension, phonological working memory, and face matching. Their studies have shown that the brain tries to match perceived facial gestures with templates or prototypes in order to recognize the emotion behind the expression.

In a study [52], Harmer, Thilo, Rothwell and Goodwin suggest that the recognition of different emotional states involves at least partly separable neural circuits. They assessed the discrimination of both anger and happiness in healthy subjects receiving transcranial magnetic stimulation (TMS) over the medial-frontal cortex or over

---

[1]Episodic memories are those that store specific events such as attending a class or flying to France. It can be thought of as mentally reliving a past event. Episodic memory is believed by many to be the system that supports and underpins semantic memory

Ioanna-Ourania Stathopoulou and George A. Tsihrintzis

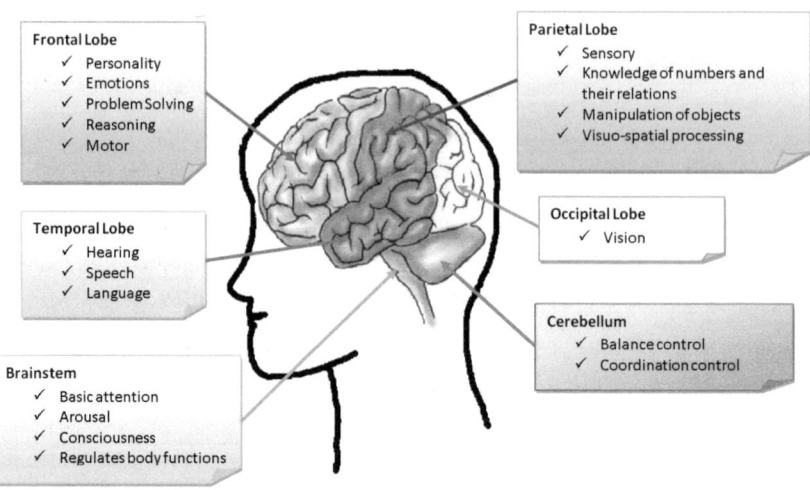

Figure 2.3: Anatomy of Cerebral Cortex

a control site (mid-line parietal cortex). The experimental task utilized sequences of face images morphed between two prototypes, e.g. angry and neutral, in 10% increments. Subjects were presented with these images and asked to differentiate between happy/neutral faces and angry/neutral faces. Recognition thresholds were established prior to the application of TMS. Recognition thresholds were defined as the level of emotional intensity at which 75% of the facial expressions were correctly identified. The recognition threshold for happiness was at a morph increment of 40% while for anger it was at an increment of 70%. Application of TMS to the medial frontal cortex was found to impair the processing of angry facial expressions but not happy facial expressions.

'Disgust' is another emotion that is considered to derive from the cerebral cortex. Specifically, anterior Insula and adjacent frontal operculum, play an important role in the perception of disgust. Studies from Gallese et al. [53] and Jabbi et al. [54] have demonstrated this assumption. During an experiment by Jabbi et al. [54], the same subjects were scanned while they (a) view actors taste the content of a cup and look disgusted (b) tasted unpleasant bitter liquids to induce disgust, and (c) read and imagine scenarios involving disgust and their neutral counterparts. They found voxels in the anterior Insula and adjacent frontal operculum to be involved in all three modalities of disgust, suggesting that simulation in the context of social perception and mental imagery of disgust share a common neural substrates.

2.3.2 Amygdala

The amygdalae (Latin, also corpus amygdaloideum, singular amygdala) are almond-shaped groups of neurons located deep within the medial temporal lobes of the brain in complex vertebrates, including humans. Shown in research to perform a primary role in the processing and memory of emotional reactions, the amygdalae are considered part of the limbic system.

The regions described as amygdalae encompass several nuclei with distinct functional traits. Among these nuclei are the basolateral complex, the centromedial nucleus and the cortical nucleus. The basolateral complex can be further subdivided into the lateral, the basal and the accessory basal nuclei. Anatomically, the amygdala and more particularly, its centromedial nucleus, may be considered as a part of the basal ganglia.

In humans, the amygdalae perform primary roles in the formation and storage of memories associated with emotional events. Research indicates that, during fear conditioning, sensory stimuli reach the basolateral complexes of the amygdalae, particularly the lateral nuclei, where they form associations with memories of the stimuli. The association between stimuli and the aversive events they predict may be mediated by long-term potentiation, a lingering potential for affected synapses to react more readily.

Memories of emotional experiences imprinted in reactions of synapses in the lateral nuclei elicit fear behavior through connections with the central nucleus of the amygdalae. The central nuclei are involved in the genesis of many fear responses, including freezing (immobility), tachycardia (rapid heartbeat), increased respiration, and stress-hormone release. Damage to the amygdalae impairs both the acquisition and expression of Pavlovian fear conditioning, a form of classical conditioning of emotional responses.

The amygdala is also involved in appetitive (positive) conditioning. It seems that distinct neurons respond to positive and negative stimuli, but there is no clustering of these distinct neurons into clear anatomical nuclei.

Amygdala is considered to play an important role in the perception of the emotion of 'fear', regardless of the different ways of expressing it (e.g masked fear, low spatial frequency fear, broad spatial frequency fear, conditioned response (CR) to fear. Many studies [55, 56, 57, 58] have prooved this assumption. In the presence of 'fear', the subject demonstrated significantly increased amygdalar response, particularly in the left hemisphere, to images of fearful expressions. Decreased response was associated with viewing of happy expressions. Amygdalar response can occur without explicit knowledge of the stimulus [57].

Ioanna-Ourania Stathopoulou and George A. Tsihrintzis

2.3.3 Superior Temporal Sulcus

The superior temporal sulcus is thought to be used by humans in making simple actions, or watching other people make actions. Several research areas claim the superior temporal sulcus (STS) as the host brain region for their particular behavior of interest. Some see it as one of the core structures for the theory of mind [2]. For others, it is the main region for audiovisual integration. It plays an important role in biological motion perception, but is also claimed to be essential for speech processing and processing of faces [60].

A common process performed by the superior temporal sulcus (STS), namely analyzing changing sequences of input, either in the auditory or visual domain, and interpreting the communicative significance of those inputs, suggests the importance of superior temporal sulcus (STS) in the acquisition of social and speech perception [61]. Studies have shown [62, 61] that because of the superior temporal sulcus' (STS) role in interpreting social and speech input, abnormalities in this area of the brain are highly implicated at the most common clinical sign of autism spectrum disorders (ASD). Autism Sspectrum Disorders (ASD) is social interaction impairment, which is associated with communication deficits and stereotyped behaviors. Base on the studies, abnormalities are characterized by decreased gray matter concentration, rest hypoperfusion and abnormal activation during social tasks.

Dynamic changes in facial displays contribute to face recognition abilities, judgment of affect, and identity. LaBar, Crupain, Voyvodic and McCarthy [63] used functional magnetic resonance imaging (fMRI) to compare brain activation to static facial displays versus dynamic changes in facial identity or emotional expression. Static images depicted prototypical fearful, angry and neutral expressions. Dynamic changes consisted of two groups: (1) identity morphs depicted identity changes from one person to another, always with neutral expressions and (2) emotion morphs depicted expression changes from neutral to fear or anger, creating the illusion that the actor was 'getting scared' or 'getting angry' in real-time. Brain regions implicated in processing facial affect, including the amygdala and fusiform gyrus, showed greater responses to dynamic versus static emotional expressions, especially for fear. Identity morphs activated a dorsal fronto-cingulo-parietal circuit and additional ventral areas, including the amygdala, that also responded to the emotion morphs. Activity in the superior temporal sulcus discriminated emotion morphs from identity morphs, extending its known role in processing biologically relevant motion. The results highlighted the importance of temporal cues in the neural coding of facial displays.

---

[2]The term 'theory of mind' refers to the influence of emotion and mental state [59]

Ioanna-Ourania Stathopoulou and George A. Tsihrintzis

2.3.4   Implicit and Explicit Perception of Emotion

The 'implicit-explicit' distinction was entered in the study of memory when Graf and Schaschter [64] wrote a paper about 'implicit' and 'explicit' measurements of the memory. In the last years, these terms have been added to the study of emotion and facial expression perception [65]. As 'implicit' emotion is considered the unconscious emotion, whereas 'explicit' is usually referred to the conscious emotion. Most of what the brain does is unconscious, but attention both amplifies and prolongs activation, which allows processing at one site to affect processing at other sites, forming a network of activation that can give rise to the experience of consciousness. Generally, 'implicit' emotions can be considered the emotions that someone feels without any further processing (as we say 'what comes first to your mind'), whereas 'explicit' require further processing and multiple factors must be considered. Sometimes, in presence of 'explicit' emotions the brain tries to match the acquired emotion with templates stored from previous experiences. The majority of studies deal with fMRI in order to examine the brain activation in the occurrence of 'implicit' and 'explicit' emotions and have reported quite contradictory results.

Several studies reported stronger activation of the amygdala-hippocampal area during unattended emotion processing, that is, implicit or passive, compared to explicit tasks, in which the depicted emotion was the focus of attention [66, 67, 68, 69, 70]. Critchley et al. [66] used fMRI in nine subjects to determine which brain areas subserve processing of high-valence expressions and if distinct brain areas are activated when facial expressions are processed explicitly or implicitly. They conducted two experiments: in the first experiment, they examined explicit processing of expressions by requiring subjects to attend to, and judge, facial expression, whereas in the second experiment, they examined implicit processing of expressions by requiring subjects to attend to, and judge, facial gender, which was counterbalanced in both experimental conditions. Processing of facial expressions significantly increased regional blood oxygenation level-dependent (BOLD) activity in fusiform and middle temporal gyri, hippocampus, amygdala-hippocampal junction, and pulvinar nucleus. Explicit processing evoked significantly more activity in temporal lobe cortex than implicit processing, whereas implicit processing evoked significantly greater activity in amygdala region. Mixed high-valence facial expressions are processed within temporal lobe visual cortex, thalamus, and amygdala-hippocampal complex. Also, neural substrates for explicit and implicit processing of facial expressions are dissociable: explicit processing activates temporal lobe cortex, whereas implicit processing activates amygdala region. Hariri et al. [67] also used fMRI to identify the neural networks underlying the 'implicit' and 'explicit' emotion processing. Their study comprised of two tasks: subjects either matched the affect of one of two faces to that of a simultaneously presented target face ('implicit' task) or identified the affect of a tar-

Ioanna-Ourania Stathopoulou and George A. Tsihrintzis

get face by choosing one of two simultaneously presented linguistic labels ('explicit' task). Matching angry or frightened expressions was associated with increased regional cerebral blood flow (rCBF) in the left and right amygdala, the brain's primary fear centers. Labeling these same expressions was associated with a diminished rCBF response in the amygdalae. This decrease correlated with a simultaneous increase in rCBF in the right prefrontal cortex, a neocortical region implicated in regulating emotional responses. Winston et al. [68] also conducted fMRI experiment in which subjects viewed morphed emotional faces displaying low or high intensities of disgust, fear, happiness, or sadness under two tasks: (1) recognize the emotion ('explicit' task) or (2) determine the gender of the displayed face ('implicit' task). The amygdala and fusiform cortex responded to high-intensity expressions of all emotions, independent of task. Ventromedial prefrontal and somatosensory cortices (right STS) showed enhanced activity during explicit emotional judgments. Keightley et al. [69] used a multivariate technique, partial least squares (PLS) to determine spatially distributed patterns of brain activity associated with different tasks and stimulus conditions, as well as the interaction between the two. Their experiments consisted of emotional faces (one face in the image plane) and emotional pictures (many faces in the image plane) The experimental conditions required the participant to perform an indirect or direct emotional processing task. When presented with emotional faces, the indirect face task was a gender discrimination task, while the direct task involved emotional processing task. Alternatively, when presented with emotional pictures, the indirect emotional task required participants to count the number of people in the picture, whereas in the direct emotional task, participants indicated if the scene depicted in the picture was positive or negative. Based on the results, the amygdala and related regions (thalamus, insula, rostral anterior cingulate, ventral and inferior prefrontal cortex) showed extensive activity in the processing of emotional stimuli with biological significance, such as fearful/angry faces. Cognitive tasks demanding increased attention have been shown to attenuate activity in these brain regions and increase activity in dorsal areas.Finally, Scheuerecker et al. [70] tried again to find specific regions for single types of emotions and for the cognitive demands of expression processing. Again they conducted fMRI experiments in twelve subjects by presenting them with an 'implicit' and 'explicit' emotional paradigm. The subjects reacted significantly faster in implicit than in explicit trials but did not differ in their error ratio. For the 'implicit' condition increased signals were observed in particular in the thalami, the hippocampi, the frontal inferior gyri and the right middle temporal region. For the 'explicit' condition increased blood-oxygen-level-dependent signals were shown in the caudate nucleus, the cingulum and the right prefrontal cortex.

The opposite, however, has also been found regarding the amygdala region: no activation during implicit processing of disgusted faces [71] or less activation during incidental emotional processing compared to explicit emotion recognition [72]. Specifically, studies by Gorno-Tempini et al. [71] in their fMRI study investigated the neural correlates of incidental and explicit processing of the emotional content of faces expressing either disgust or happiness. Subjects were examined while they were viewing neutral, disgusted, or happy faces. The incidental task required subjects to decide about face gender, the explicit task to decide about face expression. In the control task subjects were requested to detect a white square in a greyscale mosaic stimulus. Results showed that the left inferior frontal cortex and the bilateral occipito-temporal junction responded equally to all face conditions. Several cortical and subcortical regions were modulated by task type, and by facial expression. Right neostriatum and left amygdala were activated when subjects made explicit judgements of disgust, bilateral orbito-frontal cortex when they made judgement of happiness, and right frontal and insular cortex when they made judgements about any emotion. Gur et al. [72] tested the hypothesis that activation of the amygdala is related to the relevance of the emotional valence of stimuli. They presented fourteen participants (7 men, 7 women) facial displays of happiness, sadness, anger, fear, and disgust as well as neutral faces obtained from professional actors and actresses of diverse ethnicity and age and asked them to discriminate the emotion (positive or negative) or the age(older or younger than 30). The results showed that limbic response was greater during the emotion than during the age discrimination conditions. The response was most pronounced in the amygdala, but was also present in the hippocampus and circumscribed voxels in other limbic regions.

The results of the aforementioned studies are presented in Table 2.1 and in Figure 2.4. Based on these studies, we can observe the following:

1. The structures involved in the perception of facial expressions include subcortical structures, primary sensory areas such as the visual and somatosensory cortices, higher level visual processing areas including the fusiform cortex and the STS, premotor areas involved in motion planning, and prefrontal areas involved in more abstract processes such as analysis and discrimination.

2. Perception of facial expressions invokes conscious and unconscious processes in parallel.

3. Understanding of emotion in others appears to involve an unconscious imitative process that simulates the observed emotional state.

4. It appears that different brain areas are deal with different emotions.

Ioanna-Ourania Stathopoulou and George A. Tsihrintzis

Table 2.1: Brain areas and emotions (Adapted from [4])

Brain Area	Activation for:	Authors:
Right Inferior Frontal Cortex	Facial expressions	Nakamura [51]
Medial Frontal Cortex	Anger	Harmer [52]
Anterior Insular Cortex	Disgust	Gallese [53]
Amygdala	Masked fear	Morris [55]
Amygdala	Disgust	Whalen [57]
Amygdala	Low spatial frequency fear, Broad spatial frequency fear	Vuillemier [58]
Amygdala	Conditioned response (CR) to fear	Morris [55]
Amygdala	Gender & Expression	Gorno-Tempini [71]
Left Inf Frontal/ Occipito-Temporal	Disgust	Gorno-Tempini [71]
Rt Neostriatum & Lt Amygdala	Disgust	Gorno-Tempini [71]
Rt Frontal & Insular Cortices	Happiness & Disgust	Gorno-Tempini [71]
Amygdala / Fusiform Cortex	Gender/Intense expression	Winston [68]
Rt STS, Ventromedial prefrontal, Somatosensory Cortex	Intense expression	Winston [68]

2.4 Expression of Emotion

HUMANS can express emotion in a variety of ways, the primary ones being written language, facial expressions, speech, and body movements (such as posture and gait).

2.4.1 Written Language

From the ancient years to nowadays, written language was used to convey messages and news between humans, especially when other means of communication were not available. In these cases it was important for the humans to express their emotion through written language. This can be done in many ways, as written language is a powerful medium for expressing emotion. First of all, people can literally state how they are feeling using emotive words such as 'happy', 'sad', 'angry' or 'surprised'. Moreover the colour, the size and the shape of the words can also demonstrate someone's emotional state. For the same purposes, these differences in colour, size and shape of letters are commonly applied in animated comic books or in advanced movie subtitles, especially for hearing impaired people. "ecstatic". Studies from graphologists in the early 20th century, report that handwriting can reveal information about a

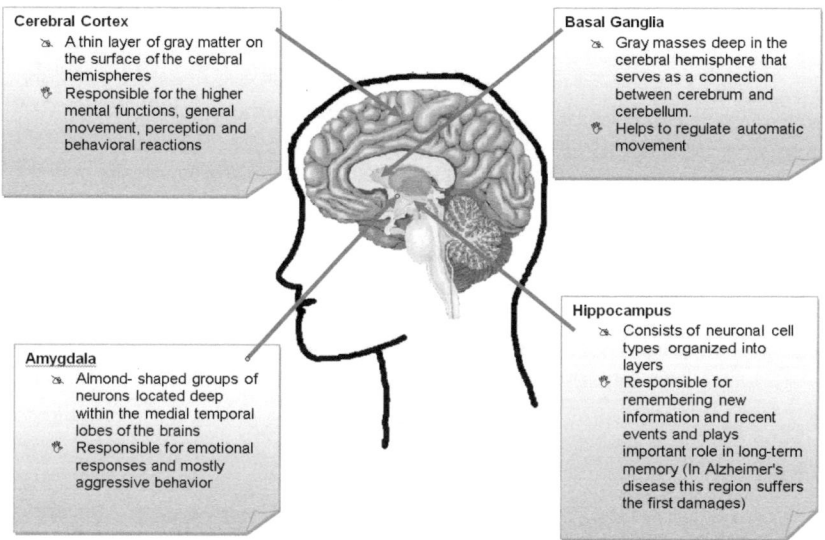

Cerebral Cortex
- A thin layer of gray matter on the surface of the cerebral hemispheres
- Responsible for the higher mental functions, general movement, perception and behavioral reactions

Basal Ganglia
- Gray masses deep in the cerebral hemisphere that serves as a connection between cerebrum and cerebellum.
- Helps to regulate automatic movement

Amygdala
- Almond-shaped groups of neurons located deep within the medial temporal lobes of the brains
- Responsible for emotional responses and mostly aggressive behavior

Hippocampus
- Consists of neuronal cell types organized into layers
- Responsible for remembering new information and recent events and plays important role in long-term memory (In Alzheimer's disease this region suffers the first damages)

Figure 2.4: Brain structures and emotion

person's character, specifically: feelings of self-worth, or pride, with size and emphasis of capital; aggressive with line quality; preoccupation with details and small filiform writing; temperament with variations in slant and alignment; and explosive-inhibit make-up with graphic complex (cited in [73]). Finally, nowadays as internet has been transformed to an important mean of information and communication, symbols such as *emoticons*, for example, ':-)' or ':-(', have been also introduced as a way to convey emotion, and are particularly popular within domains such as email, instant messaging or text messaging. Regarding the online messaging, studies have also shown that animating text can also convey information regarding the emotional state [74].

2.4.2 Speech

Besides written language, another powerful method for communication and emotion expression is through speech. In interpersonal relationships, speech is the most common mean of communication and along with facial expressions and gestures can reveal the speaker's emotional state. Also speech is used when other means of communication are not available (for example, telephone conversations). Speech can also provide other information about a speaker such as their identity, age and gender. Like written

Ioanna-Ourania Stathopoulou and George A. Tsihrintzis

language, people can also use speech to simply communicate the emotions they are experiencing using the same emotive words such as 'happy', 'sad', 'angry' or 'surprised'. Pitch (level, range and variability), tempo and loudness are considered the most influential parameters for expressing emotion through speech [75]. McNair et al. [5] have defined the general characteristics of a range of basic emotions (Table 2.2).

Table 2.2: Summary of emotional effects in speech (Adapted from [5])

	Anger	Happiness	Sadness	Fear	Disgust
Speech rate	slightly faster	faster or slower	slightly slower	much faster	very much slower
Pitch average	very much higher	much higher	slightly lower	very much higher	very much lower
Pitch range	much wider	much wider	slightly narrower	much wider	slightly wider
Intensity	higher	higher	lower	normal	lower
Voice quality	breathy, chest tone	breathy, blaring	resonant	irregular voicing	wide, downward
Articulation	tense	normal	slurring	precise	normal

2.4.3 Facial Expressions

Facial expressions are one of the primary ways in which we can detect emotions in others and is the main research in this monograph. The importance and the ways of expressing and understanding emotions through facial expressions is further analyzed in Section 2.5.

2.4.4 Body movements and Hand gestures

The question whether body movements and body postures are indicative of specific emotions is a matter of debate. While some studies have found evidence for specific body movements accompanying specific emotions, others indicate that movement behavior (aside from facial expression) may be only indicative of the quantity (intensity) of emotion, but not of its quality. Generally, the relationship between emotions and body movements is regarded not as strong compared to other nonverbal communication such as facial expressions [76]. Thus, expressive body movement reflect certain basic emotion. In particular, Meijer [77] and Wallbott [78] claim that certain body movement helps a person to cope with an experiencing an emotion and perhaps it is also possible to recognize the underlying emotion through the recognition of the associated body movement. Specifically, Meijer [77] conducted an experiment in which

Eighty-five adult subjects were shown ninety-six videotaped body movements, performed by three actors. Each movement was determined by seven general dimensions: trunk movement, arm movement, vertical direction, sagittal direction, force, velocity and directness. The subjects were asked to give the compatibility of each movement with each of twelve emotion categories. The results showed which movement features predicted particular ratings. Emotion categories differed as to the amount, type, and weights of predicting movement features. Three factors were extracted from the original ratings and interpreted as Rejection-Acceptance, Withdrawal-Approach, and Preparation-Defeatedness. Moreover, the experiment results showed that features like force, velocity and spatial orientation provide a tangible description of movement and can be used to discriminate one movement from the other. Wallbott [78] also tried to demonstrate that body movements and postures to some degree are specific for certain emotions. They analyzed 224 video takes, in which actors and actresses portrayed the emotions of elated joy, happiness, sadness, despair, fear, terror, cold anger, hot anger, disgust, contempt, shame, guilt, pride, and boredom. For the analysis of body movements and postures, they used coding schemata. Based on their results, some emotion-specific movement and posture characteristics seem to exist, but that for body movements differences between emotions can be partly explained by the dimension of activation. Alternatively, Shaarani and Romano [79] tried to relate the parameters for movements of the whole body to emotion, at least for the six basic Ekman's emotions. Their aim was to create believable virtual humans that are able to express emotions in a manner that is recognized by human spectators. In their study, they used 3-D computer animated virtual human that expressed body movements of certain emotions and asked human subjects to judge the quality of the expression of emotion.

2.5 Facial Expression of Emotion

THE question of how to best characterize perception of facial expressions has clearly become an important concern for many researchers in affective computing. Ironically somehow, this growing interest is coming at a time when the established knowledge on human facial affect is being strongly challenged in the basic research literature. In particular, recent studies have thrown suspicion on a large body of long-accepted data, even on studies previously presented by the same people.

In the past, two main studies regarding facial expression perception have appeared in the literature. The first study is the classic research by psychologist Paul Ekman and colleagues [40, 38, 37, 35, 32, 33, 26] in the early 1960s, which resulted in the identification of a small number of so-called 'basic' emotions: anger, disgust, fear, happiness, sadness and surprise (contempt was added only recently). In Ekman's theory, the basic emotions were considered to be the building blocks of more complex feeling states [26]. In newer studies, however, Eckman is sceptical about the possibility of two basic emotions occurring simultaneously [32, 33]. Following these studies, Ekman and Friesen [29] developed the, so-called, 'facial action coding system (FACS)', which quantifies facial movement in terms of component muscle actions. Recently automated, the FACS remains one of the most comprehensive and commonly accepted methods for measuring emotion from the visual observation of faces.

The second study by psychologist James Russell and colleagues [44, 80, 81, 82, 83, 84, 85, 86, 87, 88] challenges strongly the classic data, largely on methodological grounds. Russell argues that emotion in general (and facial expression of emotion in particular) can be best characterized in terms of a multidimensional affect space, rather than in terms of discrete emotion categories. More specifically, Russell claims that two dimensions, namely 'pleasure' and 'arousal', are sufficient to characterize facial affect space. The multidimensional affect space of James Russell is depicted in Figure 2.5.

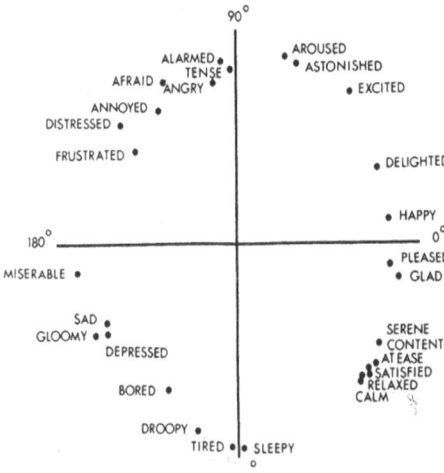

Figure 2.5: The multidimensional affect space of James Russell [82, 85, 86, 87, 84, 88]

Despite the fact that divergent studies have appeared in the literature, most scientists agree that:

- Humans experience emotions in subjective ways.

- The 'basic emotions' deal with fundamental life tasks.

- The 'basic emotions' mostly occur during interpersonal relationships, but this does not exclude the possibility of their occurring in the absence of others.

- Facial expressions are important in revealing emotions and informing other people about a person's emotional state. Indeed, studies have shown that people with congenital (Mobius Syndrome) or other (e.g. from a stroke) facial paralysis report great difficulty in maintaining and developing interpersonal relationships.

- Each time an emotion occurs, a signal will not necessarily be present. Emotions may occur without any evident signal, because humans are, to a very large extent, capable of suppressing such signals. Also, a threshold may need to be exceeded to bring about an expressive signal and this threshold may vary across individuals.

- Usually, emotions are influenced by two factors, namely social learning and evolution. Thus, similarities across different cultures arise in the way emotions are expressed because of past evolution of the human species, but differences also arise which are due to culture and social learning.

- Facial expressions are emotional signals that result into movements of facial skin and connective tissue caused by the contraction of one or more of the forty four bilaterally symmetrical facial muscles. These striated [3] muscles fall into two groups:

    - four of these muscles, innervated by the trigeminal (5th cranial) nerve, are attached to and move skeletal structures (e.g., the jaw) in mastication

    - forty of these muscles, innervated by the facial (7th cranial) nerve, are attached to bone, facial skin, or fascia and do not operate directly by moving skeletal structures but rather arrange facial features in meaningful configurations.

---

[3]Striated muscle is a form of fibers that are combined into parallel fibers. More specifically, it can refer to:

- Skeletal muscle

- Cardiac muscle (cardiac referring to the heart).

In practice, the term 'striated muscle' is sometimes used to refer exclusively to skeletal muscle when distinguishing it from smooth muscle. However, different medical dictionaries report different usages of the terms. Cardiac muscle is a different type of muscle, but has almost the same structure as skeletal muscle.

Ioanna-Ourania Stathopoulou and George A. Tsihrintzis

2.5.1 Previous Attempts to Facial Emotion Quantification and Classification

In the recent years, research work has been done that attempted at quantifying facial emotion and automating facial expression classification. Neurologists have made progress in demonstrating that emotion is one or the most important factor in a person's decision making process. Recent studies have shown that automated emotion recognition can play an important role in the development of more effective and friendlier methods in multimedia interactive services and human-computer interaction systems, because how people feel may play an important role on their cognitive processes as well [89]. Picard points out that one of the major challenges in affective computers is to try to improve the accuracy of recognising people's emotions [90].

Ekman and Friesen first defined a set of universal rules to 'manage the appearance of particular emotions in particular situations' [32, 33, 30, 29, 26]. Unrestrained expressions of anger or grief are strongly discouraged in most cultures and may be replaced by an attempted smile rather than a neutral expression; detecting those emotions depends on recognizing signs other than the universally recognized archetypal expressions. D. Goren et al. made an attempt to measure emotion intensity based on a metric of deviation from a neutral face [91]. Reeves and Nass [92], [93] have shown that people's interactions with computers, TV and similar machines/media are fundamentally social and natural, just like interactions in real life. Studies have also shown that the facial expression recognition process is configural and entails an obligatory computation of gaze direction [94]. Picard, in her work in the area of affective computing, states that 'emotions play an essential role in rational decision-making, perception, learning, and a variety of other cognitive functions' [95], [90]. De Silva et al. performed an empirical study and reported results on human subjects' ability to recognize emotions [96]. They showed video clips of facial expressions to human subjects, while they had them listen to corresponding synchronised emotional speech clips in languages unfamiliar to them, namely spanish and sinhala. Then, they compared human recognition results in three tests: video only, audio only, and combined audio and video. Finally, M. Pantic et al. [97] performed a survey of past work in solving emotion recognition problems by computer and provided a set of recommendations for developing the first part of an intelligent multimodal human-computer interaction interface.

2.5.2 External Factors in Facial Emotion Perception

Social factors impact the perception of emotional expression. Based on studies [98, 99], the person's gender affects the way he/she are considered to express. Generally, men's and women's emotion displays differ in many ways. Firstly, women report smiling more and are considered by others to smile more than men, and second, men's displays of anger have been reported to be both more pervasive and are generally more acceptable [100, 101]. These stereotypic expectations are present even to children of 5-years-old who tend to consider a crying baby as 'mad' when the baby is a boy but not when it is a girl [102]. The difference on how people of different gender express affects also the interpersonal relationships and especially the marriage life, as husbands tend to interpret the simple absence of smiling during a marital dispute as a sign of hostility on the part of their wives, whereas wives tend to interpret the simple absence of hostility displays by their husbands in such disputes as a sign of love [103]. There also a difference in the perception of the expression's intense depending on the person's gender. Women expression of happiness are perceived as more intense and their expressions of anger and disgust as less intense than expressions of the same physical intensity shown by men [98].

Another important factor in emotion perception is the orientation and the posture of the head. Mignault and Chaudhuri [104] conducted two experiments showing 3-D models of faces to 64 participants. The results confirmed that when a head is bowed, the face is perceived as submissive, sad, displaying inferiority emotions (i.e., shame, embarrassment, guilt, humiliation, and respect). In contrary a raised head is perceived as more dominant and displaying greater superiority emotions (i.e., contempt and pride). Regarding the head orientation, based on our studies (Chapter 5), people tend to bend their head left or right when their are feeling bored or sleepy.

2.5.3   Face and Facial Expressions: Their Role

Face and facial expressions play an important role in interpersonal relationships. As people interact with each other, they express their emotions through their face and, at the same time, they try to understand the other person's emotions which are depicted in his/her facial expression. That is why facial expression represents an essential element in social interactions. The origin of human sociality and ultimately, human culture is one of the most important questions in the research field of human evolution. Many anthropologists focus their research in social intelligence on the evolution of the human brain and consciousness and refer to millions of years of evolution, in order to explain the human behaviour [105, 106, 107]. Schmidt and Cohn [108] disagree and consider that social intelligence is not reflected only in the brain but in every adaptation that allows successful interaction in social groups. They believe that the face is the most visibly social part of the human body, as it is a visible signal of others' social intentions and motivations, and facial expression continues to be a critical variable in social interaction. Regarding, emotion interpretation, the task is facilitated by the assumption that others' minds are like our own. The inference of emotion and mental state is known as the theory of mind [59].

Another important role of the face in interpersonal relationships, lies in the fact that personality characteristics are depicted through the facial characteristics. Usually, people tend to acquire some first impressions regarding someone from his/her face. This process is called '*physiognomy*' which derives from the Greek word '*φυσιο-γνωμία*'. '*Φυσιογνωμία (physiognomy)*' is composed by two Greek words: (1) '*φύση (physis)*', which means 'nature', and (2) '*γνώμη (gnomon)*', which means 'judge' or 'interpreter'. '*Physiognomy*' is the assessment of a person's character or personality from their outer appearance, especially the face and dates back to ancient Greece. Regarding physiognomy, researches have shown that people agree in their social judgments from faces [109, 110, 111], which indicates that faces provide information that is interpreted consistently across perceivers. Moreover, researches have shown that people acquire some first impressions for a person from his/her face almost instantly without further mental effort [112, 113]. Specifically, Willis and Todorov [113] conducted five experiments which have shown that 100 ms are sufficient for a person to judge a face, whereas 100 to 500 ms, participants' judgments became more negative, response times for judgments decreased, and confidence in judgments increased. When exposure time increased from 500 to 1,000 ms, trait judgments and response times did not change significantly, but confidence increased for some of the judgments; this result suggests that additional time may simply boost confidence in judgments. More recent studies of Todorov et al. [114] showed that only 33 ms exposure to a face is sufficient for people to decide whether the face looks trustworthy or not. Finally, the process of social judging from faces plays an important role in social outcomes like sentencing decisions [115, 116] or electoral success [117].

Regarding personality attribution, facial attractiveness is considered to affect this task. Usually, positive characteristics are more frequently attributed to attractive people, while negative characteristics are more frequently attributed to unattractive people [118, 119]. Regarding the attractiveness of the face, studies by Scheib et al. [120] and Valentine et al. [121] have shown that a face is considered attractive when it is symmetric and close to the average, depending on the person's sex. The preference for symmetry may extend to a preference for symmetry in movement, as shown by Schmidt and Cohn [108]. Moreover, the symmetry of a face plays an important role at signaling: (1) spontaneity in expressions, and (2) health information. Specifically, based on studies by Gazzaniga and Smylie [122] and Rinn [123] more spontaneous facial expressions are under the control of a different neural pathway, and therefore more symmetric. Moreover, based on studies by Rhodes et al. [124] facial averageness and symmetry plays an important role in order for a person to be considered healthy. In their study, they investigated whether the attractive facial traits of averageness and symmetry can signal health, examining two aspects of signalling: whether these traits are perceived as healthy, and whether they provide accurate health information. They conducted two experiments. In the first experiment they morphed images to alter the averageness and symmetry of individual faces. Increases in both symmetry and averageness were found to result in higher perceived health ratings, whereas increased distinctiveness were found to result in lower perceived health ratings. In the second experiment, they examined whether these traits signal real, as well as perceived, health, in a sample of individuals for whom health scores, based on detailed medical records, were available. Perceived health correlated negatively with distinctiveness and asymmetry, like the first experiment. Facial asymmetry was not found to be associated with actual health, in contrast to facial distinctiveness which was associated with poor childhood health in males, and poor current and adolescent health in females, although the last association was only marginally significant. Furthermore, since their experiments included 17-year-olds, a prime age for mate choice, their results can suggest that more subtle deviations may also provide cues to the health of potential mates. A preference for average faces may be the reason because it enhanced reproductive success, either because healthy mates provide better parental care or because they confer genetic benefits on their offspring if disease resistance is heritable, or both. This assumption is further supported by studies by Penton-Voak and Perrett [125] which showed that women prefer more masculine (closer to the male average) faces during the high-fertility phase. In contrast, more feminine faces were preferred during the low-fertility phase.

With respect to the attractiveness of the face, large and widely spaced eyes, light-colored hair, high forehead, small nose, full lips, and wide cheekbones are also though as attractive facial characteristics [126, 109]. Also, adults who have babyish features (i.e., large eyes, small chin, high forehead, and high eyebrows) may usually be considered youthful or/and immature by the others. Paunonen et al. [126] conducted experiments in order to investigate the effects of: (1) eye size and spacing, and (2) eye size and mouth fullness on observer's perceptions and personality understanding. They showed to participants images that had previously modified in order to change the relative size and spacing of the eyes as well as fullness of the lips and asked them to rate the images on four physical traits: attractiveness, babyfacedness, masculinity, and physical strength and on thirteen personality variables: nurturance, extraversion, popularity, dominance, likeability, honesty, empathy, agreeableness, intelligence, ambition, conscientiousness, culture, and neuroticism. Results have shown that personality attribution is not affected by eye spacing and mouth fullness, in contrary to eye size, which affected the ratings ratings of masculinity/femininity, babyfacedness, and attractiveness.

Ioanna-Ourania Stathopoulou and George A. Tsihrintzis

2.6 The Importance of Understanding Emotions

ACcording to psychologists, the fulfilment of emotional needs is essential and necessary to human well-being, as living with unmet emotional needs may cause pain, anxiety, depression, or violence eruptions [90], [127], [89], [128]. Indeed, several of the best known problems that plagued human societies in the twentieth century, such as drug and alcohol abuse, violence and criminality, derive from inability to meet such basic emotional needs. The first step in order for someone to fulfil his/her emotional needs is to be aware of them and recognize them, while the next step is to be able to meet them. Emotional needs are often categorized into two main categories: The first category consists of 'emotional skill needs' and refers to awareness of emotions, both one's own and those of others, and the ability to manage them [129], [130].

The second category is referred to as 'experiential emotional needs' and tends to follow the Webster Dictionary definition of a need: 'a physiological or psychological requirement for the well-being of an organism.' When one or more of these needs go unmet, an individual may suffer pain. In extreme cases, chronic failure to meet these needs can have very severe effects.

Below are indicative lists of the two aforementioned categories of emotional skill and experiential needs. Specifically, emotional skill needs [129], [130], [131], [89] are needs for basic skills and abilities for handling emotions, such as:

- Emotional self-awareness: a need to learn to appraise and express what one is feeling;

- Managing emotions: the need to handle and regulate feelings so that they are appropriate;

- Self-motivation: a need to learn to harness one's emotions in the service of a goal, for example by delaying gratification;

- Affect perception: a need to accurately appraise what others are feeling as they are feeling and expressing it;

- Empathy: a need to learn to appreciate what others are feeling (closely linked in the literature to emotional self-awareness);

- Handling relationships, primarily via managing the emotions of others: This skill is a necessary component of friendship, intimacy, popularity, and leadership.

Experiential emotional needs [132], [133], [134] are mostly inherently social needs and are, therefore, usually met only with the assistance or presence of others. These include needs:

- for attention, which is strong and constant in children and fades to varying degrees in adulthood

- to feel that one's current emotional state is understood by others, particularly during strong emotional response

- to love and feel reciprocity of love;

- to express affection and feel reciprocated affection expressed;

- for reciprocity of sharing personal disclosure information;

- to feel connected to others;

- to belong to a larger group;

- for intimacy;

- to feel that one's emotional responses are acceptable to others;

- to feel accepted by others;

- to feel that emotional experience and responses are 'normal';

- for touch, to be touched;

- for security.

2.7 Meeting Emotional Needs with the Help of Advanced Human-Computer Interaction Techniques

TECHNOLOGICAL advances may help people meet their emotional needs, at least during a human-computer interaction session. Although computers cannot replace interpersonal relations, they can assist humans to fulfil their needs. Such a case may arise, for example, during e-learning, where the teacher is not present, but the encouragement of the student or the reward is needed.

Indeed, computers offer great potential for supporting human emotional needs, because of the abilities of modern computational media. More specifically, interactive media:

Ioanna-Ourania Stathopoulou and George A. Tsihrintzis

- are increasingly portable, smaller, and cheaper; therefore, they are increasingly able to be with their users at all times;

- soon they will be able to sense emotion via a variety of traditional means such as facial expression, tone of voice, and gesture;

- are able to be eternally attentive, particularly valuable for applications with young children;

- are sometimes treated by humans as real people;

- have the potential not only to support educational needs and enable social interaction, but can also help people to partially meet their emotional needs. Some of such opportunities are identified below.

2.7.1 Supporting emotional skill needs

Meeting someone's emotional needs is very important during a human-computer interaction process, especially within the framework of educational technology. This way, the computer program can enable learners to acquire academic skills and knowledge. It is conceivable that similar tools can be designed to address emotional skill needs. Software tutors could be built today for students of any age to learn about emotions; other tools could help build emotional awareness and management skills.

Emotional self-awareness is one of the basic emotional skill needs and a system able to recognize and record a person's needs is basic to modern human-computer interaction techniques. A simple way to build such a system is by prompting the user to record emotions, possibly via selection from a list of pre-specified emotions, at random moments of the day. Work on such a tool is in investigation at the MIT Media Laboratory [90], [128].

Another important task is real-time emotion sensing and recognition. This can be achieved, either by facial expression recognition, speech recognition, or gesture recognition or by combining two or three of these techniques. The realization of this technology may represent a fundamental advancement in human-computer interaction. For example, it may enable the development of an emotion-sensitive 'active listener'. Active listening is a simple, yet powerful skill used extensively by experienced therapists, and involves providing non-judgmental feedback, often about a speaker's emotional expression during conversation. While such a tool would probably rely on still-primitive speech processing capabilities, the potential benefit of such a tool is enormous.

2.7.2 Supporting experiential needs

While it is commonly assumed that experiential needs can only be met with the help of other humans, this assumption is not entirely true. People may satisfy several of these needs via other means, such as pet dogs or cats. In fact, people are able to establish relationships with a wide variety of organisms of various degrees of interactivity. During a human-computer interaction session, the system should be able to provide a bonding with the user and enable him to emotionally express himself. This, as an example, can be seen in recent products featuring computational simulations of pets, which demonstrate that interactive media can stimulate pet-like emotional bonding for both children and adults [90], [128]. Again, this conceptualization does not suggest that machines would substitute for interpersonal or even inter-organism contact, but offers a dramatic expansion in the availability and interactivity of non-human companions.

Speech and gesture recognition and facial expression classification can help machines to meet human emotional needs. It is clear that humans can and do meet many of their experiential emotional needs on a daily basis using speech or facial expressions. Computational media has much to offer today and in the future to assist in their provision, but such products require research and development.

Ioanna-Ourania Stathopoulou and George A. Tsihrintzis

3

Studies and Systems on Emotion Recognition

3.1 Face Databases

THE first step in order to develop a facial analysis system is to acquire an adequate face database. This database can be used for training and testing the system under development. So, it is very important that this database meets the needs and requirements set during development. In this section, we set the requirements of an ideal facial expression database. Based on these requirements, we review the facial expression databases that are currently publically available. This review helps us to decide whether to use any of these databases or to develop our own facial expression database.

3.1.1 Specifying Requirements for an Ideal Facial Expression Database

For use in the development, training, and testing of facial expression classifiers, appropriate extensive facial databases are required. These databases are non-trivial to create, as they need to be sufficiently rich in both facial expression variety and representative samples of each expression. Moreover, the creators of the database need to make sure that the human models form their true facial expressions when posing.

The first thing that a facial expression classification system developer must take into account is the quality of the input media of the databases. The input media of the databases are usually either static images or image sequences (video). Also, depending on when the database was created, the input media is usually in grayscale format (as in earlier databases) or in color. Moreover, an ideal database of facial expressions should address the following issues:

- It is very important that the facial expression database should cover all the possible emotions. In many cases, the subjects in some databases are asked to form any of the Facial Auctions of the Facial Action Coding System (FACS), proposed by Paul Ekman [27]

- Another important factor that it must be taken into consideration, is the human subjects' background. As there are cultural variations in the way in which humans express emotion, an ideal facial expression database should include subjects of any culture. Moreover, as there are changes in the texture of the human skin depending on the age and the gender of the human, the facial expression database should also cover cases of different age and gender.

- The conditions during photo shooting or video acquisition should also be taken into account. In order to build a facial expression classification system that works independent of external factors, a complete facial expression database in needed for training and testing. Specifically, the facial expression database should include face images under different illumination conditions, and poses, as well as cases of faces which are partially occluded by glasses, scarfs, hats or moustache and/or beard.

- The facial expression database should be extensive enough to be used for training and testing the facial expression classification system. In order to fulfill this requirement, an adequate number of input media, static images or video, should be included in this database.

- As, in some cases, the aim is to build a user dependent facial expression classification system, there is a need of a facial expression database where the subjects are repeatedly forming the same facial expressions and repeated shots are taken.

- Finally, an ideal facial expression image database should include all the expressions formed by each subject.

The aforementioned requirements for an ideal facial expression database are summarized in the following Table 3.1.

3.1.2 Previous Facial Expression Databases

In the recent years, only a relatively small number of relevant face databases have been presented in the literature, including: (1) The AR Face Database [135], which

Table 3.1: Requirements for an ideal facial expression database

	Input media quality
1	Input media should be either images or image sequences (video)
2	Input media quality (grayscale or color)
	Emotion Categorization
3	Number of emotion' classes depicted by subjects
4	The subjects depict the FACS
5	Emotion' classes names
	Human Subjects' Categorization
6	Number of subjects
7	Subjects of any age?
8	Subjects of any gender?
9	Subjects of any culture?
	Conditions during photo shooting
10	The number of sessions that the photo shooting was repeated for each subject
11	Photo shooting in various illuminations
12	Photo shooting of subjects in different poses
13	Photo shooting in cases of partial occlusion of faces
14	Total number of data
15	Complete emotion sequences for all the subjects?

contains over 4,000 front-view color images of 126 persons' faces, forming different facial expressions under various illumination conditions and occlusion (e.g., wearing sun glasses and/or a scarf). The main disadvantage of this database is its limitation to containing only four facial expressions, namely 'neutral', 'smile', 'anger', and 'scream'. (2) The Japanese Female Facial Expression (JAFFE) Database [136, 137], which contains 213 images of the neutral and 6 additional basic facial expressions, as formed by 10 Japanese female models. (3) The Yale Face Database [138], which contains 165 gray-scale GIF-formatted images of 15 individuals. These correspond to 11 images per subject of different facial expression or configuration, namely, center-light, with glasses, happy, left-light, without glasses, normal, right-light, sad, sleepy, surprised, and wink. (4) The Cohn-Kanade AU-Coded Facial Expression Database [139], which includes approximately 2000 image sequences from over 200 subjects and is based on the Facial Action Coding System (FACS) first proposed by Paul Ekman [27]. (5) The MMI Facial Expression Database [140], which includes more than 1500 samples of both static images and image sequences of faces in front and side view, displaying various expressions of emotion and single and multiple facial muscle activation.

The aforementioned databases are reviewed in Table 3.2, based on the requirements set on Table 3.1.

Ioanna-Ourania Stathopoulou and George A. Tsihrintzis

Table 3.2: Review of the facial expression databases

Reference	1	2	3	4	5	6	7	8	9	10	11	12	13	14	15
AR Face Database [135]	Img	C	3	x	'neu', 'joy', 'ang', 'scr'	126	x	x	x	2	✓	x	✓	4.000	✓
JAFFE Database [136, 137]	Img	C	7	x	b.em., 'neu'	10	x	x	x	1	x	x	x	213	✓
Yale Face Database [138]	Img	G	6	x	'neu', 'joy', 'sad', 'sle', 'sur', 'wink'	15	x	x	x	1	✓	x	✓	165	✓
Cohn-Kanade Database [139]	Vid, Img	C	6	✓	b.em., 'neu'	182	✓	✓	✓	1	x	≈	x	2.105	x
MMI Database [140]	Vid, Img	C	6	✓	b.em., 'neu'	19	✓	✓	✓	1	≈	≈	✓	2894*	≈

*1395 AUs and 197 emotions

Legend:

✓ : 'Yes'	**Img** : Static Image	**C** : Color Images
x : 'No'	**Vid** : Image sequences (Video)	**G** : Grayscale Images
≈ : 'Partially available'		

Emotions/Expressions : 'neu':'neutral', 'ang':'anger', 'scr':'scream', 'sle':'sleep', 'sur':'surprise'
b.em. : 6 Basic Emotions ⇒ anger', 'disgust', 'fear', 'happiness', 'sadness' and 'surprise'

3.1.3 Section Summary - Results

Our study revealed the following problems:

- Many of the aforementioned databases do *not* contain an adequate number of human subjects. Specifically, most databases have been acquired by photo shooting of fewer than 20 subjects, and only two of them, namely the AR Face Database [135] and the Cohn-Kanade Database [139], contain more than 100 subjects. The use of such databases will constrain our system performance, as the facial expression recognition task would be person-dependent and, thus, will not be able to generalize for new persons.

- On the other hand, the two databases that contain more than 100 subjects, and, thus, could lead to the development of a more user independent system, have some problems, specifically: (1) the AR Face Database [135] is constrained to only four emotions/expressions, namely 'neutral', 'happiness', 'anger', and 'scream', (2) the Cohn-Kanade Database [139] is based on Facial Action Units

Ioanna-Ourania Stathopoulou and George A. Tsihrintzis

and not on emotion classes, which is the aim of our system. Moreover, although we could construct some emotion classes using the Cohn-Kanade Database [139], it is not complete in terns of each subject depicting all the sequence of emotions.

- Additionally, most of these databases do *not* cover the range of face expressions recognized by our system and, therefore, were found insufficient for its development.

Although we used some of these databases (the AR Face Database [135] and the Cohn-Kanade Database [139]) for the early development and testing of our system, eventually we were forced to create our own face image database which is described in the following Chapter 4.

3.2 Face Detection

3.2.1 Specifying Requirements for an Ideal Face Detection System

FACE detection is one of the visual tasks which humans can do effortlessly. However, in computer vision terms, this task is not trivial to perform. A general statement of the problem can be defined as follows: Given a still or video image, detect and localize an unknown number (if any) of faces. The solution to the problem involves segmentation, extraction, and verification of faces and possibly facial features from an uncontrolled background. As a visual front-end processor, a face detection system should also be able to achieve the task regardless of illumination, orientation, and camera distance.

When building a face detection system, the first thing to be taken into consideration is the type of the input media that will be used to perform the face detection. The input media of the databases are usually either static images or image sequences (videos). Also, another important factor is the format of the input media. Some systems perform face detection based on the skin color, so the input media should be in color format, but, in other cases, the input media can be in grayscale format. Also, an ideal face detection system should adhere the following rules:

- It is very important that the face detection system would be able to perform well regardless of the conditions during image or video acquisition. Specifically, some of the conditions that should be taken into account are the following:

  - Changes in illumination

  - De-focus and noise problems

Ioanna-Ourania Stathopoulou and George A. Tsihrintzis

- Partially occluded faces

- Rotated faces

- Faces in side view

- Complex background

- Faces of different sizes and portions of image plane

- Subjects form different facial expressions

- Subjects of any culture and, especially, any color of the face

• As face detection is usually the first processing step of a fully automated facial analysis system, another important factor that should be taken into account is the ability to perform in real time.

The aforementioned requirements for an ideal face detection system can be summarized in the following Table 3.3.

Table 3.3: Requirements for an ideal face detection system

	Input media quality
1	Input media should be either images or image sequences (video)
2	Input media quality (grayscale or color)
	Conditions during photo shooting
3	Perform well regardless of changes in illumination
4	Perform well regardless of de-focus and noise problems
5	Perform well in cases of partially occluded faces
6	Perform well in cases of different poses: rotated faces
7	Perform well in cases of different poses: faces in side view
8	Perform well in cases of complex backgrounds
9	Perform well in different face sizes
10	Perform well for different facial expressions
11	Perform well regardless of the subject's culture
12	Real time face detection
13	Success rate (%)
14	False rate (%)

3.2.2 Previous Works on Face Detection

The goal of face detection is to determine whether or not there are any faces in an image and, if so, return the location and extent of each face. To address this problem, a number of works have appeared in the literature (e.g. [141, 142, 143, 144, 145, 146, 147, 148, 149, 150, 151, 152, 153, 154, 155, 156, 157, 158, 159, 160, 161, 162, 163]). As discussed above, the key issue and difficulty in face detection is to account for the wide range of facial pattern variations in images.

There are four main approaches to address this problem: (1) knowledge-based methods, (2) feature - or image - invariant methods, (3) template matching methods and, (4) appearance-based methods. Knowledge-based methods [142, 155], encode human knowledge of what constitutes a typical face. Usually, rules capture relationships between facial features. On the other hand, approaches based on feature - or image - invariants, aim at finding structural features that exist even when pose, viewpoint and lighting conditions vary, and then use them to detect faces. Template matching methods can be divided in two subcategories which use: (1) correlation templates and, (2) deformable templates. In approaches where correlation templates are used, we compute a difference measurement between one or more fixed target patterns and candidate image locations and the output is thresholded for matches. Deformable templates are similar in principle to correlation templates, except that the latter are more rigid. To detect faces, in this approach we try to find mathematical and geometrical patterns that depict particular regions of the face and we fit the template to different parts of the images and threshold the output for matches. Finally, approaches based on appearance can be considered the reverse of template matching methods. In this case, the models (or templates) are learnt from a set of training images which should capture the representative variability of facial appearance. These learnt models are then used for detection.

In the past years, several systems have been developed that implement the previous approaches. The system proposed by Colmenarez et al. [141] is template-based; they try to encode face images in a particular prototype. Yang et al. [142] and Lee et al. [143] proposed systems that are knowledge-based; they encode human knowledge of what constitutes a face. Leung et al. [144], applied a local feature detector to find faces in an image. Many systems (Rowley et al [145],[146],Yang et al [147], Sung and Poggio [150] and Juell et al [148]), use artificial neural networks to find faces. Lin et al. [149], proposed a system that searches for potential face regions, based on the triangle that form the eyes and the mouth. Sung et al. [150] used a two distance metrics that measure the distance between the input image and the cluster of faces and non-faces. Lin Lin Huang et al. [151] designed three detection experts which employ different feature representation schemes of local image and then use a polynomial neural network to determine whether or not there is a face in an image. Castrillon et

Ioanna-Ourania Stathopoulou and George A. Tsihrintzis

al. [152], developed a system to real time detect faces in video sequences, by means of cue combination. S. Phimoltares et al. [153] developed a two-stage system, which, first, detected the faces from an original image by using Canny edge detection and their proposed average face templates, and, next, use a neural visual model (NVM) to recognize all possibilities of facial feature positions. Kadoury and Levine [154] proposed a novel technique which used locally linear embedding (LLE) to determine a locally linear fit so that each data point can be represented by a linear combination of its closest neighbors and used this representation to train Support Vector Machines to detect faces. A fairly detailed survey on the methods used for face detection is given on [164],[165]. Liu [159] developed a Bayesian discriminating feature method for face detection, in which the likelihood density was estimated by considering both the projection weights and the residual components in the eigenspace. Papageorgiou et al. [156] proposed an over-complete wavelet model to present an object class for object detection. Finally, Viola and Jones [157] presented a real-time front-view face detection system featuring a cascade of boosting classifiers based on an over-complete set of Haar-like features. Li et al. [161] modified the monotonic assumption of the Adaboost algorithm proposed by Viola and Jones in [157] to develop the so-called Floatboost algorithm for the training of face and nonface classifiers. By implementing these classifiers using a coarseto- fine and simple-to-complex pyramidal structure, the authors successfully developed a computationally-efficient multi-view multi-face detection system. However, the proposed classifiers used in such boosted cascades operate independently of one another and therefore discard useful information between layers, resulting in convergence problems during the training process

All the studies on face detection are reviewed in Tables 3.4, 3.5 and 3.6 based on the requirements set on Table 3.3.

3.2.3   Section Summary - Results

In the recent years, some interesting studies on face detection have appeared in the literature with good success rates. Despite that fact, the majority of the studies on face detection have some major drawbacks: (1) they have not been tested in order to cover cases of de-focus and noise problems. (2) They usually have a size limit on the detected face, which must usually be bigger than 30-by-30 pixels. (3) They cannot detect many faces (more than 3 faces) in complex backgrounds. (4) They cannot all address the problem of partial occlusion of mouth or wearing sunglasses. (5) Although some of the approaches presented above, try to deal with multi-view face images, it is not easy to detect faces in side view. Although there are some researches that can solve two or three of these problems, there is still no system that can solve all of them. Moreover, some of them can only detect faces in color images, as the use skin extraction techniques to achieve this task. Finally, many of the aforementioned methods cannot perform in real time.

Table 3.4: Review of the face detection approaches - 1* (Before 2000)

Reference	1	2	3	4	5	6	7	8	9	10	11	12	13	14
Yang [142]	Img	G	-	-	-	-	-	✓	48*60-200*280	-	-	60-120sec	83%	n/a
Leung [144]	Img	A	nt	nt	✓	✓	X	✓	n/a	✓	nt	n/a	75%	n/a
Dai [166]	Img	C	nt	nt	✓	✓	-	✓	16*20, 20*26	✓	x	n/a	100%	0,34%
Tankus [167]	Img	n/a	✓	nt	nt	nt	nt	nt	≥64*96	nt	nt	x	92,77%	n/a
Colmenarez [141]	Img	G	✓	-	-	✓	x	✓	≥11*11	-	✓	x	86,8%-98%	0,2%-2,2 %
Kotropoulos [155]	Vid	n/a	✓	-	-	-	-	-	n/a	-	-	n/a	86,5%	n/a
Rowley [145, 146]	Img	G	✓	-	-	✓	x	✓	≥20*20	-	-	n/a	86%	n/a
Sung [150]	Img	G	✓	✓	nt	✓	x	✓	n/a	nt	nt	n/a	88,1%	n/a
Saber [168]	Img	C	nt	nt	nt	✓	nt	nt	x	x	nt	✓	n/a	n/a
Jeng [169]	Img	n/a	nt	nt	nt	✓	nt	✓	≥80*80	nt	nt	av.	86%	n/a
Wang [170]	Img	C	nt	nt	nt	x	nt	x	≥128*128	nt	nt	av.	94%	n/a
Wei [171]	Img	C	nt	nt	nt	✓	nt	✓	n/a	nt	nt	n/a	70%-80%	n/a
Miao [169]	Img	G	nt	nt	✓	✓	nt	✓	✓	nt	nt	x	83,8%	3,62%

*The review is made based on what the authors have written in the cited articles
*If not otherwise stated in the paper, the false rate, if possible, is calculated as: (false detections):(total faces tested) (%)

✓ : 'Yes'	nt : Not tested	Img : Static Image
x : 'No'	n/a or '-' : Not available	Vid : Video
		av. : Not tested, but could be available

C : Color Images
G : Grayscale Images
A : Images of any color

3.3 Facial Expression Classification System

3.3.1 Specifying Requirements for our Facial Expression Classification System

In the first step before developing a facial expression classification system, we should specify the requirements and decide on its functionality. A very interesting and important study regarding this issue was made by Pantic and Rothkrantz [6]. In this section we discuss corresponding requirements and further enhance them with our own observations.

Firstly, there are some questions/statements we need to set:

1. Facial expression understanding was firstly used by humans during interpersonal relationships. So, the first known system which is considered to have the best performance is the human. Some questions derive from this fact:

Ioanna-Ourania Stathopoulou and George A. Tsihrintzis

Table 3.5: Review of the face detection approaches - 2* (2000-2004)

Reference	1	2	3	4	5	6	7	8	9	10	11	12	13	14
Han [172]	Img	G	✓	nt	nt	✓	nt	✓	≥50*50	✓	nt	18sec	94%	n/a
Schneiderman [160]	Img	G	✓	nt	nt	✓	✓	✓	n/a	✓	✓	5sec	92,3%	n/a
Wang [173]	Img	G	✓	nt	nt	✓	nt	✓	n/a	nt	nt	n/a	84,96%	3,47%
Chen [174]	Img	G	✓	nt	nt	✓	nt	✓	n/a	✓	nt	n/a	88,2%	1,58%
Viola [157, 158]	Img	G	✓	nt	nt	✓	✓	✓	≥24*24	✓	✓	0,067sec	81,1%-93,7%	1,97% -32,9%
Yao [175]	Img	C	✓	nt	nt	nt	nt	✓	n/a	✓	nt	n/a	95,4%	n/a
Wang [176]	Img	C	x	nt	nt	✓	nt	✓	≥30*20	nt	✓	n/a	91,1%	6,67%
Ayinde [177]	Img	A	nt	✓	nt	nt	nt	✓	n/a	nt	nt	x	85,7%	n/a
Zhou [178]	Img	A	nt	nt	nt	✓	nt	✓	≥80*80	nt	nt	324sec	80%	7%
Hock Koh [179]	Any	C	✓	nt	nt	✓	nt	nt	≥16*16	nt	nt	n/a	95,8%	n/a
Liu [159]	Img	G	✓	✓	✓	✓	x	✓	n/a	✓	nt	1sec	97,4%	0,44%
Hsieh [180]	Img	C	✓	nt	✓	nt	nt	✓	≥30*30	nt	nt	6,16sec	80,73%	n/a
Huang [181]	Img	A	✓	nt	nt	nt	nt	✓	≥18*18	✓	✓	n/a	91,45%	n/a
Wu [182]	Img	G	✓	nt	x	✓	nt	✓	n/a	✓	nt	✓	95,85%	n/a
Wong [183, 184]	Img	C	✓	nt	✓	✓	nt	✓	≥30*30	nt	nt	n/a	91,10%	9,94%

*The review is made based on what the authors have written in the cited articles
*If not otherwise stated in the paper, the false rate, if possible, is calculated as: (false detections):(total faces tested) (%)

✓ : 'Yes'	**nt** : Not tested	**Img** : Static Image	**C** : Color Images
x : 'No'	**n/a or '-'** : Not available	**Vid** : Video	**G** : Grayscale Images
		Any : Image or Video	**A** : Images of any color

(a) Has the human system truly the best performance?

(b) In which cases, are people prone to errors when classifying an expression?

(c) Should we try to understand the human system and mimic it through our application?

(d) Can we use the success rates of this system as a metric for our system?

2. It is necessary that our system is fully automated. In order to achieve this, all of the stages of the facial expression analysis are to be performed automatically, namely, face detection or localization, facial expression information extraction (feature extraction or feature model extraction), and facial expression classification. Based on this assumptions, the first step of a facial expression classification system is to detect the face in a scene. This process in the case of static images, is referred to as *face localization*. Whereas, in the case of facial image sequences, this process is referred to as *face tracking*. The next step is to extract from the face the necessary information that will help in the following

Ioanna-Ourania Stathopoulou and George A. Tsihrintzis

Table 3.6: Review of the face detection approaches - 3* (2005 to present)

Reference	1	2	3	4	5	6	7	8	9	10	11	12	13	14
Bae [185]	Img	C	✓	nt	nt	✓	nt	nt	40*40-80*80	nt	nt	✓	98%	n/a
Kubleck [186]	Vid	C	nt	nt	nt	nt	nt	nt	-	nt	nt	✓	94,3%	3,6%
Shih [187]	Img	A	nt	nt	nt	✓	nt	✓	≥16*16	nt	nt	10,5sec	98,2%	0,7%
Kondo [188]	Img	A	✓	nt	nt	nt	nt	nt	≥40*48	nt	nt	n/a	97,78%	n/a
Wang [189]	Vid	C	nt	nt	nt	✓	✓	✓	-	nt	nt	200msec	84,5%	n/a
Lin [190]	Img	C	✓	nt	✓	✓	✓	nt	n/a	✓	✓	✓	98,2%	n/a
Phimoltares [153]	Img	A	✓	✓	✓	✓	nt	✓	≥24*24	✓	nt	20sec	97,5%	10,25%
Meynet [191]	Vid	A	✓	nt	✓	✓	nt	✓	n/a	nt	nt	n/a	90,93%	13,75%
Kadoury [154]	Img	G	✓	nt	✓	✓	nt	✓	n/a	✓	nt	n/a	97%	0,0004%
Castrillon [152]	Video	Colorn/a	nt	n/a	✓	✓	✓	✓		✓	nt	✓	99,9%	8,07%
Juang [192]	Image	Color✓	nt	✓	✓	nt	✓	n/a		✓	nt	n/a	95,55%	15,26%

*The review is made based on what the authors have written in the cited articles
*If not otherwise stated in the paper, the false rate, if possible, is calculated as: (false detections):(total faces tested) (%)

✓ : 'Yes'	nt : Not tested	Img : Static Image	C : Color Images
x : 'No'	n/a or '-' : Not available	Vid : Video	G : Grayscale Images
		Any : Image or Video	A : Images of any color

face recognition step. Regarding this information, it can be divided in the following two categories: (1) *facial features* and (2) *face model features*. The facial features are the prominent features of the face, such as eyebrows, eyes, nose, mouth, and chin. The face model features are the features used to represent (model) the face. The face can be represented in various ways, e.g., as a whole unit (holistic representation), as a set of features (analytic representation) or as a combination of these (hybrid approach). Depending on the input image and the face model representation, different mechanisms for automatic extraction of facial expression information are applied. The final step is facial expression classification. In this step, the input image is classified in one of the classes of the expressions that have been defined before building the system.

3. Based on the assumptions made in Chapter 2, besides the 'basic emotions' which, according to the theory of evolution and the fact that are universally common regardless culture of the subject, there are also cultural variations in the way in which humans express emotion. An ideal system should take this into account.

4. Also, the system should work regardless of external factors when acquiring a face image or a sequence of face images. This means, that the system should

perform robustly despite changes in lightning conditions and distractions such as glasses, changes in hair style, and facial hair like moustache, beard and eyebrows that have grown together.

5. Another important factor is setting the classes of emotion that the system is ideally expected to recognize. In our case, we will use our system for advanced human computer interaction techniques, so the corresponding set of emotions should result from those emotions that are present during a typical human computer session. Until now, the majority of the facial expression classification systems, deal with one of the following sets:

   (a) the six 'basic emotions'

   (b) some other set of emotions, usually a subset of the six 'basic emotions'

   (c) FACS: there are no distinctive classes emotion but, rather, facial action movements

Regarding the last statement, the classes of emotion that our system should recognize depends highly from its use [6]. Specifically, if the system is to be used for behavioral science research purposes it should perform facial expression recognition based on the FACS encoding system. In this case, the system should accomplish multiple quantified expression classification in terms of 44 AUs (Auction Units) defined in FACS (Facial Action Coding System) [193, 194]. Alternatively, if the system is to be used for advanced multimodal human-computer interaction techniques, the system should be able to understand the shown facial expressions and map them to the respective emotion. In this case, the system may classify the six 'basic emotions' or some other set of emotions. Another approach would be the system to be able to adapt the classification mechanism according to the user's subjective interpretation of expressions, e.g., as suggested in [195], because, as stated in the previous chapter, there use also a subjective way on how someone expresses an emotion. Also, it must be taken into account that in some cases not every facial expression can be classified to only one emotion class [27].

The requirements for an ideal facial expression classification system were first set by Pantic and Rothkrantz [6], based on which the following Table 3.7 has resulted.

3.3.2   Facial Expression Classification Approaches

Previous attempts to address problems of facial expression classification in images fall within one of two main directions in the literature:(1) methods that use image sequences (video) ([196, 197, 198, 198, 199]) and (2) methods that use static images.

Table 3.7: Requirements for an ideal facial expression classification system (Adapted from [6])

1	Automatic facial image acquisition
2	Subjects of any age, ethnicity and outlook
3	Deals with variation in lightning
4	Deals with partially occluded faces
5	No special markers / make-up required
6	Deals with rigid head motions
7	Automatic face detection
8	Automatic facial expression data extraction
9	Deals with inaccurate facial expression data
10	Automatic facial expression classification
11	Distinguishes all possible expressions
12	Deals with unilateral facial changes
13	Obeys anatomical rules
14	Distinguishes all 44 facial actions (FACS)
15	Quantifies facial action codes
16	# interpretation categories unlimited
17	Features adaptive learning facility
18	Assigns quantified interpretation labels
19	Assign multiple interpretation labels
20	Features real-time processing

Approaches that use image sequence often apply optical flow analysis to the image sequence and rely on pattern recognition tools to recognize optical flow patterns associated with particular facial expression. This approach requires acquisition of multiple frames of images to recognize expressions and, thus, has limitations in real-time performance and robustness. Facial expression recognition using still images can be divided in two main categories: (1) methods based on face features ([200, 201, 30, 202, 203, 194]), and (2) methods that utilize image-based representations of the face ([204, 205, 206, 207]). Methods that use facial features for facial expression recognition have fairly fast performance, but the challenge in this approach is to develop a feature extraction method that works well regardless of variations in human subjects and environmental conditions. Methods that utilize image-based representation have as an input the entire facial image which is preprocessed in various ways (e.g. Gabor Filters) or is given to a classifier that recognizes the facial expression. The aforementioned methods usually work well in generalizing for other face images, not in the database, but it is fairly difficult to train such classifier. Finally, with the advances in technology, there are some new methods based on thermal imagery (e.g. [208]), but, in this cases,

Ioanna-Ourania Stathopoulou and George A. Tsihrintzis

there is a need for a more sophisticated hardware, which makes it difficult to use in everyday human-computer interaction.

Another fundamental issue about facial expression classification is to define a set of expression categories we are interested in. A related issue is to devise mechanisms of categorization. Facial expressions can be classified in various ways: (1) Methods that try to classify the image face in discrete facial emotions (e.g. [209, 210, 211]) and, (2) Methods that try to classify the image in terms of facial actions that cause an expression (e.g. [212, 213, 207, 214]). The majority of these methods use the Facial Action Coding System (FACS) [28]. An extended survey about all the aforementioned methods can be found in [6].

Early Years of Facial Expression Recognition

In the early years of facial expression classification, which can be identified as the period between 1990 and 1995, three main approaches can be identified and summarized as follows: Cottrell et al. [215], Rahardja et al [216] and Matsuno et al. [217] use holistic spatial analysis to classify the expression. Whereas, Mase et al. [218], Moses et al. [219], Rosenblum et al. [220] and Yacoob et al. [221] use techniques based on spatio-temporal analysis and Kearney et al. [195], Kobayashi et al. [222], Ushida et al. [223] and Vanger et al. [224] use analytic spatial analysis.

The resulting evaluation of the aforementioned systems has already been done by Pantic and Rothkrantz [6] and is shown in Table 3.8.

Table 3.8: Review of the facial expression approaches (Early Years) (Adapted from [6])

Reference	1	2	3	4	5	6	7	8	9	10	11	12	13	14	16	17	18	19	20
Input media: Static images																			
Cottrell [215]	X	✓	X	X	✓	-	X	-	-	✓	X	✓	-	x	8	X	X	X	X
Kearney [195]	X	✓	X	X	✓	-	X	X	-	✓	X	✓	✓	36	n	✓	X	✓	X
Kobayashi [222]	X	✓	X	X	✓	-	X	X	-	✓	X	✓	✓	x	6	X	✓	✓	X
Matsuno [217]	X	X	✓	X	✓	-	X	X	-	✓	X	✓	✓	x	4	X	X	X	X
Rahardja [216]	X	-	X	-	-	-	X	-	-	✓	X	-	-	x	6	X	X	X	X
Ushida [223]	X	✓	X	X	✓	-	X	X	-	✓	X	X	✓	x	3	X	X	X	X
Vanger [224]	X	✓	X	X	✓	-	X	X	-	✓	X	✓	✓	x	7	X	X	X	X
Input media: Image Sequences (Video)																			
Mase [218]	X	-	X	X	✓	X	X	✓	X	✓	X	✓	✓	x	4	X	X	X	X
Moses [219]	✓	-	✓	X	✓	✓	✓	✓	✓	✓	X	✓	✓	5	5	X	X	X	X
Rosenblum [220]	X	-	-	X	✓	✓	X	✓	✓	✓	X	✓	✓	x	2	X	X	X	X
Yaccob [221]	-	-	-	X	✓	✓	X	✓	✓	✓	X	✓	✓	x	7	X	✓	X	X

✓ : 'Yes' x : 'No' '-' : Not available

Ioanna-Ourania Stathopoulou and George A. Tsihrintzis

Mid-years of Facial Expression Recognition (1996-2000)

Between 1996 and 2000, related works can be summarized in the following categories:

- In terms of the form of input data: (1) Static images [225, 226, 227, 228, 229, 202, 230, 213, 231, 205] and, (2) Image sequences [232, 201, 233, 234, 235, 236].

- In terms of facial expression information extraction: (1) template-based methods [225, 226, 227, 228, 229, 202, 232, 201, 233, 234, 235, 205, 136] and, (2) feature-based methods [230, 213, 231, 236].

- In terms of the method used for the classification to the respective expression: (1) template-based methods [225, 226, 227, 136, 229, 201, 233, 234, 235], (2) Neural network-based [230, 228, 202, 231, 205] and, (3) Rule-based methods [213, 232]

The aforementioned categorization of the previous studies is summarized in the following Table 3.9.

Table 3.9: Categorization of the approaches based on the techniques and the input media

Input media: Static Images	
Used techniques	
Template-based	*Feature based*
Edwards [225]	Kobayashi and Hara [230]
Hong [226]	Pantic [213]
Huang [227]	Zhao [231]
Padgett [228]	Dailcy [205]
Yoneyama [229]	
Zhang [202]	
Lyons [136]	
Input media: Image Sequences (Video)	
Used techniques	
Template-based	*Feature based*
Black [232]	Cohn [236]
Essa [201]	
Kimura [233]	
Otsuka [234]	
Wang [235]	

Ioanna-Ourania Stathopoulou and George A. Tsihrintzis

Facial Expression Recognition on static images:

Edwards et al. [225] presented a framework for interpreting face images and image sequences using an Active Appearance Model (AAM). The AAM contains a statistical, photo-realistic model of the shape and grey-level appearance of faces. The process in rder to construct the AAM is described in [237]. Shape and grey-level models are used together to describe the overall appearance of each face; collectively they referred to the model parameters as appearance parameters. When a new image is presented to their system, facial features are located automatically using Active Shape Model (ASM) search [238] based on the flexible shape model obtained during training. The resulting automatically located model points are transformed into shape model parameters. Grey-level information at each model point is collected and transformed to local grey-level model parameters. The statistical model of the grey-level appearance, was built by warping each training image, by using a triangulation algorithm, so that its control points match the mean shape. By applying PCA to the grey-level information extracted from the warped images, they obtained a mean normalized grey-level vector. Then the face is deformed to the mean face shape and the grey-level appearance is transformed into the parameters of the shape-free grey-level model. By building the AAM, their goal was to identify the subject regardless of the conditions during photo acquisition (such as pose and facial expression). They first used the AAM as a basis for face recognition and obtained good results for difficult images. For the facial expression recognition task, they used 200 images of six basic emotional expressions and 'neutral' emotion categories to train a linear classifier and other 200 images for testing. The system was tested against the answers of 25 human observers and achieved an accuracy of 74% with respect to the human answers. The method was tested for subjects already in the database and the maximum accuracy was measured based on the accuracy of the human observers. Base on the researchers, there were very few cases in which all the human observers agreed.

Kobayashi and Hara [230] tried to build an animated 3-dimensional face robot for communicative interaction with human beings which would give the impression of a realistic human-like response. So, the face robot could produce human-like facial expressions and recognize human facial expressions using facial image data obtained by a CCD camera mounted inside the left eyeball. The camera gives the brightness distributions of the face and, thus, helps in locating the face and the iris of the subject. They normalized the input image by using an affine transformation so that the distance between these irises became 20 pixels. They used 13 vertical lines and their length was computed empirically based on the distance between the irises. The range of the acquired brightness distributions is normalized to [0,1] and these data were given further to a trained neural network for expression emotional classification. They used a 243-by-50-by-6 layered neural network and achieved the correct recognition rate of 85% for six typical human computer interaction expressions of 15 subjects in 55ms.

Hong et al. [226] made an online facial expression recognition system based on personalized galleries. This system is built on the framework of the PersonSpotter system, which is able to track and detect the face of a person in a live video sequence. By utilizing the recognition method of Elastic Graph Matching, the most similar person is found, whose images are stored in the gallery. Then, the personalized gallery of this person is used to recognize the expression on the probe face. A personalized gallery consists of images of the same person showing different facial expressions. Node weighting and weighted voting in addition to Elastic Graph Matching are applied to identify the expression. The personalized galleries of nine people have been utilized, where each gallery contained 28 images (four images per expression). The personalized gallery of the best matching person is used to make the judgement on the category of the observed expression. The method has been tested on images of 25 subjects. The achieved recognition rate was 89% in the case of the familiar subjects and 73% percent in the case of unknown persons.

Huang et al. [227] introduced an automatic facial expression recognition system which consists of two parts: facial feature extraction and facial expression recognition. They first used a Canny edge detector to obtain a rough estimate of the face location in the image. The face should be without facial hair and glasses, no rigid head motion may be encountered and illumination variations must be linear for the system to work correctly. The system applies the point distribution model and the gray-level model to find the facial features. Then the position variations of certain designated points on the facial feature are described by 10 action parameters (APs). There are two phases in the recognition process: the training phase and the recognition phase. In the training phase, given 90 training image samples of six classes representing six basic emotional expressions, the system classifies the principal components of the APs of all training expressions into six different clusters. In the recognition phase, given a facial image sequence, the system identifies the facial expressions by extracting the 10 APs, analyzes the principal components, and finally calculates the AP profile correlation for a higher recognition rate. The proposed method has been tested on another 90 images shown by the same subjects. The achieved correct recognition ratio was 84.5%. It is not known how the method will behave in the case of unknown subjects.

Lyons et al. [136] proposed a method for automatically classifying facial images based on labeled elastic graph matching, a 2-D Gabor wavelet representation, and linear discriminant analysis. Their method synthesized aspects of two major approaches to facial image processing: Gabor-wavelet labeled elastic graph matching [239] and eigenface or Fisherface algorithms [240] based on statistical representation of face space. Specifically, in their approach, they combined the advantages of the Gabor wavelet representation with the ability to train the system simply and quickly from examples in a manner similar to the Fisherface algorithm. Their algorithm can be divided into two steps: registration of a grid with the face and face classification based on feature values extracted at grid points. The facial grids are registered either automatically, using labeled elastic graph matching or by manually clicking on points of the face. A multiscale, multiorientation Gabor filter is applied and then, the grid is registered with the face. They considered two types of grid: a rectangular grid and a fiducial grid with nodes located at easily identifiable landmarks of the face. The amplitude of the complex valued Gabor transform coefficients are sampled on the grid and combined into a single vector, the labeled graph vector (or LG vector). The ensemble of LG vectors from a training set of images are subjected to principal components analysis (PCA) to reduce the dimensionality of the input space. LG vectors project into the lower dimensional PCA space (LG-PCA vectors). The ensemble of LG-PCA vectors from the training set are then analyzed using linear discriminant analysis (LDA) in order to separate vectors into clusters having different facial attributes. Input vectors in the original LG space may then be analyzed using the same LDA to determine their attributes. Six binary classifiers, one for each of the six fundamental facial expressions (happy, sad, angry, fearful, surprised, disgusted), were trained independently and combined to build a facial expression categorizer. An input image that is not positively classified for any category is classified as 'neutral'. They used 10-fold cross validation of 193 images of different facial expressions displayed by nine Japanese females (Zhang et al. [202]) to train and test the classifier. The generalization rate was 92% for subjects in the database, whereas it was 75% for recognition of expression of a novel subject.

Padgett and Cottrell [228] used three different face images which are fed to an artificial neural network classifier: full face projections of the dataset onto their eigenvectors (eigenfaces); a similar projection constrained to eye and mouth areas (eigenfeatures); and, finally, a projection of the eye and mouth areas onto the eigenvectors obtained from 32-by-32 random image patches from the dataset. They adopted the third approach which achieved better results. The neural network consisted of: (1) a single hidden layer with 10 nodes using as activation function the nonlinear sigmoid function and, (2) the output layer of seven units, each of which corresponds to one emotion category of the six basic emotions and the 'neutral'. They trained using the backpropagation algorithm with images of 11 subjects and tested it on the images of the 12th subject. The system achieved 86% generalization on novel face images (individuals the networks were not trained on).

Pantic and Rothkrantz [213] developed an expert system called Integrated System for Facial Expression Recognition (ISFER), which performs recognition and emotional classification of human facial expression from a still full-face image. The system consisted of two major parts: (1) the ISFER Workbench, which forms a framework for hybrid facial feature detection by applying multiple feature detection techniques in parallel and, (2) its inference engine called HERCULES, which converts low level face geometry into high level facial actions, and then this into highest level weighted emotion labels. The multidetector performs locates the contours of the facial features, from which the model features are extracted. The difference between the currently detected model features and the same features detected in an expressionless face of the same person is computed. They use rules based on the knowledge acquired from FACS, to classify the calculated model deformation into the appropriate 31 AUs-classes. The performance of the system in automatic facial action coding from dual-view images has been tested on a set of 496 dual views (31 expressions of separate facial actions shown twice by eight human experts). The average recognition rate was 92% for the upper face AUs and 86% for the lower face AUs.

Zhang et al. [202] used two types of features extracted from 256-by-256 face images for recognizing facial expressions: (1) geometric positions of a set of 34 facial points on a face and, (2) a set of multi-scale and multi-orientation Gabor wavelet coefficients extracted from the face image at 34 facial points. These two types can be used either independently or jointly. In order to classify the expressions, they built a two-layer perceptron. The recognition performance with different types of features has been compared, which shows that Gabor wavelet coefficients are much more powerful than geometric positions. The finally conclude to a 680-by-7-by-7 neural network, which classifies the six basic emotions and the 'neutral' emotion. The neural network performs a nonlinear reduction of the input dimensionality and makes a statistical decision about the category of the observed expression. Each output unit gives an estimation of the probability of the examined expression belonging to the associated category. The network has been trained using a resilient propagation. The input to the network consists of the geometric position of the 34 facial points and 18 Gabor wavelet coefficients sampled at each point. The neural network' output is a 7-by-1 vector where each output unit gives an estimation of the probability of the examined expression belonging to the associated category. The network has been trained using the 10-fold cross validation algorithm with resilient propagation for 213 images of different expressions displayed by nine Japanese females. has been used to train and test the used network. So, the database has been partitioned into ten segments. Nine segments have been used to train the network while the remaining segment has been used to test its recognition performance. The achieved recognition rate was 90.1%. The performance of the network is not tested for recognition of expression of a novel subject.

Yoneyama et al [229] compute the outer corners of the eyes, the height of the eyes, and the height of the mouth in an automatic way. Once these features are identified, the examined face image is divided into 8 x 10 regions. Accordingly, 8 x 10 ternary values [+1 (moving upward), 0 (no movement), -1 (moving downward)] computed from averaged value of the optical flows tn each region are used as the feature parameters. They use two kinds of discrete type Hopfield neural networks in order to recognize four facial expressions, namely:'surprise', 'anger', 'happiness' and 'sadness' The two neural networks trained by different learning data are cascade-connected to compensate each other. As the experimental result, the averaged recognition rate for those four expressions was obtained 92.2%.

Zhao and Kearney [231] also use artificial neural network classifiers. They manually extract and compute 10 facial distances from 94 images from the Ekman and Friesen database [27] which feature the six basic emotions. The difference between a distance measured in an examined image and the same distance measured in an expressionless face of the same person was normalized. Then, each such measure was mapped into one of the eight signaled intervals of the appropriate standard deviation from the corresponding average. These intervals formed the input to the neural network. The output of the neural network represents the associated emotion (e.g., the string '001' is used to represent happiness). The neural network was trained and tested on the whole set of data (94 images) with 100% recognition rate. It is not known how the method will behave in the case of an unknown subject.

Dailey et al [205] also use artificial neural networks. The model begins by computing a biologically plausible representation of its input, which is a static image of an actor portraying a prototypical expression of the six basic emotions plus the 'neutral'. The input data are computed using the Gabor Lattice Representation which first computes the basic feature which is a 2-D Gabor wavelet filter and, secondly, combines two filters to get phase insensitivity, modeling complex cell responses in primary visual cortex. The dimensionality of the resulting vector is further reduced using Principal Component Analysis (PCA). The resulting feature vector consists of 50 inputs which are fed to a 6-unit softmax neural network with no hidden layers. The network was trained with a dataset of 12 actors forming the seven expressions, whereas the 13th was used for testing between the training epochs to test the network's performance and adjust its weights. The expression formed by the 14th actor was used for the final testing. In total, the build 182 networks and applied different combinations of the datasets for training and testing. In average, the neural networks achieved an accuracy of 85.9%.

Facial Expression Recognition on image sequences:

Black and Yacoob [232] use local parametrized models of image motion for recovering and recognizing the non-rigid and articulated motion of human faces. The assume that within local regions in space and time, such models not only accurately model non-rigid facial motions but also provide a concise description of the motion in terms of a small number of parameters. The recovered image motion parameters correspond simply and intuitively to various facial expressions and are used to derive mid-level predicates describing the image motion of the facial features. High-level recognition rules describe the temporal structure of a facial expression in terms of these mid-level predicates. For each of six basic emotional expressions, they developed a model represented by a set of rules for detecting the beginning and ending of the expression. The rules are applied to the predicates of the midlevel representation. The method has been tested on 70 image sequences containing 145 expressions shown by 40 subjects ranged in ethnicity and age. The expressions were displayed one at the time. The achieved recognition rate was 88%.

Kimura and Yachida [233] not only did-they recognize some kind of facial expressions which is associated with human emotion but also they estimated its degree. Their method was based on the idea that facial expression recognition can be achieved by extracting a variation from expressionless face with considering face area as a whole pattern. For the purpose of extracting subtle changes in the face such as the degree of expressions, it is necessary to eliminate the individuality appearing in the facial image. Using a elastic net model, a variation of facial expression is represented as motion vectors of the deformed Net from a facial edge image. Then, by applying K-L expansion, the change of facial expression represented as the motion vectors of nodes is mapped into low dimensional eigen-space, and estimation is achieved by projecting input images on to the Emotion Space. They constructed three kinds of expression models: 'happiness', 'anger', 'surprise'. To test the system, they prepared 10 sequential images consisting of 20 frames for these three kinds of expression. These input images were from the same person as these from model images. The system showed good results in recognizing the expressions of the same person but failed to recognize the expressions of an unknown person.

Otsuka and Ohya [241] used Hidden Markov Model for facial expression recognition. They proposed a method that can be used for spotting segments that display facial expression. The motion of the face is modeled by Hidden Markov Model in such a way that each state corresponds to the conditions of facial muscles, e.g., relaxed, contracting, apex and relaxing. The probability assigned to each state is updated iteratively as the feature vector is obtained from image processing. A spotted segment is placed into a certain category when the probability of that category exceeds a threshold value. The Hidden Markov Models was trained on 120 image sequences, shown by two male subjects. Then, the method was tested with image sequences formed by the same two male subjects. based on the studies, the recognition performance was good, but it is not known how the method will behave in the case of an unknown expresser.

Cohn et al. [236] developed and implemented an optical-flow-based approach (feature point tracking) that is sensitive to subtle changes in facial expression. They use a model of facial landmark points localized around the facial features. This model is first marked by hand with a mouse device in the first image frame of the subject, and, afterwards, uses an hierarchical optical flow method to track the optical flows of 13-by-13 windows surrounding the landmark points. The displacement of each landmark point is calculated by subtracting its normalized position in the first frame

Ioanna-Ourania Stathopoulou and George A. Tsihrintzis

from its current normalized position. This displacement is used as a feature vector to classify the expression. In order to do this, they apply separate discriminant function analyzes within facial regions of the eyebrows, eyes, and mouth. For training and testing, they used the image sequences of 100 human subjects depicting 872 facial actions. They used two discriminant functions for three facial actions of the eyebrow region, two discriminant functions for three facial actions of the eye region. Feature point tracking demonstrated high concurrent validity with human coding using the Facial Action Coding System (FACS).

Essa and Pentland [201] developed a computer vision system for observing facial motion by using an optimal estimation optical flow method coupled with geometric, physical and motion-based dynamic models describing the facial structure. First, by modeling the elastic nature of facial skin and the anatomical nature of facial muscles they developed a dynamic muscle-based model of the face, including FACS-like [29] control parameters. In order to use this model, they needed to locate and extract the position of the facial features. Initially they started their estimation process by manually translating, rotating and deforming their 3-D facial model to fit a face in an image. To automate this process, in more recent efforts, they used the view-based and modular Eigenspace methods of Pentland and Moghaddam [242]. They compute the eigenfaces to automatically track the face in the scene and extract the positions of the eyes, nose, and mouth. These feature positions are used to wrap the face image to match a canonical face mesh. This allowed them to extract the additional 'canonical feature points' on the image that correspond to the fixed (non-rigid) nodes on their mesh. After the initial registering of the model to the image the coarse-to-fine flow computation methods presented by Simoncelli [243] and Wang et al. [244] are used to compute the flow. The model on the face image tracks the motion of the head and the face correctly as long as there is not an excessive amount of rigid motion of the face during an expression. They tested with 52 front-view image sequences of eight people showing six distinct expressions and a correct recognition rate of 98% has been achieved.

Wang et al. [235] used a 19-point (12 of them are used for facial expression recognition) labeled graph to track the facial features in an input image sequence. To represent the relationship between the motion of features and change of expression, they constructed expression change models by using B-spline curves. Each curve describes the relationship between the expression change and the displacement of the corresponding facial feature point in the labeled graph. The model of each expression was constructed based on the data acquired by 10 image sequences formed by 5 subjects. The category of an expression is decided by determining the minimal distance between the actual trajectory of the 12 points and the trajectories defined by the models. They tested their approach on 29 image sequences of three emotional expressions. The expression were formed by 8 young subjects of Asian ethnicity. During photo shooting, the subjects didn't have a moustache, a beard or wear glasses and the photos were acquired under constant illumination. The average recognition rate was 95%.

Lien, Kanade and Cohn [198] developed a computer vision system that is sensitive to subtle changes in the face. The system included three modules to extract feature information: dense-flow extraction using a wavelet motion model, facial feature tracking, and edge and line extraction. The feature information thus extracted was fed to discriminant classifiers or hidden Markov models that classify it into FACS [29] action units. The system was tested on image sequences from 100 male and female subjects of varied ethnicity (65% female, 35% male, 85% European-American, 15% African-American or Asian, ages 18 to 35 years). Subjects sat directly in front of the camera and performed a series of facial expressions that included single action units and combinations of action units. Each expression sequence began from a neutral face. Each frame in the sequence was digitized into a 640 by 490 pixel array with 8-bit precision for gray scale. In the brow region, three action units or action unit combinations were analyzed, 92% were correctly classified by dense flow extraction with HMM, 91% by facial-feature tracking with discriminant analysis, 85% by facial feature-tracking with HMM, and 88% by high-gradient component detection with HMM. In the eye region, analysis was limited to facial-feature tacking with discriminant analysis. Three action units were classified with 88% accuracy. There was some disagreements between two action units, but the authors claimed that there is also difficulty to discriminate for manual FACS coders as well. In the mouth region, 6 action units were analyzed by dense-flow extraction with HMM, 9 action units by facial-feature tracking with discriminant analysis, 6 action units by facial-feature tracking with HMM, and two action units by high-gradient component detection. Accuracy was above 80% for each module. The percentage correctly classified by dense-flow extraction with HMM was 92%. The percentage correctly classified by facial-feature tracking with discriminant analysis was 81% and by facial-feature tracking with HMM was 88%. The percentage correctly classified by high-gradient component detection with HMM was 81%. In conclusion, agreement with manual FACS coding was strong for the results based on dense-flow extraction and facial feature tracking, and strong to moderate for edge and line extraction.

All the aforementioned methods are evaluated based on the requirements set by Pantic and Rothkrantz [6] and this evaluation is summarized in the following Table 3.10 [6].

Recent studies on Facial Expression Recognition (2001-present)

In the final section of this survey, we will discuss the more recent studies in facial expression recognition, from 2001 until the time of preparation of this monograph

Ioanna-Ourania Stathopoulou and George A. Tsihrintzis

Table 3.10: Review of the facial expression approaches (Middle Years) (Adapted from [6])

Reference	1	2	3	4	5	6	7	8	9	10	11	12	13	14	16	17	18	19	20
Input media: Static images																			
Edwards [225]	✓	-	✓	-	✓	✓	x	✓	-	✓	x	✓	✓	x	7	x	x	x	x
Hara [230]	✓	1	-	-	✓	x	✓	✓	-	✓	x	✓	-	x	6	x	x	x	✓
Hong [226]	✓	-	x	-	✓	✓	✓	✓	✓	✓	x	✓	✓	x	7	x	x	x	✓
Huang [227]	✓	1	x	-	✓	x	✓	✓	-	✓	x	✓	✓	x	6	x	x	x	x
Lyons [136]	x	✓	x	-	✓	-	x	x	-	✓	x	✓	✓	x	7	x	x	x	x
Padget [228]	x	✓	x	-	✓	-	x	x	-	✓	x	✓	✓	x	7	x	x	x	x
Pantic [213]	✓	3	x	-	✓	✓	✓	✓	✓	✓	x	✓	✓	31	6	x	✓	✓	x
Yoneyama [229]	✓	1	-	-	✓	x	✓	✓	-	✓	x	✓	✓	x	4	x	x	x	-
Zhang [202]	x	✓	x	-	✓	-	x	x	-	✓	x	✓	✓	x	7	x	✓	✓	x
Zhao [231]	x	✓	x	-	✓	-	x	x	-	✓	x	✓	-	x	6	x	x	x	x
Dailey [205]	x	-	-	-	✓	-	x	x	-	✓	x	-	x	x	7	x	x	x	x
Input media: Image Sequences (Video)																			
Black [232]	✓	-	✓	-	✓	✓	x	✓	x	✓	x	✓	✓	-	6	x	✓	x	x
Cohn [236]	✓	3	x	-	✓	x	x	✓	x	✓	x	✓	✓	15	-	x	x	x	-
Essa [201]	✓	✓	✓	-	✓	-	✓	✓	✓	✓	x	✓	✓	2	4	x	x	x	✓
Kimura [233]	✓	x	✓	-	✓	x	✓	✓	✓	✓	x	✓	✓	x	3	x	✓	x	-
Otsuka [234]	✓	-	-	-	✓	✓	-	✓	x	✓	x	x	✓	x	6	x	x	x	x
Wang [235]	✓	1	x	-	✓	x	x	✓	-	✓	x	✓	✓	x	3	x	✓	x	x

✓ : 'Yes' x : 'No' '-' : Not available

(May 2009). The techniques used in these studies fell within the same categories as in previous studies, so, in terms of facial expression information extraction, some of the studies use template-based methods, whereas other studies use feature-based methods. For classification, more sophisticated classifiers are also used, such as Hidden Markov Models (HMMs) [199, 245, 246] and Support Vector Machines (SVMs) [194, 208, 247] and only one uses Artificial Neural Network classifiers [248].

Cohen et al. [199] developed a real time facial expression classification system for human-computer intelligent interaction (HCII), which classified the expression into the six classes of the basic emotions, plus the 'neutral'. They first track the face in real time and afterwards use the features extracted from the face tracking for facial expression recognition. They build several different classifiers for recognizing the facial expressions. In the first class of classifiers, they used the features extracted for each frame in the video sequence to produce a classification result for that frame. In the second type of classifiers, they developed a multi-level Hidden Markov (HMM) classifier, combining the temporal information to both automatically segment the video sequence to the different expressions and perform the classification of each segment to the corresponding facial expression. Their face tracking system was based on a system developed by Tao and Huang [249] called the Piecewise Bézier Volume Deformation (PBVD) tracker. This face tracker uses a model-based approach where an explicit 3-D wireframe model of the face is constructed. In the first frame of the image sequence, landmark facial features such as the eye corners and mouth corners are selected interactively. The generic face model is then warped to fit the selected facial features. The face model consists of 16 surface patches embedded in Bézier volumes. Once the model is constructed and fitted, head motion and local deformations of the facial features such as the eyebrows, eyelids, and mouth can be tracked. First, the 2-D image motions are measured using template matching between frames at different resolutions. Image templates from the previous frame and from the very first frame are both used for more robust tracking. The measured 2-D image motions are modeled as projections of the true 3-D motions onto the image plane. In the first class of classifiers, they built SNoW (Sparse Network of Windows), SNoW-NB(SNow-Naive-Bayes (NB) classifiers), NB-Gaussian (Naive-Bayes Gaussian classifiers), NB-Cauchy (Cauchy Naive Bayes classifiers), and TAN (Tree-Augmented-Naive Bayes classifiers). In another approach, they used temporal information displayed in the video to discriminate different expressions, with Hidden Markov Models (HMM). They tested all the approaches for persons in the database and new persons forming the expressions. For persons already in the database, the average facial expression recognition accuracies were 78.53%, 86.45%, 79.36%, 80.05% and 83.31%, by using SNoW, SNoW-NB, NB-Gaussian, NB-Cauchy and TAN classifiers, respectively, whereas the average accuracy was 78.49% with Single HMM and 82.46% with Multilevel HMM. For persons not in the database, the average facial expression recognition accuracies were 57.69%, 61.31%, 58.94%, 63.58% and 65.11%, by using SNoW, SNoW-NB, NB-Gaussian, NB Cauchy and TAN classifiers, respectively, whereas the average accuracy was 55% with Single HMM and 58% with Multilevel HMM.

Bartlett et al. [194] developed a facial expression classification system to be used with computer animated agents and robots for 'face to face communication'. The system automatically detects front-view faces in the video stream and codes them with respect to seven dimensions in real time which represent the six basic emotions, plus the 'neutral'. The face finder employs a cascade of feature detectors trained with boosting techniques. The expression recognizer receives image patches located by the face detector. A Gabor representation of the patch is formed and then processed by a bank of SVM classifiers. A novel combination of Adaboost and SVM"s enhances performance. The system was tested on the Cohn-Kanade dataset [139]of posed facial expressions. The real time system has been deployed in the Aibo robot and the RoboVie robot.

Ioanna-Ourania Stathopoulou and George A. Tsihrintzis

Busiu, Kotsia and Pitas [207] investigated the facial expression recognition task in cases where the face is partially occluded (e.g. a person wears glasses or a mouth mask). They worked with the six basic facial expressions and their main goal was to find the part of the face that contains sufficient information in order to correctly classify these six expressions. (1)the Japanese female facial expression (JAFFE)[136, 137], where ten expressers posed three or four examples of each of the six basic facial expressions (anger, disgust, fear, happiness, sadness, surprise) plus neutral pose, for a total of 213 images of facial expressions (2) the Cohn-Kanade AU-coded facial expression database [139] that contains single or combined action units. In the images of these two databases, they superimposed a black rectangle around the eyes and mouth regions to occlude them partially. Each image from the database was convolved with a set of Gabor filters having various orientations and frequencies. The new feature vectors are classified by using a maximum correlation classifier and the cosine similarity measure approaches. They found that, overall, the facial expression recognition method provides robustness against partial occlusion, the classification accuracy only decreasing from 89.7 % (no occlusion) to 84 % (eyes region occlusion) and 83.5 % (mouth region occlusion) for the first database and from 94.5 % (no occlusion) to 91.5 % (eyes region occlusion) and 87.2 % (mouth region occlusion) for the second database, respectively.

Hernández et al. [208] presented an illumination independent approach for facial expression recognition based on long wave infrared imagery. Until now, all the studies we have presented for facial expression recognition are designed considering the visible spectrum and consist of three major steps: (1) Region of Interest Selection, (2) Feature Extraction, and (3) Image Classification. This makes the recognition process not robust enough to be deployed in poorly illuminated environments. In this study, a Visual Learning approach based on Evolutionary Computation is proposed, which solved the first two tasks, mentioned above, simultaneously using a single evolving process. The first task consisted of the selection of a set of suitable regions where the feature extraction is performed. The second task consisted of tuning the parameters that defines the extraction of the Gray Level Co-occurrence Matrix used to compute region descriptors, as well as the selection of the best subsets of descriptors. The output of these two tasks is used for classification by a SVM cassifier. A data-set of thermal images with three different expression classes was used to validate the performance. They used 33 images for 'surprise' emotion, 26 images for 'happy' emotion and 33 images for 'angry' emotion, in total 92 images for training/validation of the classifier. The experimental results showed 77% of accuracy of the three expressions. Although this is a quite novel approach, the system's performance was only measured for only three classes of emotions, which are very discriminative. Also, a major drawback is that a specific, more advanced hardware is required, which is a thermal camera.

Hammal et al. [209] proposed a method for facial expression classification, which is based on the Transferable Belief Model (TBM) framework. This fusion method is well suited for the problem of facial expression classification: this model facilitates the integration of a priori knowledge and can deal with uncertain and imprecise data which could be the case with data measures resulting from video-based segmentation algorithm. In addition, it is able to model intrinsic doubt which can occur between facial expressions in the recognition process. It allows the classification of different expressive states like 'pure' expression and allows the doubt between pairs of expressions. Their emotion classes were the six basic emotions plus the neutral. The proposed classifier relied on data coming from a contour segmentation technique, which extracted an expression skeleton of facial features (mouth, eyes and eyebrows) and derived simple distance coefficients from every face image of a video sequence. The characteristic distances were fed to a rule-based decision system that relies on the TBM and data fusion in order to assign a facial expression to every face image. They compared their system's performance with the results given by human classifiers. In order to do this, they conducted an empirical study, where they presented the skeleton images corresponding to contours of permanent facial features to 60 subjects and asked them to classify by means of emotions. Humans achieved a 60% correct classification rate, whereas this rate was further improved to 80% when the original image was also showed to them. For the TBM method, they identified that there are some emotions that they can be combined together in terms of facial expression, for this reason, besides the emotion classes, they created 2 more classes which corresponded to 'Joy and/or Disgust' and 'Surprise and/or Fear', and after classification, these images will further processed and re-classified. The system showed good results in recognizing some of the basic emotions plus the two classes mentioned above.

Kim et al. [210] extended their face detection system in order to perform facial expression recognition. They first detect the face using the AdaBoost face detection algorithm proposed by Viola and Jones [157], which guarantees real-time computation. If an initial face is detected, a face search window is set to reduce the searching region on the whole image and the system locates the face within the window. After face detection, face tracking is operated using the mean shift algorithm. Whenever a face region is extracted, first, a determination of whether the face is a front-view face is performed. After face detection, if the size of the face is sufficient for facial expression recognition (in this case 50 x x50 pixels), two pre-processing algorithms are applied to the input image: (1)illumination, and (2)geometry normalization, in order to reduce false recognition rates caused by illumination changes and size changes, respectively. For facial expression data extraction, the extended the form of the 3 x 1 AdaBoost rectangle feature to all possible rectangle features in a 3 x 3 matrix form, which included: 2 two-rectangle features, 6 three-rectangle features, 5 four-rectangle features, 58 six-rectangle features, and 249 nine-rectangle features for a total of 320 rectangle features. In order to reduce the computation time for selecting weak classifiers, the best five-rectangle features for each facial expression were chosen from among the 320 rectangle features. Each rectangle feature is selected by the AdaBoost algorithm, then the error rate is measured and the top five-rectangle features, that is those which have the lowest error rate among the total 320 rectangle features, are selected. The classification is made by applying the top five features for each expression to the input image.

Wang et al. [247] were also based their study on the AdaBoost face detection algorithm proposed by Viola and Jones [157]. Like Kim et al. [210], they first detect the face using the AdaBoost face detection algorithm proposed by Viola and Jones [157]. Afterwards, they extract three key points of human face: the pair of eyes and the mouth center, using a Simple Direct Appearance Model (SDAM) method [250] based on the texture. A weak classifier pool of simple features should was configured. The weak classifier' s construction was based on the Haar feature, which is a kind of simple rectangle feature proposed by Viola and Jones [157], and can be calculated very fast through the integral image. For each Haar feature, one weak classifier is configured. Their method was tested with by using the JAFFE database [136, 137] and was compared to SVM classifiers and demonstrated an average accuracy of 92,4% in 0.11 ms in correctly classifying the expressions, in comparison to SVM classifiers which demonstrated 91,6% accuracy in 28.7 ms. In cases where subject was already in the database, the accuracy was 98,9%.

Liang et al. [211] developed a facial expression recognition system which was based on Supervised Locally Linear Embedding (SLLE). The system consists of three modules: face detection, feature extraction with SLLE and classification. In face detection module, two independent characteristics, skin color characteristic and motion characteristic are used to detect face region, and a trained Support Vector Machine (SVM) classifier is used to verify candidate regions. In feature extraction module, SLLE, a supervised learning algorithm that can compute low dimensional, neighborhood-preserving embeddings of high dimensional data is used to reduce data dimension and extract features. In classification module, minimum-distance classifier is used to recognize different expressions. Their method was tested with by using the JAFFE database [136, 137] and was compared to PCA-based method. The results showed up to 95% accuracy for subjects already in the database and up to 85% for new subjects in the database.

Zhou et al. [245] used Hidden Markov Models (HMM) to build a real - time facial expression recognition system which could be used in a role playing game. Their work was based on the HMM proposed by Nefian et al. for face recognition [251]. First, they detect the face using the AdaBoost face detection algorithm proposed by Viola and Jones [157]. Second, face alignment is used in facial expression environment. The embedded HMM uses observation vectors that are composed of two-dimensional Discrete Cosine Transform (2D-DCT) coefficients opposite to previous HMM approaches which use pixel intensities to form the observation vectors. The system was tested for the classification of five emotions/states, namely: 'normal', 'laugh', 'anger', 'sleep' and 'surprise'. The results showed 92% accuracy for subjects already in the database and up to 84% for new subjects in the database.

Xiang et al. [212] proposed a fuzzy spatio-temporal approach for real time facial expression recognition in video sequences. The proposed system first employed the Fourier transform to convert a facial expression sequence of images (displaying one expression) from the spatio-temporal domain into the spatio-frequency domain. This was followed by a fuzzy C means classification [252] for expression representation. Their system classified the input images in the six basic emotion classes. Unknown input expressions are matched to the models using the Hausdorff distance to compute dissimilarity values for classification. Since the proposed algorithm used Fourier transform, it is robust, in terms of lighting changes during image acquisition. Also, by using fuzzy C means classification, quantified interpretation labels are assigned with degrees varied from 0 to 1. Since some expressions might look alike, these degrees represent the membership of the input image to the respective class, rather than using hard boundaries between the expressions. Moreover, the system needs only the positions of two eyes that can be detected accurately in current technology. Since fewer landmarks are needed, the system is less affected by the inaccuracy of facial features detection. The system was trained and tested using the Cohn-Kanade AU-Coded Facial Expression Database [139], as follows: they used the data of all but one subject as training data, and tested on the sequences of the subject that was left out. Each input sequence was compared with model for each of the six basic expressions. A dissimilarity score was computed to measure the dissimilarity degree for each comparison. The results showed 88,8% accuracy for new subjects in the database.

Ma and Khorasani [248] built a neural network-based facial expression recognition system. In their proposed technique, the 2-dimensional discrete cosine transform (2-D DCT) is applied over the entire difference face image for extracting relevant features for recognition purpose. In order to find a proper network size, they propose to use the constructive one-hidden-layer feed forward neural networks (OHL-FNNs). The constructive OHL-FNN will obtain in a systematic way a proper network size which is required by the complexity of the problem being considered. Furthermore, the computational cost involved in network training can be considerably reduced when compared to standard back- propagation (BP) based FNNs. So, in this study, the lower frequency 2-D DCT coefficients obtained are then used to train a constructive OHL-FNN. The proposed technique is applied to a database consisting of images of 60 men, each having 5 facial expression images (neutral, smile, anger, sadness, and surprise). Images of 40 men are used for network training, and the remaining images are used for generalization and testing. Confusion matrices calculated in both network training and testing for 4 facial expressions (smile, anger, sadness, and surprise) are used to evaluate the performance of the trained network. The results showed 93,75% accuracy for new subjects in the database.

Pardas et al. [246] were based on the modeling of the expressions by means of Hidden Markov Models for building their facial expression recognition system. The observations used to create the models are the MPEG-4 standardized facial animation parameters (FAPs). The FAPs of a video sequence are first extracted and then analyzed using semi-continuous Hidden Markov Model. They trained and tested their system for recognizing the six basic emotions using the Cohn-Kanade AU-Coded Facial Expression Database [139]. The database consisted of 90 subjects depicting the six expressions. They trained the system using all subjects except one, and, then, tested the recognition rate with the subject that had not participated in the training process. This process was repeated 90 times, as the number of subjects. Results showed 84% recognition rate. They also tested their system in 'talking videos', where the subject was talking while forming the expression. The recognition rate in this case was 64%.

Kobayashi et al. [253] proposed a method of expression learning by imitating the process of a baby's learning process. A baby cannot know what an expression means but he/she can be affected by the action that people do to him or her, and then he/she remembers this facial expression. In their system, a robot starts learning facial expression by recognizing human actions. The system detects the face regions and extracts the facial features using four direction features: horizontal, vertical and diagonally in both directions. For face detection they used two methods: (1) skin-color information and (2) template matching. Since, in previous works, they had found skin-color information-based face detection weak in some environments, they adopted template matching methods for face detection. The system was trained and tested for three emotions: 'anger', 'happiness' and 'neutral/normal'. They collected the data 12 days in several locations and the data was taken 3 times per day, in morning, afternoon, and evening. For each learning time, they got 30 flames for each expression. The number of images of experimental data totals 3,240 images (3 expressions x 12 days x 3 times x 30 frames). They used 6 days of the data for learning (half of data). The other were used as unknown data for testing. The system achieved a recognition rate of 97,5%, for a single subject.

Abboud and Davoine [254] proposed bilinear factorization based representations for facial expression recognition and compared this method with previously investigated methods such as linear discriminant analysis and linear regression. In order to perform facial expression recognition, they used a test set of 108 unknown face image showing each of the seven basic facial expressions and ran Active Appearance Mode (AAM) optimization to extract the corresponding appearance parameters. Their aim was to extract from each appearance vector a subset of relevant parameters that represent facial expression information. Towards this goal, searching for the vectors that best discriminate among classes, the compared Linear Discriminant Analysis (LDA) techniques and Bilinear Factorization techniques. The predictive learning is performed on a training set containing 70 images which represent 10 different persons showing each of the 7 basic facial expressions. The correct recognition rate, when using LDA, for 108 unknown test persons was 67.59%. LDA was also tested for a training set containing 26 images per class and achieved an optimal correct recognition rate of 84.34%. When trained with the same training set of 70 images, the asymmetric bilinear factorization expression classifier achieved a correct recognition rate of 83,33%, for 108 unknown test persons.

All the aforementioned methods are evaluated based on the requirements set by Pantic and Rothkrantz [6] and this evaluation is summarized in the following Table 3.11.

Table 3.11: Review of the facial expression approaches (Recent Years)

Reference	1	2	3	4	5	6	7	8	9	10	11	12	13	14	15	16	17	18	19	20
Input media: Static images																				
Busiu [207]	X	3	X	✓	✓	X	X	✓	✓	✓	X	✓	✓	X	X	7	X	-	-	✓
Hernández [208]	✓	-	✓	X	✓	X	✓	✓	-	✓	X	X	X	X	X	3	X	-	-	-
Kim [210]	X	✓	✓	✓	✓	X	✓	✓	-	✓	X	-	-	X	X	7	X	-	-	✓
Wang [247]	✓	-	X	X	✓	X	✓	✓	-	✓'	X	✓	-	X	X	7	X	-	-	✓
Liang [211]	X	X	X	X	✓	X	✓	✓	X	✓	X	✓	-	X	X	7	X	-	-	-
Ma [248]	X	X	X	X	✓	X	X	✓	X	✓	X	-	-	X	X	4	X	-	-	X
Kobayashi [253]	X	age	X	X	✓	X	✓	✓	X	✓	X	-	-	X	X	3	X	✓	-	✓
Abboud [254]	X	X	X	X	✓	X	X	✓	X	✓	X	-	-	X	X	7	X	-	-	X
Input media: Image Sequences (Video)																				
Cohen [199]	✓	X	X	X	✓	✓	✓	✓	-	✓	X	✓	✓	X	X	7	X	-	-	✓
Bartlett [194]	✓	3	X	X	✓	✓	✓	✓	-	✓	X	✓	-	X	X	7	X	-	-	✓
Hammal [209]	X	3	X	X	✓	X	X	✓	-	✓	X	✓	✓	X	X	7	X	-	-	-
Zhou [245]	✓	-	X	X	✓	X	✓	✓	-	✓	X	-	-	X	X	5	X	-	-	✓
Xiang [212]	✓	3	✓	X	✓	X	-	✓	✓	✓	X	-	-	X	X	6	X	✓	-	✓
Pardas [246]	X	3	X	X	✓	X	X	✓	X	✓	X	X	X	X	X	6	X	-	-	X

✓ : 'Yes' x : 'No' '-' : Not available

Based on the previous survey, many studies included the recognitions of different facial expressions or facial action units. Moreover, many studies were centered in the development of a user dependent facial expression recognition system. This task is quite easier rather than a facial expression recognition system which would be able to perform well regardless of the subject. The evaluation of the aforementioned studies,

Ioanna-Ourania Stathopoulou and George A. Tsihrintzis

based on those criteria, are summarized in Table 3.12 and Table 3.13, where the input data are static images or image sequences, respectively.

Table 3.12: Performance evaluation and generalization of recent systems - 1

Study reference	Success Rate (User dependent)	Success Rate (User independent)	User independent tests?	Number of emotion classes
Input media: Static images				
Busiu [207]	88,96% (no occlusion), 83,46% (mouth occlusion), 85,45% (eye occlusion)	-	-	6 b.em. + 'neu'
Hernández [208]	-	77%	✓	3
Kim [210]	n/a	n/a	✓	6 b.em. + 'neu'
Wang [247]	98,9%	92,46%	✓	6 b.em. + 'neu'
Liang [211]	95%	85%	✓	6 b.em. + 'neu'
Ma [248]	-	93,75%	✓	4: 'joy', 'sur', 'ang', 'sad'
Kobayashi [253]	93,75%	X	-	3: 'ang', 'joy', 'neu'
Abboud [254]		83,33%	✓	6 b.em. + 'neu'

Legend:
✓ : 'Yes'
- : 'No'/ 'Not available'
n/a : 'Not available'
Emotions/Expressions : 'neu':'neutral', 'ang':'anger', 'scr':'scream', 'sle':'sleep', 'sur':'surprise', 'lau':'laughter'
b.em. : 6 Basic Emotions ⇒ anger', 'disgust', 'fear', 'happiness', 'sadness' and 'surprise'

Table 3.13: Performance evaluation and generalization of recent systems - 2

Study reference	Success Rate (User dependent)	Success Rate (User independent)	User independent tests?	Number of emotion classes
Input media: Image Sequences (Video)				
Cohen [199]	80,66%	59,95%	✓	6 b.em.
Bartlett [194]	n/a	n/a	n/a	6 b.em. + 'neu'
Hammal [209]	-	-	-	6 b.em. + 'neu'
Zhou [245]	92%	84%	✓	5: 'neu', 'lau', 'ang', 'sle', 'sur'
Xiang [212]	-	88,8%	✓	6 b.em.
Pardas [246]	-	84%(Cohn Database), 64%(subject is talking)	-	6 b.em

Legend:
✓ : 'Yes'
- : 'No'/ 'Not available'
n/a : 'Not available'
Emotions/Expressions : 'neu':'neutral', 'ang':'anger', 'scr':'scream', 'sle':'sleep', 'sur':'surprise', 'lau':'laughter'
b.em. : 6 Basic Emotions ⇒ anger', 'disgust', 'fear', 'happiness', 'sadness' and 'surprise'

Ioanna-Ourania Stathopoulou and George A. Tsihrintzis

3.3.3 Section Summary - Results

Some of the aforementioned methods have achieved good results, but there are some drawbacks. Firstly, the majority of these methods use some of the facial expression databases described in Section 3.1, mostly the JAFFE, the Cohn-Kanade and the MMI. However, as research shows, cultural exposure increases the chances of correct recognition of facial expressions indicating cultural dependence ([255], [49], [256]). This point has become more noticeable for the expressions formed by Greek people, in following Chapter 5, where we present two different questionnaires. In the first questionnaire we used images of people forming facial expressions gathered from the web, whereas in the second we used facial expression images from our own facial expression database. The difference between the error rates of the two different questionnaires is quite noticeable. In our system we used our own facial expression database which consists of Greek people forming seven different expressions. Secondly, the methods which attempt to classify the expression in discrete emotions, usually assume six emotions, namely: 'neutral', 'anger','happiness','sadness', 'disgust' and 'fear'. Our system has been designed to be implemented in human computer interaction. Again, based on our studies, which are pointed out in following Chapter 5, the emotions that are most commonly observed during a typical human computer interaction session are namely: 'neutral', 'anger','happiness','sadness', 'disgust' and 'bored-sleepiness' which are the categories used by our system.

Ioanna-Ourania Stathopoulou and George A. Tsihrintzis

4

Face Image Databases

Every man builds his world in his own image. He has the power to choose, but no power to escape the necessity of choice.

—*Ayn Rand (1905–1982)*

OUR review on previous facial expression databases, as described on Section 3.1, led us to the assumption that we must create our own facial expression database [9, 11]. Our work to the creation of two different databases:

1. The database of low quality images: this database consists of many subjects, depicting many expressions, but the image quality is quite low as we used web cameras to acquire the data

2. The database of high quality images: this database consists again of many subjects, depicting the expressions recognized by our system, and the image quality is quite high as we we used digital cameras to acquire the data

In this chapter, we present thoroughly these two databases and the means of developing them.

4.1 The Database of Low Quality Face Images (DBLQFI)

THE first database was created by photographing individuals aged 19-35 years old while they were forming various expressions. To acquire image data, we built a three-camera system, as in Fig. 4.1. Specifically, three identical cameras of 320-by-240 pixel resolution were placed with their optical axes on the same horizontal plane and successively forming 30-degree angles. Subjects were placed in front of the camera configuration and formed facial expressions, which were simultaneously photographed by the three cameras.

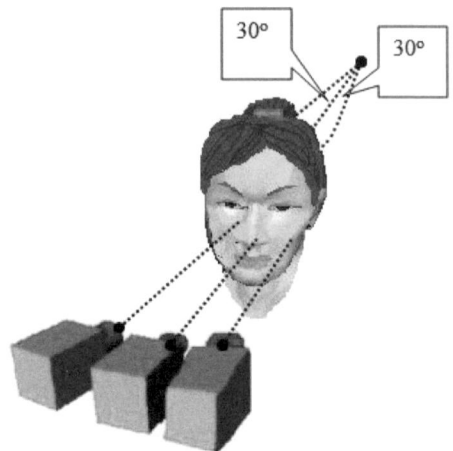

Figure 4.1: Three Camera Configuration

The database consisted of 300 subjects: 233 male and 67 female. All participants and expression-forming subjects were Greek, so they were used to the Greek culture and the Greek ways of expressing emotions. The study participants aged 19 to 45 years old and their majority were either under-graduate or graduate students in the University of Piraeus. A small number of the participants were employees of the University. They were asked to form the 10 following expressions/emotions: *'neutral, 'happiness', 'sadness', 'surprise' 'boredom-sleepiness', 'disappointment', 'scream', 'anger', 'disgust' and 'talking expression'.*

The resulting database consisted of **300 by 10 by 3 = 9000 color images**. The database details are summarized in the following Table 4.1, while some samples of the database are shown in Table 4.2 at the end of this Chapter.

4.2 The Database of High Quality Face Images (DB-HQFI)

THE first efforts in building a facial expression database resulted to the 'Database of Low Quality Face Images (DBLQFI)', which, although complete in terms of subjects and facial expressions, contains images of such low quality that is not useful for the purpose of building our system. Specifically, because of the low quality, many details of the expressions (such as the texture of the skin) were not clearly distinguishable in these images. Based on these assumptions, DBLQFI could only be

Table 4.1: Low quality Database

Emotions/Expressions	
Number of emotions	10
Emotion Classes	'neutral, 'happiness', 'sadness', 'surprise' 'boredom-sleepiness', 'disappointment', 'scream', 'anger', 'disgust' and 'talking expression'
Subjects	
Number of subjects	300
Subjects' culture	Greek
Subjects' age	19-45
Subjects' sex	Male: 77,66% and Female: 22,44%
Image Quality	
Image resolution	320-by-240
Image color	RGB
Data acquisition	
Camera	Webcamera
Front view	✓
Right Side view	✓
Left Side view	✓
Total images: 9000	

used for testing the generalization of the system in cases of low quality images. This led us to the development of a new database of high quality images captured with digital cameras.

The process of developing the new database consisted of three steps:

1. *Observation of the user's reactions* during a typical human-computer interaction session: From this step, we concluded that the facial expressions corresponding to the **'neutral', 'happy', 'sad', 'surprised', 'angry', 'disgusted' and 'bored-sleepy'** psychological states arose quite commonly in human-computer interaction sessions and, thus, form the corresponding classes for our classification task.

2. *Data acquisition:* We created our own database of facial expressions, by photographing individuals aged 19-35 years old while they were forming various expressions. To ensure spontaneity, each subject was presented with pictures on a screen behind the camera. To acquire image data, we built a two-camera system, as in Fig. 4.2. Specifically, two identical cameras of 1600-by-1200 pixel resolution were placed with their optical axes on the same horizontal plane

Ioanna-Ourania Stathopoulou and George A. Tsihrintzis

Table 4.2: Sample images of our low quality facial expression database

Emotions	Views		
	Left Side	Front	Right Side
Neutral			
Happiness			
Sadness			
Anger			
Surprise			
Disgust			
Boredom-Sleepiness			
Disappointment			
Scream			
Speaking			

Ioanna-Ourania Stathopoulou and George A. Tsihrintzis

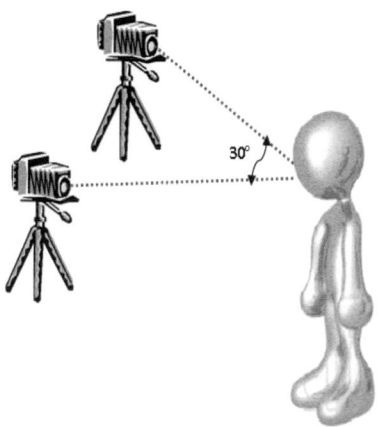

Figure 4.2: Two Camera Configuration

and successively forming 30-degree angles. Subjects were placed in front of the camera configuration and formed facial expressions, which were simultaneously photographed by the two cameras.

These pictures were expected to generate those emotional states that would map on the subject's face as the desired facial expression. For example, to have a subject assume a 'happy' expression, we showed him/her a picture of funny content. We photographed the resulting facial expression and then asked him/her to classify this expression. If the image shown to him/her had resulted in the desired facial expression, the corresponding photographs were saved and labeled; otherwise, the procedure was repeated with other pictures. The final dataset consists of the images of 250 different individuals, each forming the seven expressions: 'neutral', 'happy', 'sad', 'surprised', 'angry', 'disgust', 'bored-sleepy' and 'screaming'.

The resulting dataset consisted of 2000 images of each view, which is the result of 250 persons forming 7 different expression, a total of **4000 high quality images**. The database details are summarized in the following Table 4.3.

Studying this dataset, we identified differences between the 'neutral' expression of a model and its deformation into other expressions. We quantified these differences into measurements of the face (such as size ratio, distance ratio, texture, or orientation), so as convert pixel data into a higher-level representation of shape, motion, color, texture and spatial configuration of the face and its components.

Ioanna-Ourania Stathopoulou and George A. Tsihrintzis

Table 4.3: Low quality Database

Emotions/Expressions	
Number of emotions	8
Emotion Classes	'neutral, 'happiness', 'sadness', 'surprise' 'boredom-sleepiness', 'scream', 'anger' and 'disgust'
Subjects	
Number of subjects	250
Subjects' culture	Greek
Subjects' age	19-45
Subjects' sex	Male: 77,66% and Female: 22,44%
Image Quality	
Image resolution	1600-by-1200
Image color	RGB
Data acquisition	
Camera	Webcamera
Front view	✓
Right Side view	✓
Left Side view	x
Total images: 4000	

Furthermore, we identified that there are some differences between the ways that people express themselves in the occurance of same emotions. For example, as we observe in Table 4.4 in the occurance of the 'Boredom-Sleepiness' emotions some people tend to yawn, others to close their eyes and others to slightly tilt their head left or right, as in the case of the second subject. Specifically, we locate and extract the corner points of specific regions of the face, such as the eyes, the mouth and the brows, and compute their variations in size, orientation or texture between the neutral and some other expression. This constitutes the feature extraction process and reduces the dimensionality of the input space significantly, while retaining essential information of high discrimination power and stability. In order to validate these facial features and understand how they are used by humans to deduce someone's emotion from his/her facial expression, we developed questionnaires where the participants were asked to determine which facial features helped them in the expression recognition/classification task.

3. *Questionnaires – empirical study by observers:* In order to understand aspects of the process of facial expression recognition by human observers and set target error rates for automated systems, we conducted two relevant empirical studies

Ioanna-Ourania Stathopoulou and George A. Tsihrintzis

based on two corresponding questionnaires, as described below. The first study was only preliminary and was based on a short ('preliminary') questionnaire. The purpose of this study was to obtain an overall idea and identify the general aspects of the facial expression recognition process in humans. The images used in this preliminary study were gathered from the Web and existing facial expression databases. The lack of a complete facial expression database, containing a sufficient number of all seven expressions of interest to us, required us to create our own database of better quality images [9, 11].We also developed a 'detailed' questionnaire, as described below, which used images of our own database. Then, we conducted a second, more detailed empirical study. Results from both empirical studies are presented in this paper and conclusions are drawn.

A sample of this database of the two persons forming the 7 expression can be seen in Table 4.4.

Table 4.4: Sample images of our facial expression database

Emotions	First Subject		Second Subject	
	Front View	Side View	Front View	Side View
Neutral				
Happiness				
Sadness				
Anger				
Surprise				
Disgust				
Boredom-Sleepiness				

Ioanna-Ourania Stathopoulou and George A. Tsihrintzis

5

Empirical Studies on Emotion Recognition

We know too much and feel too little. At least we feel too little of those creative emotions from which a good life

spring.

—*Bertrand Russell (1872–1970)*

IN our attempts to understand the facial expression recognition task and set the requirements for our facial expression recognition system, we conducted two empirical studies involving human subjects and observers [9, 10, 11, 12]. The first study, as described in Section 5.1, was simpler than the second and aimed at setting an error goal for our system. We used images from facial expression databases gathered from World Wide Web [135, 139] and asked people to map the emotion based on the subject's expression. Our second empirical study, which is described in Section 5.1, was more complicated and aimed not only at an error goal, but also, at understanding how facial expression recognition works in humans. In this study, we used our own facial expression database [9, 10, 11, 12]. The two studies are described in detail in this Chapter, whereas in the final Section 5.4 we draw conclusions, from these studies.

5.1 Preliminary Questionnaires

TO obtain a preliminary idea of facial expression classification by humans, we developed a preliminary questionnaire in which we asked 300 study participants to classify the facial expressions that appeared in 36 images. Each participant could choose from 11 of the most common facial expressions, such as: 'angry', 'happy', 'neutral', 'surprised', or specify any other expression that he/she thought appropriate. Next, the participant had to decide which emotion he/she thought that the facial expression indicated. Our dataset consisted of 3 subsets of images, typically depicted in Table 5.1, namely:

- various images of individuals placed in a background and forming a facial expression,

- a sequence of facial expressions of the same person without a background, and

- face images of different persons without a background.

Table 5.1: Typical face image subsets in our questionnaire

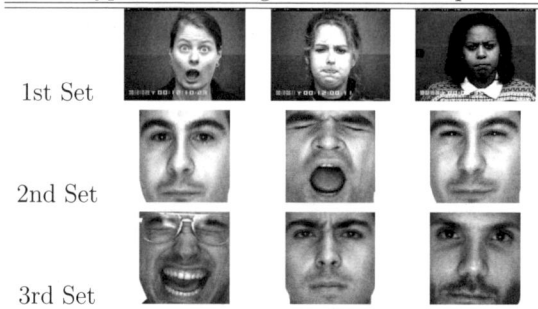

1st Set

2nd Set

3rd Set

From the results of the questionnaire, we observed that the 'surprised' expression was the one most easily recognized, as the corresponding error rate of 22% was the lowest among all error rates. The 'happy' and 'neutral' expressions were recognized with corresponding error rates of 30% and 35%, respectively. The expression recognized with the highest difficulty was the 'sad' expression, as its corresponding error rate reached 88%. The 'angry' and 'disappointed' expressions had a corresponding error rate of 80% and 76%, respectively. These are summarized in Figure 5.1.

Clearly, the facial expression classification task in images is quite challenging. The reasons why humans could not achieve low classification error rates for specific expressions such as 'angry', 'sad' and 'disappointed', may be found in the fact that these expressions seem to differ significantly from person to person or some people may be too shy to form them clearly. This finding corroborates similar findings in previous psychological studies [20], which we discussed in Chapter 2, Section 2.2.2.

5.2 Newer (Detailed) Questionnaires

IN the newer questionnaires, we used images of subjects of the facial expression database we created ourselves [9, 10, 11, 12]. Our aim was to identify those facial features which help humans to classify a facial expression. Moreover, we wanted to know the degree to which it is possible to map a facial expression into an emotion.

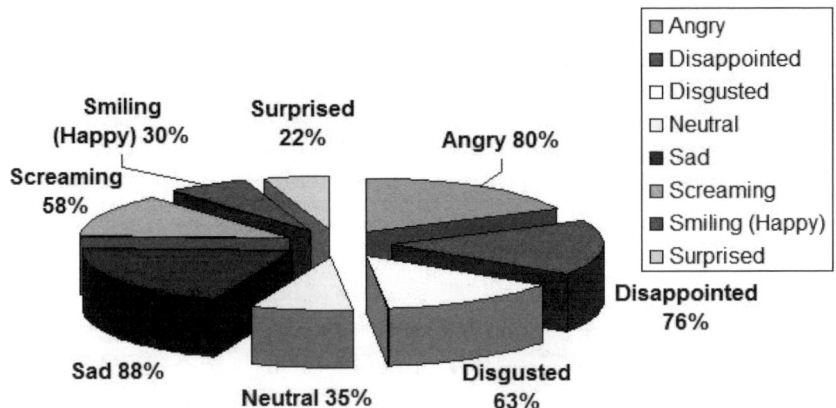

Figure 5.1: Error rates in recognizing the expressions in our preliminary questionnaire

A third goal was to determine whether a human observer could recognize a facial expression from only portions of the face (e.g., eyes, mouth, etc.), as we expect the artificial classifier to do. Thus, we had to redesign the structure of the questionnaires. This led to detailed questionnaires, which are more significantly complex than the preliminary questionnaire and described next.

5.2.1 The detailed questionnaire structure

In order to understand how humans classify someone else's facial expression and set a target error rate for automated systems, we developed a questionnaire filled again by 300 study participants. These were not the same participants as those who filled the preliminary questionnaire.

Specifically, the questionnaire consisted of three parts:

1. In the first part of the questionnaire, each participant was asked to map into facial emotions the facial expressions that appeared in 14 images. Each participant could choose from the 7 common emotions 'angry', 'happy', 'neutral', 'surprised', 'sad', 'disgusted', 'bored-sleepy', or specify any other emotion that he/she thought appropriate. Next, the participant had to specify the degree (0-100%) of his/her confidence in the identified emotion. Finally, he/she had to indicate which features (such as the eyes, the nose, the mouth, the cheeks, etc.) had helped him/her make that decision. A typical print-screen of the first part of the questionnaire is depicted in Figure 5.2.

Ioanna-Ourania Stathopoulou and George A. Tsihrintzis

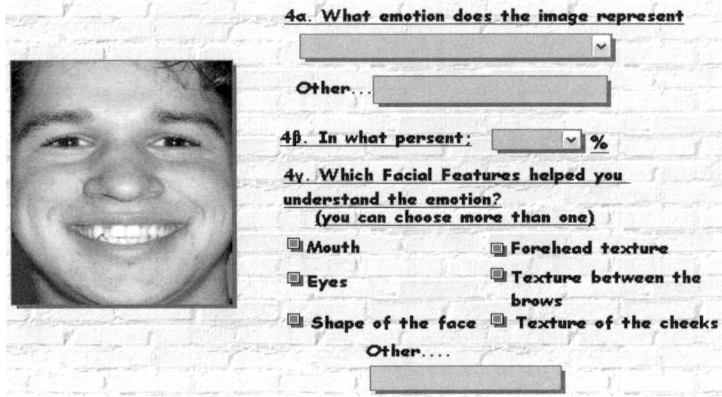

Figure 5.2: The first part of the detailed questionnaire

2. In the second part of the questionnaire, each participant had to classify the emotion from portions of the face. Specifically, we showed the participant the 'neutral' facial image and an image of some facial expression of a subject. The latter image was cut into the corresponding facial portions, namely, the eyes, the mouth, the forehead, the cheeks, the chin and the brows. A typical print-screen of this part of the questionnaire is shown in Figure 5.3.

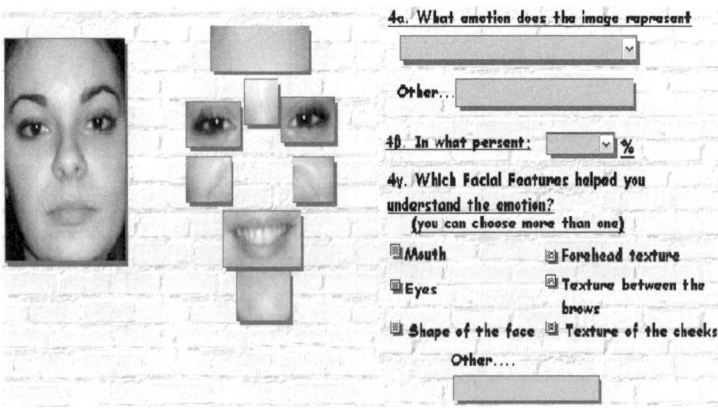

Figure 5.3: The second part of the detailed questionnaire

Ioanna-Ourania Stathopoulou and George A. Tsihrintzis

Again, each participant could choose from the 7 emotions or specify any other emotion that he/she thought appropriate. Next, the participant had to specify the degree (0-100%) of his/her confidence in the identified emotion. Finally, he/she had to indicate which features (such as the eyes, the nose, the mouth, the cheeks, etc.) had helped him/her make that decision.

3. In the third part of the questionnaire, we collected background information (e.g. age, interests, etc.) about the study participants. Additional information provided by the participants at this stage included:

   - The level of difficulty of the questionnaire, with regards to the facial expression classification task

   - Which emotion they considered the most difficult to classify

   - Which emotion they considered the easiest to classify

   - The degree (0-100%) to which an emotion maps into a facial expression

5.2.2 The observer and subject backgrounds

A total number of 300 participants participated in our study and filled up the detailed questionnaires. All participants and expression-forming subjects were Greek, so they were used to the Greek culture and the Greek ways of expressing emotions. The study participants aged 19 to 45 years old and their majority were either under-graduate or graduate students in the University of Piraeus, along with a small number of the participants were employees of the University.

5.3 Results from Statistical Analysis

5.3.1 Statistical Analysis per Expression

Angry

The 'angry' expression was recognized at an error rate of 23,86% in the first part of our detailed questionnaire, in which the entire facial image was depicted. The corresponding error rate was 30,30% in the second part of the questionnaire, in which only portions of the faces were depicted.

The participants mistook the 'angry' emotion mostly for the 'neutral' and the 'sad' expressions. The percentages to which the participants mistook the 'angry' emotion for some other emotion are shown in Figure 5.4 for both parts of the questionnaire. Specifically, as 'other' emotions, the participants indicated 'sceptical', 'confused', 'concerned', 'wondering', or 'suspicious', most of which are considered as 'neg-

Ioanna-Ourania Stathopoulou and George A. Tsihrintzis

ative' emotions. As the 'angry' emotion is considered as a negative one, one might come to the conclusion that even though the specific emotion was not recognized, a broader class of perhaps similar emotions was recognized.

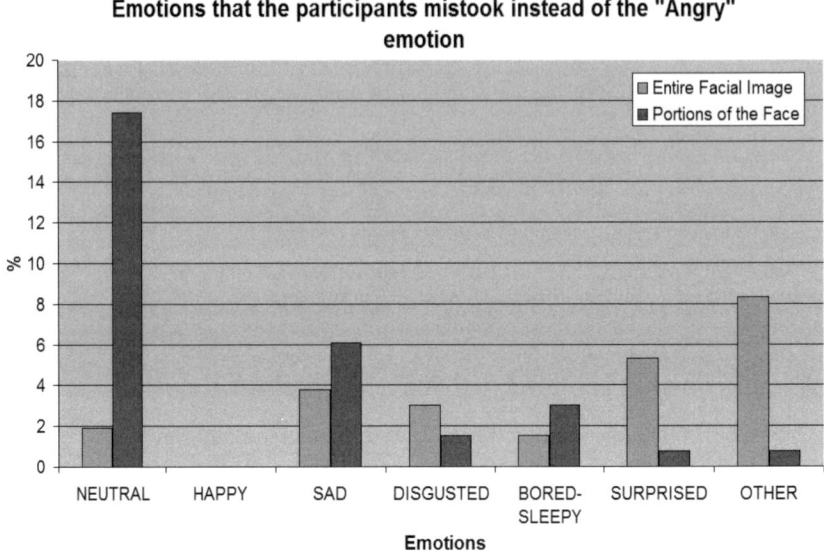

Figure 5.4: Graph of the percentage to which the participants mistook the 'angry' emotion for other emotions

The facial portions that helped the participants recognize this expression were mostly the 'eyes', the 'mouth' and the 'cheeks'. Specifically, the participants assigned percentages of significance of each facial portion as in Figure 5.5.

Finally, regarding the percentage to which the 'angry' expression maps the equivalent emotion, the participants' answers are shown in Figure 5.6. Specifically, 26,24% of the participants indicated that it maps only 10% percent of the strength of the emotion, whereas 21,82% of the participants believe that the expression maps 60% of the strength of the emotion. Moreover, the majority of the participants (67,4%) thought that the 'angry' expression maps more than 50% of the emotion, as opposed to 32,6% of the participants who thought that the 'angry' expression maps less than 50% of the emotion. This may again be in line with the fact that 'angry' is a negative emotion that people would tend to mask.

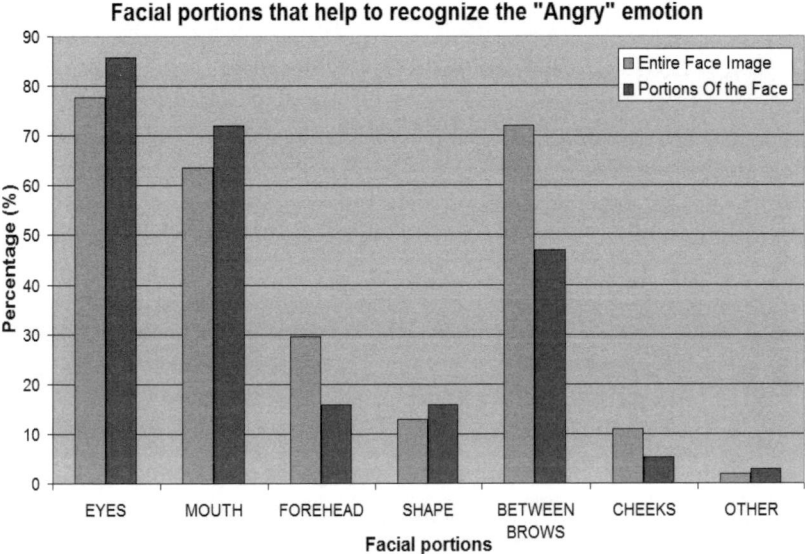

Figure 5.5: Graph of the percentage to which the 'angry' expression maps the equivalent emotion, based on the correct answers of the participants

Bored - Sleepy

The 'bored-sleepy' expression was recognized at an error rate of 49,24% in the first part of our detailed questionnaire, in which the entire facial image was depicted. The corresponding error rate was 21,96% in the second part of the questionnaire, in which only portions of the faces were depicted. The 'angry' expression was recognized at an error rate of 23,86% in the first part of our detailed questionnaire, in which the entire facial image was depicted. The corresponding error rate was 30,30% in the second part of the questionnaire, in which only portions of the faces were depicted.

The participants mistook the 'bored-sleepy' emotion mostly for the 'sad' expression. The percentages to which the participants mistook the 'bored-sleepy' emotion for some other emotion are shown in Figure 5.7 for both parts of the questionnaire. Specifically, as 'other' emotions, the participants indicated 'sceptical', 'disappointed', and 'distrustful'. Some of these emotions, especially, disappointment and the distrust may eventually lead to boredom.

The facial portions that helped the participants recognize this expression were mostly the 'eyes', the 'mouth' and the 'region between the brows'. Specifically, the participants assigned percentages of significance of each facial portion as in Figure 5.5.

Ioanna-Ourania Stathopoulou and George A. Tsihrintzis

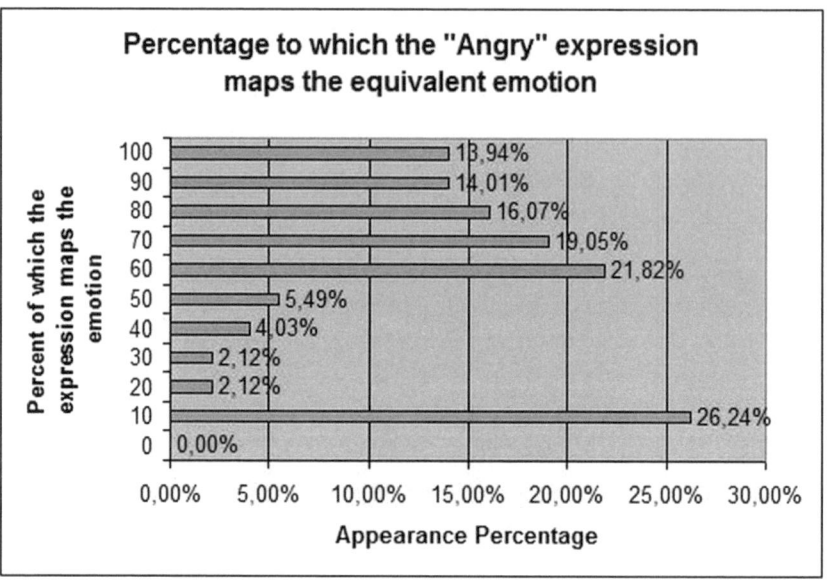

Figure 5.6: Graph of the percentage to which the 'angry' expression maps the equivalent emotion, based on the correct answers of the participants

Finally, regarding the percentages to which the 'bored-sleepy' expression maps the equivalent emotion, the participants' answers are shown in Figure 5.9. Specifically, 24,95% of the participants indicated that it shows the 80% percent of the strength of the emotion. Moreover, the majority of the participants thought that the 'angry' expression maps more than 60% of the emotion.

Disgusted

The 'disgusted' expression was recognized at an error rate of 81,26% in the first part of our detailed questionnaire, in which the entire facial image was depicted. The corresponding error rate was 86,36% in the second part of the questionnaire, in which only portions of the faces were depicted. The participants mistook the 'disgusted' emotion mostly for the 'happy' expression. The percentages to which the participants mistook the 'disgusted' emotion for some other emotion are shown in Figure 5.10 for both parts of the questionnaire. Specifically, as 'other' emotions, the participants indicated 'teasing' and 'bitter'.

Ioanna-Ourania Stathopoulou and George A. Tsihrintzis

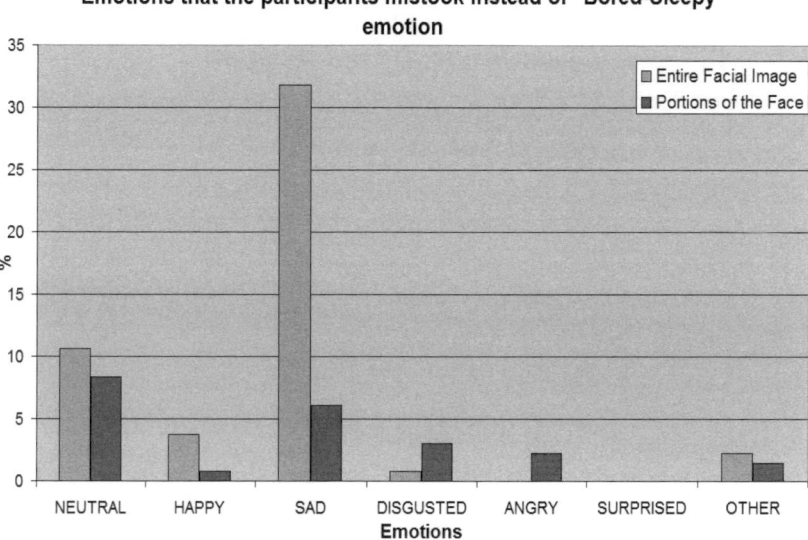

Figure 5.7: Graph of the percentage to which the participants mistook the 'bored - Sleepy' emotion for other emotions

The facial features that helped the participants classify the expression were mostly the 'eyes' and the 'mouth'. The percentage (%) of each facial feature is shown in Figure 5.11.

Regarding the percentage to which the 'disgusted' expression maps the equivalent emotion, the majority of the participants (76,47%) agreed that the expression maps the emotion with accuracy varying between 50% to 70%, as in Figure 5.12.

Happy

The 'happy' expression was recognized at an error rate of 31,06% in the first part of our detailed questionnaire, in which the entire facial image was depicted. The corresponding error rate was 3,78% in the second part of the questionnaire, in which only portions of the faces were depicted.

The participants mistook the 'happiness' emotion state mostly for the 'boredom-sleepiness' state. The percentages to which the participants mistook the 'happiness' for some other emotion state are shown in Figure 5.13 for both parts of the question-naire. Specifically, as 'other' emotions, the participants indicated 'ironic', 'satisfied',

Ioanna-Ourania Stathopoulou and George A. Tsihrintzis

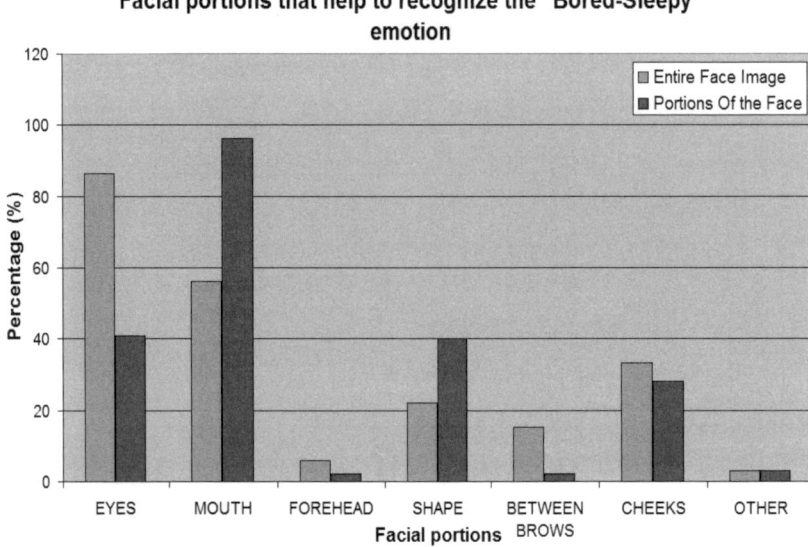

Figure 5.8: Graph of the percentage to which the 'bored - Sleepy' expression maps the equivalent emotion, based on the correct answers of the participants

'drunk', and 'pleased', most of which are considered as 'positive' emotions. As the 'happiness' emotion is considered as positive, one might come to the conclusion that when it comes to a broader class of somehow similar emotions, the error rate was even lower.

The facial portions that helped the participants classify the expression were mostly the 'eyes', the 'mouth' and the 'cheeks'. Specifically, the participants assigned percentages of significance of each facial portion as in Figure 5.14.

Finally, regarding the percentage to which the 'happy' expression maps the equivalent emotion, the participants' answers are shown in Figure 15. Specifically, 18,40% of the participants indicated that it shows 90% percent of the emotion. Moreover, the majority of the participants (77,7%) thought that the 'happy' expression maps more than 60% of the emotion. Regarding the percentage to which the 'disgusted' expression maps the equivalent emotion, the majority of the participants (76,47%) agreed that the expression maps the emotion with accuracy varying between 50% to 70%, as in Figure 5.15.

Ioanna-Ourania Stathopoulou and George A. Tsihrintzis

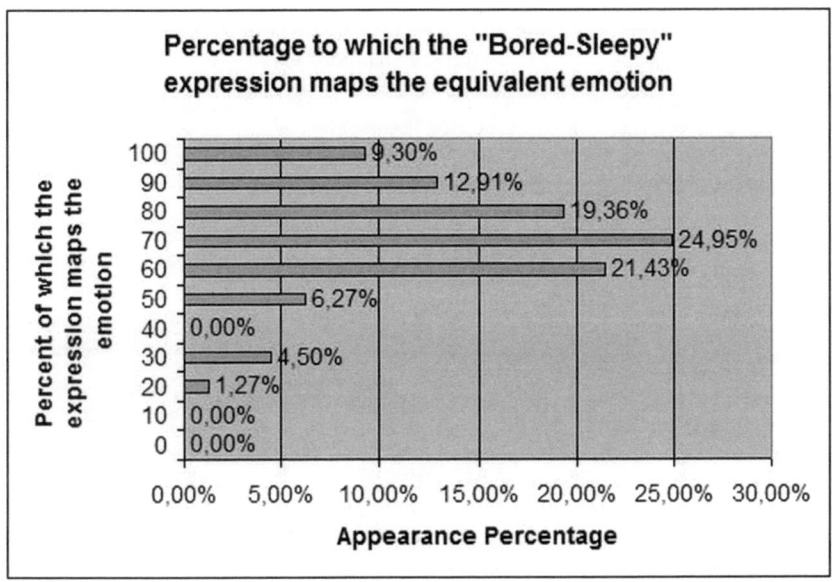

Figure 5.9: Graph of the percentage to which the 'bored - Sleepy' expression maps the equivalent emotion, based on the correct answers of the participants

Neutral

The 'neutral' expression was recognized at an error rate of 61,74% in the first part of our detailed questionnaire, in which the entire facial image was depicted. We did not use this expression in the second part of our questionnaire, as we considered other expressions as deviations from it.

The participants mistook the 'neutral' emotion mostly for the 'happy' expression. The percentages to which the participants mistook the 'neutral' emotion for some other emotion are shown in Figure 5.16 for both parts of the questionnaire. Specifically, as 'other' emotions, the participants indicated 'sceptical', 'sleepy', 'slightly happy' and 'uneasy'.

The facial portions that helped the participants classify the expression were mostly the 'eyes' and the 'mouth'. Specifically, the participants assigned percentages of significance of each facial portion as in Figure 5.17.

Finally, regarding the percentage to which the 'neutral' expression maps the equivalent emotion, the participants' answers are shown in Figure 5.18 Specifically, 54% of the participants indicated that it shows 70-80% percent of the emotion. Moreover,

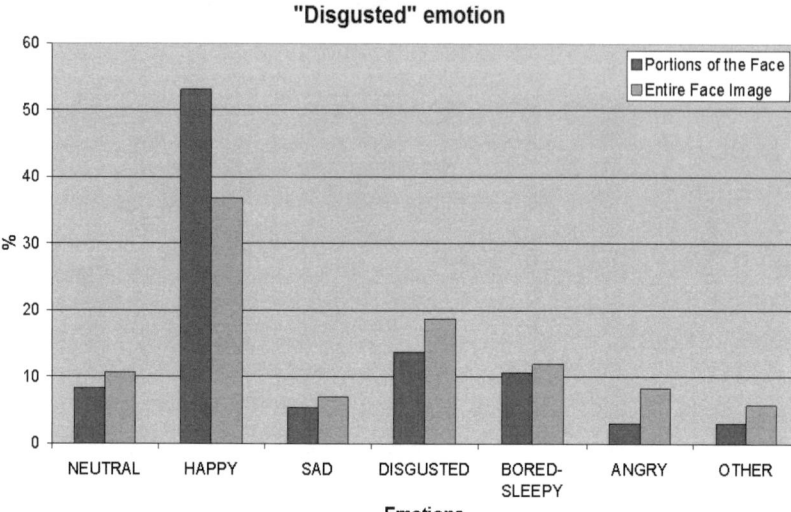

Figure 5.10: Graph of the percentage to which the participants mistook the 'disgusted' emotion for other emotions

the majority of the participants thought that the 'happy' expression maps more than 60% of the emotion.

Sad

The 'sad' expression was recognized at an error rate of 65,9% in the first part of our detailed questionnaire, in which the entire facial image was depicted. The corresponding error rate was 17,42% in the second part of the questionnaire, in which only portions of the faces were depicted.

The participants mistook the emotion state of 'sadness' mostly for the 'neutral' and 'anger' states. This might have happened because sometimes anger causes sadness. Also, as the 'sadness' is a negative emotion that humans tend to disguise and the equivalent facial expression may not be strongly formed. The percentages to which the participants mistook the 'sad' emotion for some other emotion are shown in Figure 5.19 for both parts of the questionnaire. Specifically, as 'other' emotions, the participants indicated 'disappointed', 'anxious', 'tired', and 'wondering'. These emotions may happen simultaneously or, even, be caused by the emotion of 'sadness'.

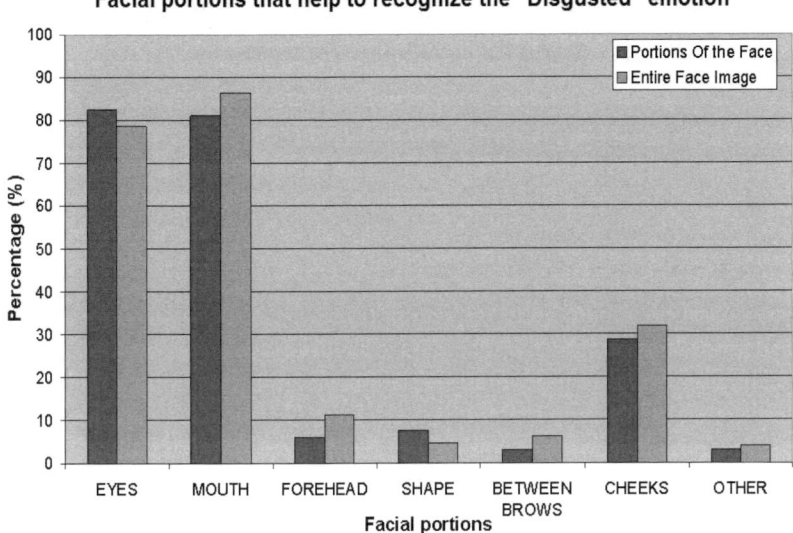

Figure 5.11: Graph of the percentage to which the 'disgusted' expression maps the equivalent emotion, based on the correct answers of the participants

The facial portions that helped the participants classify the expression were mostly the 'eyes' and the 'mouth'. Specifically, the participants assigned percentages of significance of each facial portion as in Figure 5.20.

Finally, regarding the percentage to which the 'sad' expression maps the equivalent emotion, the participants' answers are shown in Figure 5.21. Specifically, the majority of the participants thought that the 'sad' expression maps more than 60% of the emotion.

Surprised

The 'surprised' expression was recognized at an error rate of 10,22% in the first part of our detailed questionnaire, in which the entire facial image was depicted. The corresponding error rate was 4,54% in the second part of the questionnaire, in which only portions of the faces were depicted.

The participants mistook the 'surprised' emotion mostly for the 'happy' expression. The percentages to which the participants mistook the 'surprised' emotion for some other emotion are shown in Figure 5.22 for both parts of the questionnaire. Specifically, as 'other' emotions, the participants indicated 'afraid', 'excited', and 're-

Ioanna-Ourania Stathopoulou and George A. Tsihrintzis

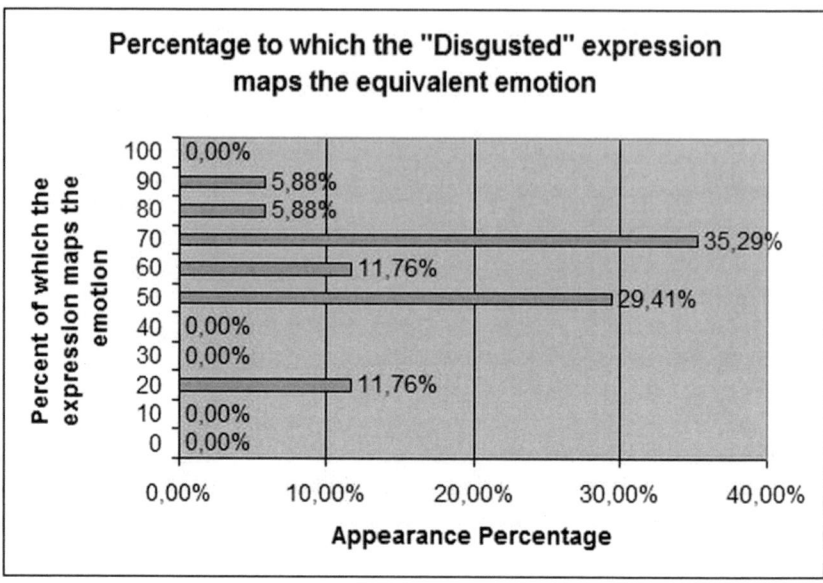

Figure 5.12: Graph of the percentage to which the 'disgusted' expression maps the equivalent emotion, based on the correct answers of the participants

lieved'. Again, some of these emotions, especially, the 'afraid' and the 'excited' can result in the formation of a facial expression of surprise.

The facial portions that helped the participants classify the expression were mostly the 'eyes', the 'mouth' and the 'shape of the face'. Specifically, the participants assigned percentages of significance of each facial portion as in Figure 5.23.

Finally, regarding the percentage to which the 'surprised' expression maps the equivalent emotion, the participants' answers are shown in Figure 5.24. Specifically, 22,32% of the participants indicated that it shows 100% percent of the emotion. Moreover, the majority of the participants thought that the 'happy' expression maps more than 70% of the emotion.

5.3.2 Difficulties of Facial Expression Classification as Outlined by the Participants

In the third (final) part of our questionnaire, we asked the participants to give their opinion regarding the difficulties when classifying an emotion. When it comes to recognizing an emotion from someone else's facial expression, the majority of the

Ioanna-Ourania Stathopoulou and George A. Tsihrintzis

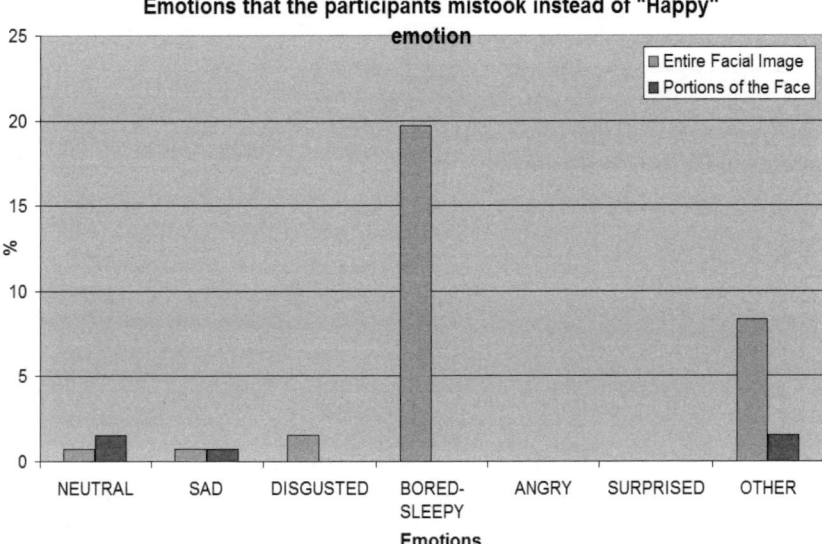

Figure 5.13: Graph of the percentage to which the participants mistook the 'happy' emotion for other emotions

participants consider this as a difficult task. Specific corresponding percentages are shown in Figure 5.25.

Regarding the most difficult emotion to recognize, the participants thought that this is the 'bored- sleepy' and the 'disgusted' emotions to percentages of 28% and 25%, respectively. However, the classification tasks in the first two parts of the questionnaire indicate the 'disgusted' and the 'sad' emotions as those identified with the highest error rates. Corresponding percentages for all emotions are shown in Figure 5.26.

The majority of participants (65%) considered the emotion of 'happiness' as the easiest emotion to recognize. Generally, 'positive' emotions were considered easier to recognize than 'negative' emotions. Corresponding percentages for all emotions are shown in Figure 5.27.

The participants' opinion regarding the easiest emotion to recognize coincided with the results of the questionnaire, as the 'happiness' and 'surprise' achieved the lowest error rates, of 17% and 7%, respectively. As for the most difficult emotion to recognize, our questionnaire showed that the 'disgusted' and the 'neutral' were the most difficult emotions to recognize. Error rates corresponding to all emotions are shown in Figure 5.28.

Ioanna-Ourania Stathopoulou and George A. Tsihrintzis

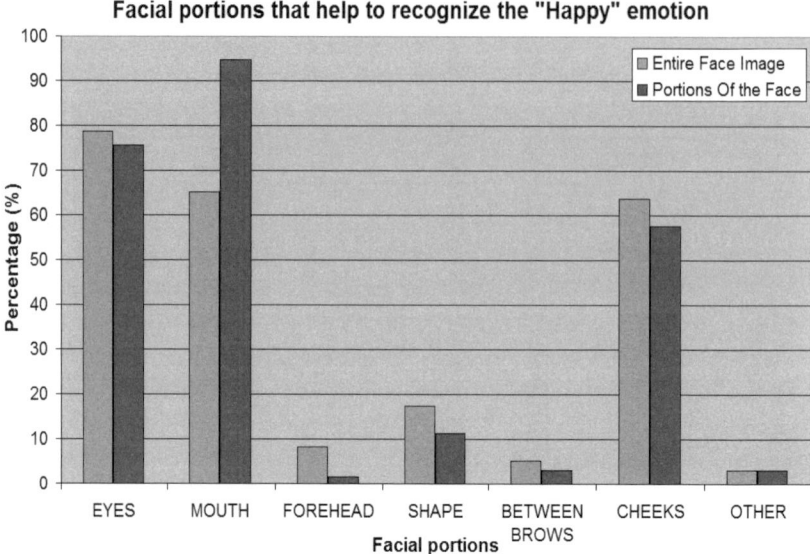

Figure 5.14: Graph of the percentage to which the 'happy' expression maps the equivalent emotion, based on the correct answers of the participants

The difference between the error rates of the preliminary and the detailed questionnaire is quite remarkable. This may be in line with the fact that for the development of the detailed questionnaire we used images of high resolution and quality from our own facial expression database. Moreover, the aforementioned databases were constructed by photographing Greeks and the expression on them were classified by Greeks, that is by people sharing the same culture and habits.

5.3.3 Statistical Significance of the Results

Most of the participants agreed that a facial expression represented the equivalent emotion with a percentage of 70% or higher. The results are shown in Table 5.2.

In the first part of the detailed questionnaire, we asked the participants to map the facial emotion from the facial expression whereas in the second part the participants were asked to perform the same task but only from portions of the face. Each participant could choose from the 7 of the most common emotions that we pointed out earlier, such as: 'angry', 'happy', 'neutral', 'surprised', 'sad', 'disgusted', 'bored-sleepy', or specify any other emotion that he/she thought appropriate. Next, the

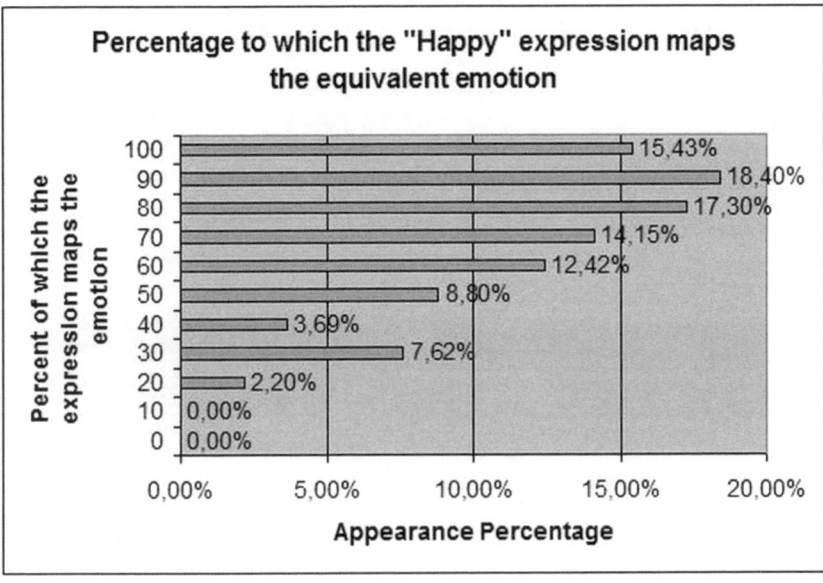

Figure 5.15: Graph of the percentage to which the 'happy' expression maps the equivalent emotion, based on the correct answers of the participants

Table 5.2: Percentage to which a facial expression represents an emotion

Percentage (%) to which an expression represents an emotion	User's answers
0%	0,00%
10%	0,00%
20%	0,76%
30%	2,27%
40%	1,52%
50%	9,85%
60%	14,39%
70%	31,06%
80%	21,97%
90%	15,91%
100%	2,27%

Ioanna-Ourania Stathopoulou and George A. Tsihrintzis

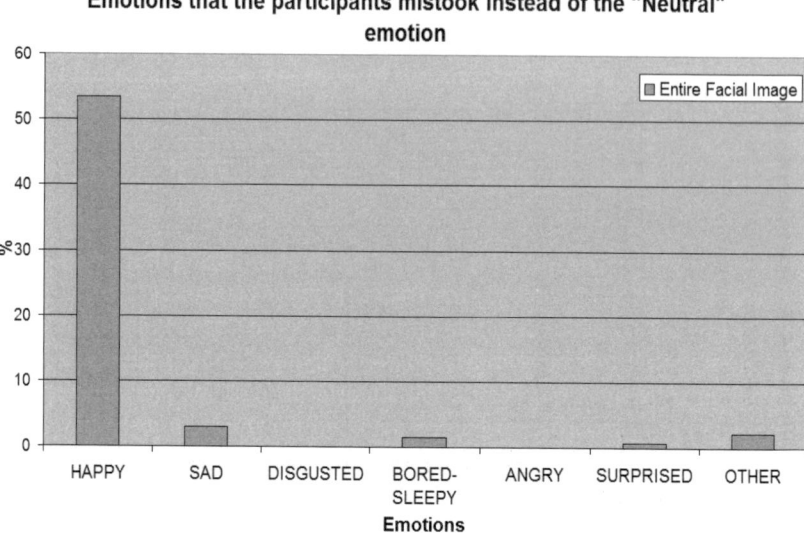

Figure 5.16: Graph of the percentage to which the participants mistook the 'neutral' emotion for other emotions

participant had to decide the degree (0-100%) of confidence to which he/she thought that the emotion was mapped from the facial image indicated. Finally, he/she had to indicate those features (such as the eyes, the nose, the mouth, the cheeks etc.) that had helped him/her make a decision.

In the second part of our questionnaire, where we had chosen specific facial portions to display to the participants, smaller emotion classification error rates were achieved than in the first part, where the entire face image was displayed. The differences in error rates are quite significant and show that the facial portions are well chosen. The differences between the error rates are shown in Table 5.3. The statistical significance of these results is shown in the last column (P-value) of Table 5.3 and is quite high.

5.3.4 Extraction of Facial Expression Classification Features

The facial portions that helped the users to understand the emotions are mostly the eyes, the mouth, and the cheeks. In some expressions, e.g. the 'angry' expression, other very important facial portions arose, such as the texture between the brows.

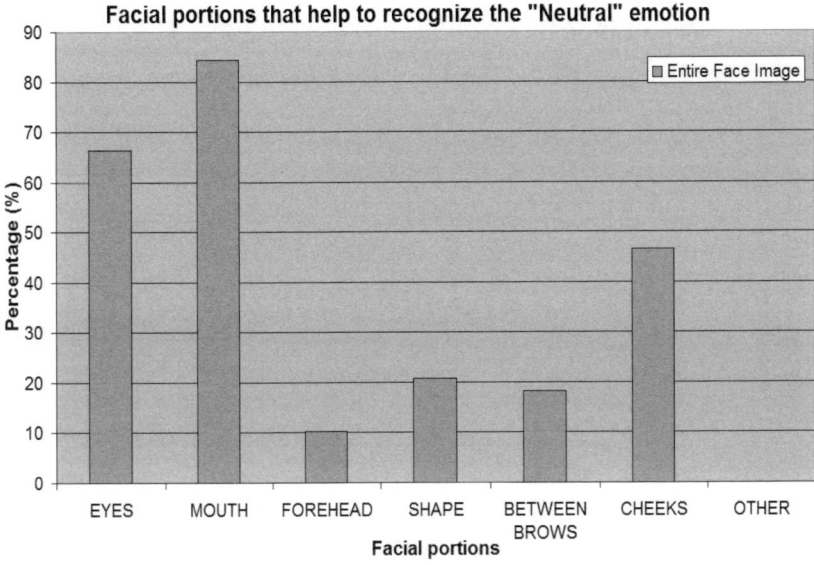

Figure 5.17: Graph of the percentage to which the 'neutral' expression maps the equivalent emotion, based on the correct answers of the participants

Table 5.3. Error rate comparison between the two parts of the questionnaire

Emotion	Error Rates 1st Part	2nd Part	Difference	P-Value
Neutral	61,74%		Not applicable	Not applicable
Happy	31,06%	3,79%	27,27%	0,000000003747
Sad	65,91%	17,42%	48,48%	0,00000000035
Disgusted	81,26%	86,36%	-5,10%	0,029324580032
Bored-Sleepy	49,24%	21,97%	27,27%	0,000012193203
Angry	23,86%	30,30%	-6,44%	0,026319945845
Surprised	10,23%	4,55%	5,68%	0,001390518291
Other	9,47%	18,18%	-8,71%	

Ioanna-Ourania Stathopoulou and George A. Tsihrintzis

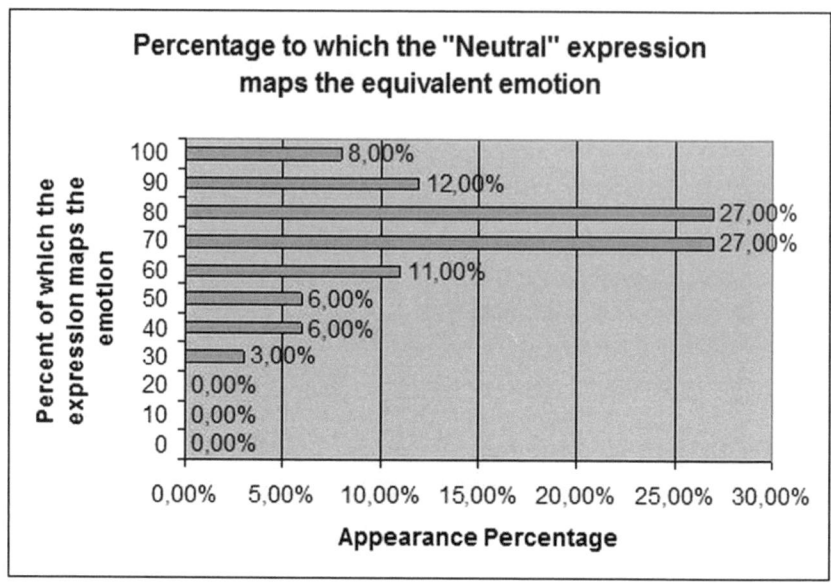

Figure 5.18: Graph of the percentage to which the 'neutral' expression maps the equivalent emotion, based on the correct answers of the participants

Table 5.4: Important features for each facial expression

	A	B	C	D	E	F	G
1	66,3	81,6	63,6	82,6	77,3	55,7	83,7
2	84,5	67,8	76,1	81,1	79,9	81,4	88,8
3	10,2	22,7	4,2	6,1 4,9	30,9	46,4	
4	20,8	14,4	31,1	7,6	14,4	10,0	11,4
5	18,2	59,5	8,7	3,0	4,2	8,9	23,7
6	46,6	8,1	30,7	28,8	60,6	21,4	5,1
7	0,0	2,5	3,0	3,0	3,0	2,3	1,5

These results are shown in Tables 5.4 and 5.5. In Table 5.4 the three most important features for the recognition of each expression are highlighted.

Based on the results in Table 4, we can identify the three most important features for the identification of each emotion. We examined such combinations of features for each expression to see whether the participants who misrecognized expressions

Ioanna-Ourania Stathopoulou and George A. Tsihrintzis

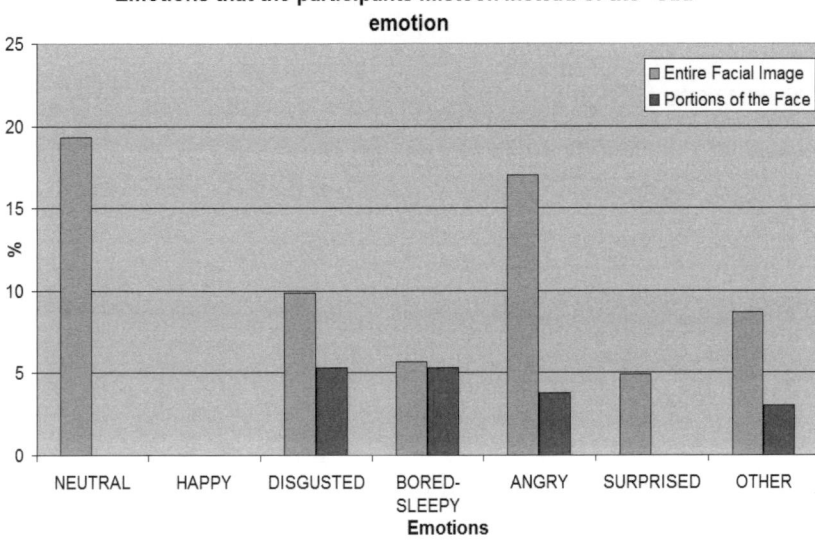

Figure 5.19: Graph of the percentage to which the participants mistook the 'sad' emotion for other emotions

Table 5.5: Mapping

1	Eyes	A	Neutral
2	Mouth	B	Angry
3	Texture of the Forehead	C	Bored-Sleepy
4	Shape of the Face	D	Disgusted
5	Texture between the brows	E	Happy
6	Texture of the cheeks	F	Sad
7	Other	G	Surprised

based their answers on different face portions than participants who recognized expressions correctly. From our studies, we can summarize the results for each emotion, as follows:

'angry': (1) The combination of the three features ('the eyes', 'the mouth' and 'the region between the brows') was used by the participants who recognized the expression correctly at a percentage of 38,31% for the first and 30,43% for the second

Ioanna-Ourania Stathopoulou and George A. Tsihrintzis

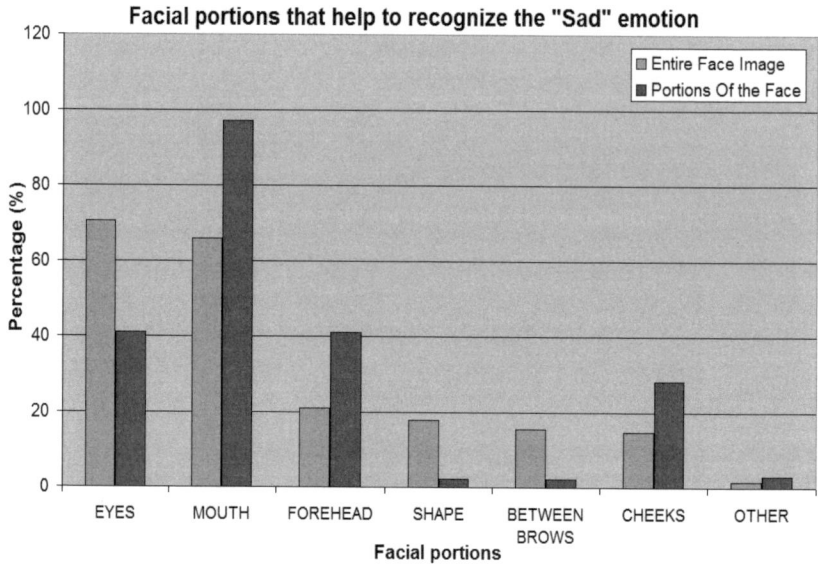

Figure 5.20: Graph of the percentage to which the 'sad' expression maps the equivalent emotion, based on the correct answers of the participants

questionnaire part. (2) In the first questionnaire part, 38,1% of the participants who recognized the expression considered only 'the eyes' as significant. (3) All the feature combinations that included the 'region between the brows' feature resulted to correct answers.

'bored-sleepy': The 'eyes' feature (alone or combined with other features) is important for the expression recognition task. Specifically: (1) The combination of 'the eyes' and 'the mouth' was used by the participants who recognized the expression correctly at a average percentage of 27,92% for the two parts of the questionnaire. (2) The 20,86% of the participants who gave the correct answers, used only 'the eyes'. (3) Finally, the combination of the three features ('the eyes', 'the mouth' and 'shape of the face' was used by the 15,98% of the participants who gave the correct answer.

'disgusted': The 'disgusted' expression achieved the highest error rate, 83,81% on average for the two parts of the questionnaire. Thus, it is difficult to indicate with safety the facial portions which led to good results, as only a relatively small number of the participants managed to recognize the emotion from the facial expression. Our

Ioanna-Ourania Stathopoulou and George A. Tsihrintzis

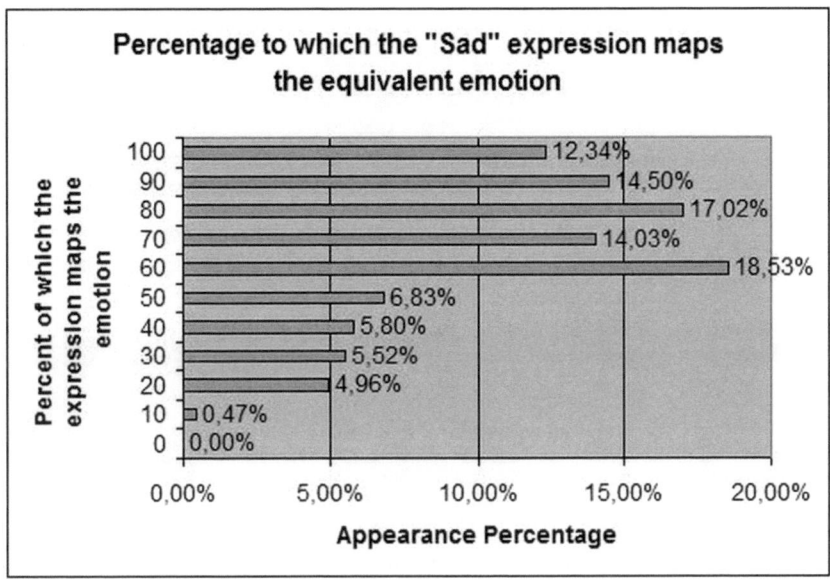

Figure 5.21: Graph of the percentage to which the 'sad' expression maps the equivalent emotion, based on the correct answers of the participants

studies concluded that: (1) The combination of 'the eyes' and 'the mouth' resulted to the best results with an average error rate of 55,56% for the two parts of the questionnaire. (2) A percentage of 16,67% of the participants who gave the correct answers used only 'the eyes'.

'happy': (1) The combination of the three features ('the eyes', 'the mouth' and 'the cheeks') was used by the participants who recognized the expression correctly at a percentage of 35,16% for the first and 41,73% for the second part of the questionnaire. (2) The participants who considered only 'the eyes' as significant for the recognition task achieved an average error rate of 24,63%, which leads us to the conclusion that the use of only 'the eyes' feature, cannot help to recognize the 'happy' expression.

'neutral': (1) The combination of the three features ('the eyes', 'the mouth' and 'the cheeks') was used by the participants who recognized the expression correctly at a average percentage of 38,45% for the two parts of the questionnaire. (2) The combination of 'the eyes' and 'the mouth' resulted to correct answers with 23,60% (3) Generally, the 'eyes' and the 'cheeks' can be considered as the most important features for the recognition task.

Ioanna-Ourania Stathopoulou and George A. Tsihrintzis

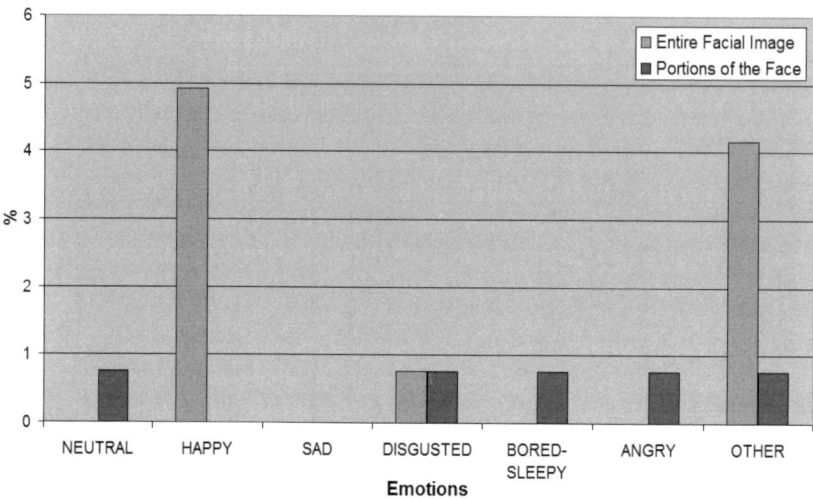

Figure 5.22: Graph of the percentage to which the participants mistook the 'surprised' emotion for other emotions

'sad': (1) The 'mouth' was the feature that was used from the users that classified correctly the 'sad' expression, at average percentage of 31,70% for the two parts of the questionnaire. (2)The combination of the 'eyes' and the 'mouth' led to good answers with average error rate of 23,16%.

'surprised': (1) The combination of the three features ('the eyes', 'the mouth' and 'the region of the forehead') was used by the participants who recognized the expression correctly at a average percentage of 63,49% for the two parts of the questionnaire. (2) The combinations of the 'forehead' with other features resulted to good answers. (3) The users that thought important only the 'mouth' feature, failed to recognize the emotion at an error rate of 12,96%.

The results are summarized in Table 5.6, where the three most important facial feature combinations are shown for each expression. This also leads to the single most important feature. Also, Table 5.6 shows the least important feature, as the one which leads to erroneous recognitions by the participants.

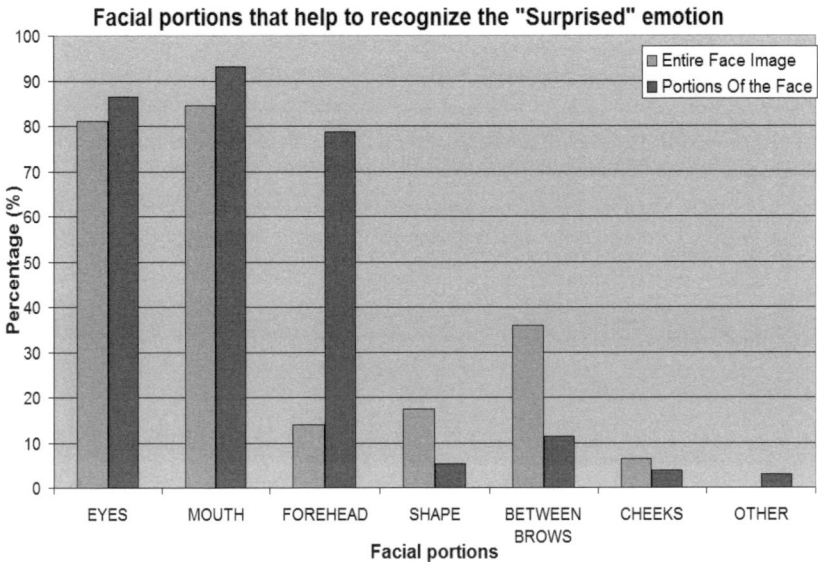

Figure 5.23: Graph of the percentage to which the 'surprised' expression maps the equivalent emotion, based on the correct answers of the participants

5.4 Summary - Conclusions

IN this Chapter, we described the two empirical studies that we conducted in order to set our error goal for our facial expression recognition system and understand how people classify an emotion. Based on the answers and the comments from the participants, we were led to the following assumptions:

1. Based on the participants' comments and the questionnaire results, classifying an emotion of an unknown person from his/hers face image,is not a easy task. During interpersonal relationships, people usually recognize the emotion of someone they know almost instantly. However, this is not the case when they are faced with an unknown person's image.

2. The cultural exposure increases the chances of correct recognition of facial expressions indicating cultural dependence in the ways people express themselves. This point is further strengthened from the results of our empirical studies. There is a big difference between the error rates of the first questionnaire, where we used images on non-Greek subjects, and the second questionnaire, where we

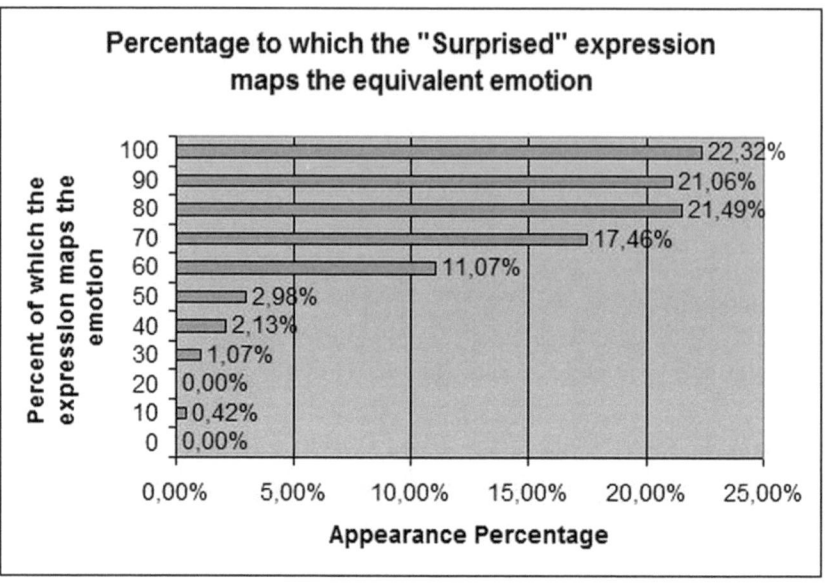

Figure 5.24: Graph of the percentage to which the 'surprised' expression maps the equivalent emotion, based on the correct answers of the participants

used images from our own facial expression database. The results for the two questionnaires are summarized in Table 5.7. As we can observe, for the majority of the expressions the success rates were extremely comparable for the second questionnaire, as they achieved a difference beginning from 13% to 46%, compared to the first questionnaire. Exceptions were observed for the 'neutral' and the 'disgust' emotion.

3. In the majority of the emotions, the participants achieved better results in classifying the emotion when they were faced with parts of the subject's face rather than the entire face image, as shown in Table 5.3

4. In the majority of the expressions, the features that helped a participant to recognize the emotion were the 'eyes' and the 'mouth'. In some cases, the 'texture of the cheeks' and the 'texture of the forehead' were also taken into account by participants of the empirical studies.

Ioanna-Ourania Stathopoulou and George A. Tsihrintzis

DIFFICULTY IN UNDERSTANDING EMOTIONS

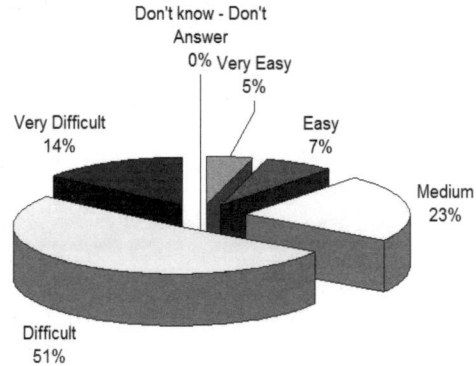

Figure 5.25: The participants' answers regarding the level of difficulty of the facial expression recognition task

MOST DIFFICULT EMOTION TO RECOGNIZE

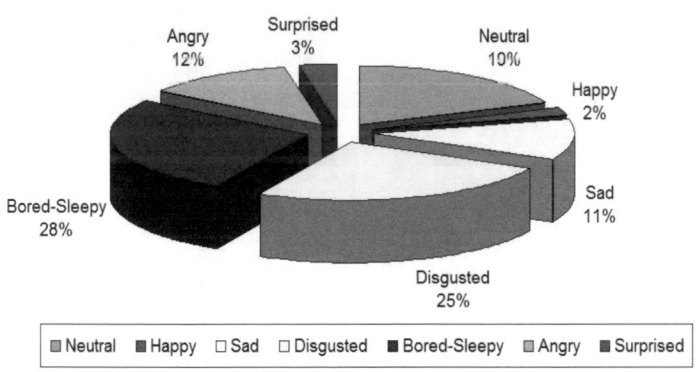

Figure 5.26: The participants' answers regarding the most difficult emotion to recognize

EASIEST EMOTION TO RECOGNIZE

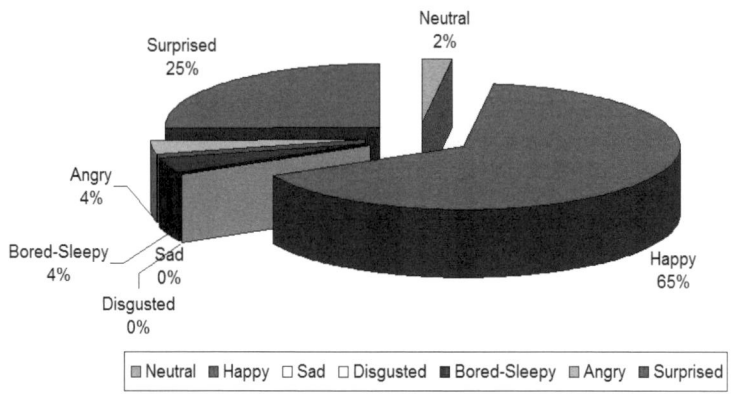

Figure 5.27: The participants' answers regarding the most difficult emotion to recognize

Average error rates for each expression for the two parts of the questionnaire

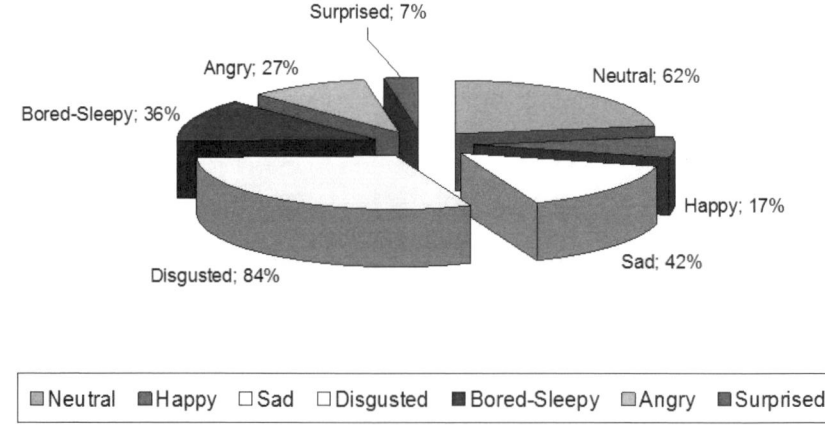

Figure 5.28: Error rates in recognizing the expressions in our detailed questionnaire

Table 5.6: Identification of the most and least important features for each expression

Most Important Features or Combinations of Features			Least Important	Single Most Important Feature
Angry				
'eyes', 'mouth' & 'rbb'	'eyes' & 'rbb'	'mouth' & 'rbb'	'eyes' & mouth	'rbb'
34,37%	14,33%	8,94%	8,94%	
Bored-Sleepy				
'eyes' & 'mouth'	'eyes'	'eyes', 'mouth' & 'shape'	'mouth'	'eyes'
27,92%	20,86%	15,98%	25,49%	25,49%
Disgusted				
'eyes' & 'mouth'	'eyes'		'cheeks'	'eyes'
16,67%				55,56%
Happy				
'eyes', 'mouth' & 'cheeks'	'eyes' & 'mouth'	'mouth' & 'cheeks'	'eyes'	'mouth' or 'cheeks'
38,45%	23,60%	13,05%	24,63%	
Neutral				
'eyes' & 'mouth'	'mouth'	'eyes'	'eyes', 'mouth'	'mouth' or 'eyes' & 'cheeks'
39,60%	14,85%	11,88%	36,81%	
Sad				
'mouth'	'eyes' & 'mouth'		'forehead'	'mouth'
31,70%	23,16%			
Surprised				
'eyes', 'mouth' & 'forehead'	'mouth' &'forehead'	'eyes' & 'forehead'	'mouth'	'forehead'
63,49%	7,50%	4,49%	12,96%	

Table 5.7: Differences between the First and the Second Questionnaire

Emotions	Average Success Rates		Difference
	1st Questionnaire	2nd Questionnaire	
Neutral	65%	38%	-27%
Happiness	70%	83%	+13%
Surprise	78%	93%	+15%
Anger	20%	73%	+53%
Disgust	37%	16%	-21%
Sadness	12%	58%	+46%
Boredom	-	64%	-

Ioanna-Ourania Stathopoulou and George A. Tsihrintzis

6

Visual-Facial Emotion Recognition System

Calm down, it's only ones and zeros!

—*Kathy Mar*

A S stated in previous sections, expressions play a significant communicative role in human-to-human interaction and interpersonal relations because they can reveal information about the affective state, cognitive activity, personality, intention and psychological state of a person and, in fact, this information may be difficult to mask. The ability of humans to analyze facial expressions of another person is one of the objects of study of the scientific areas of pattern recognition and computer vision and the results of this study are applied in the design of interactive systems for more efficient and friendlier human-computer interfaces, multimedia services, security control systems, criminology etc.

When attempting to mimic human-to-human communication, human-computer interaction systems must determine the psychological state of a computer user, so that the computer can react accordingly. This may be exploited in the design of advanced human-computer interfaces, which attempt to take into consideration the variations of the emotions of human users during the interaction and make the computer react accordingly. Thus, vision-based human-computer interactive systems with the ability to process computer user face images and extract information about the user"s identity, state and intent would prove very effective and friendly. Similar information can also be used in multimedia interactive services, security control systems or in criminology to uncover possible criminals.

Most works in automated facial expression analysis assume that the conditions under which a facial image or an image sequence is acquired are known and controlled. Usually, the image has the face in front view and the background is fairly simple, usually uniform in color. In the majority of previous works, the location and the extend of the face is known or easily computed. However, in real environments, this is not the case. Determining the exact location of the face in a digitized facial image is a more complex problem. First, the scale and the orientation of the face can vary from image to image. Also, if the photos are taken from a fixed camera, there is no way to know a priori the size and the angle of the face. For the above reasons and in order to fully automate the procedure of facial expression recognition, a two-step task is required: (1) a face detection step in which the system determines whether or not there are any faces in an image and, if so, returns the location and extent of each face and, (2) a facial expression classification step, in which the system attempts to recognize the expression formed on a detected face.

The development of such fully automated face image analysis systems, capable of detecting a face and classifying a person"s facial expression without errors, is quite challenging. Some of the challenges that have to be addressed in developing such a system arise from the facts that faces are non-rigid and have a high degree of variability in size, shape, color and texture. Furthermore, variations in pose, image orientation and conditions add to the level of difficulty of the problem. Moreover, the variability in the ways people express themselves, depending on their culture, psychological state and habits, make it even more difficult to determine one"s psychological condition through his/her face image. These facts can make the analysis of the facial expressions of another person difficult and often ambiguous.

In previous sections, we tried to understand how scientists and ordinary people interpret and understand the emotions. Our study concluded to the following assumptions:

1. There is on-going debate about how psychologists understand the emotions and the facial expressions in general. Many studies have pointed to six basic emotions, namely 'anger', 'disgust', 'fear', 'happiness', 'sadness' and 'surprise'. Despite this fact, studies have also shown that there is a cultural specificity regarding the emotion expression and understanding.

2. This assumption was further strengthened by our own studies. As stated in Chapter 4, we developed two different questionnaires. During this process, Greek people were asked to map an image to an respective emotion. The first questionnaire contained subjects of other cultures, besides the Greek, who were expressing an emotion, in contrary to the second questionnaire which contained Greek people forming an expression. The success rates for the two questionnaires are extremely different. Specifically, the average success rate for the first questionnaire is 47% in contrary to the second, which scored 60,72%. This led us to the assumption that emotions are culturally specific.

3. We also studied previous attempts towards the development of: (1) a facial expression database, (2) a face detection system and (3) a facial expression recognition system. We set the requirements for an ideal result for each of the

aforementioned three occasions, respectively. Our study concluded to the fact that there are some interesting attempts but there is none that can cover all the requirements.

4. Moreover, as our aim is to build a facial expression recognition system which can be used in more advance human-computer interaction techniques, there was a need for the system to recognize expressions that are common during a human-computer interaction session. Indeed, based on our studies, facial expressions corresponding to the 'neutral', 'happiness', 'sadness', 'surprise', 'anger', 'disgust' and 'boredom-sleepiness' psychological states arise very commonly during a typical human-computer interaction session, as stated in Chapter 4.

5. Finally, as there was no facial expression database that could cover our requirements, we developed our own facial expression database as described in Chapter 4

Based on these assumptions, we developed our own fully automated facial expression recognition system. The system consists of two modules: (1) a face detection module that determines whether a face is present in an image [257, 258, 259, 11, 260] and, if so, estimates its location and extent, and (2) a facial expression classification module that classifies the expression on a face that has been detected by the first module. We will present these two modules extensively in the following sections.

6.1 Face Detection

6.1.1 P. Sinha's Template

The face detection module follows a feature-based approach, which combines template matching and image invariant approaches. This approach relies on an observation that P. Sinha made while aiming at finding a model that would satisfactorily represent some basic relationships between the various regions of a human face [147]. Specifically, P. Sinha found that the *relative* brightness of different parts of a face, such as the eyes, the cheeks, the nose and the forehead, remains unchanged, even when variations in illumination change the *individual* brightness of these parts. This relative brightness between facial parts is captured by an appropriate set of pairwise brighter-darker relationships between sub-regions of the face, as in Figure 6.1.

6.1.2 The Face Detection Algorithm - Image Preprocessing

The face detection algorithm is built upon the P. Sinha template and preprocesses an image in order to enhance the relationships implied by the template and, subsequently,

111

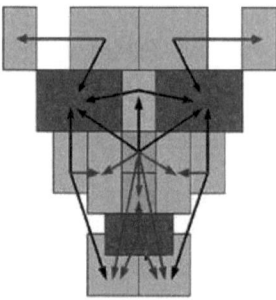

Figure 6.1: The P. Sinha Template

feeds the image into an artificial neural network to determine the presence and location of faces in the image. Specifically, the algorithm steps are as follows:

1. *Load image, which can be 3-dimensional (color or grayscale image)*

2. *Scan through image with a 35-by-35 pixel window. The image region contained in the window constitutes the 'window pattern', which is examined to determine whether it contains a face. The window size is gradually increased, so as to cover all the possible face sizes in the image.*

3. *Preprocess the window pattern as follows:*

   (a) *Apply Histogram Equalization techniques to enhance the contrast within the window pattern.*

   (b) *Compute the eigenvectors of the image using the Principal Component Analysis, a sample of the eigenfaces can be seen in Figure refeigenfaces and use the Nystrom Algorithm [261] to compute the normalized cuts.*

   (c) *Compute three clusters of the image using the k-means algorithm and color each cluster with the average color.*

   (d) *Convert the image from colored to grayscale (2-dimensional).*

4. *Resize image into dimensions of 20-by-20 pixels and feed it into the artificial neural network-based detectors described in the the following section.*

The resulting three clusters and the the grayscale image which is fed to an artificial neural network can be seen in Table 6.1 for three face and three non-face images. Specifically, in the first column we can observe the input image, whereas, in second column we have the three clusters. Usually, each cluster of a face consists of:

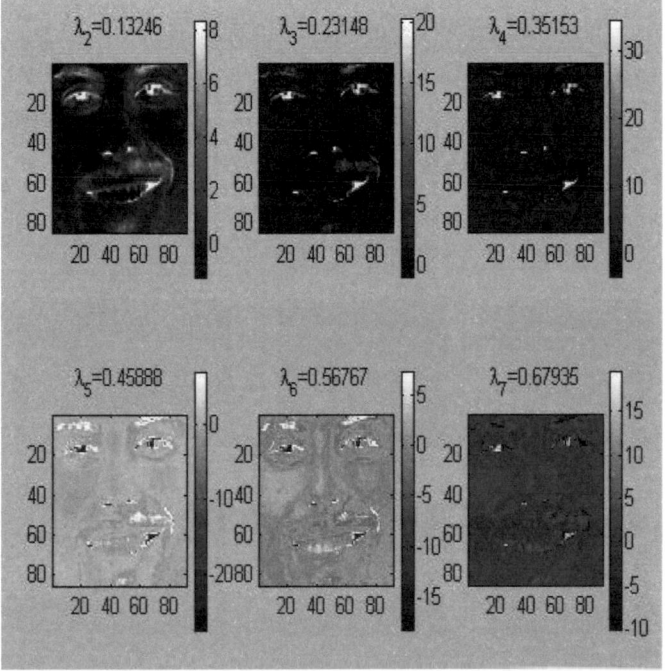

Figure 6.2: The eigenfaces of a face image

1. In the first cluster we have parts of the face: such as the eyes, the mouth and the nostrils

2. In the second cluster we have parts around the facial features located in the first cluster: regions around the eyes, the mouth and the nostrils

3. In the third cluster we have all the other face region that has been excluded from the above other two clusters

Finally, in the third column, we can observe the resulting grayscale clustered image which is fed to the artificial network classifiers.

6.1.3   Artificial Neural Network-Based Face Detectors

We have developed and tested various neural network-based face detectors, two of which are presented next. To train the neural network, we used a set of 285 images

Table 6.1: The computed three clusters

of faces and non-faces, which were gathered from sources in the World Wide Web. We paid special attention to include in the training image set, non-face images that resemble human faces, such as dog, monkey and other animal images. All training images were preprocessed as described in the previous Section 6.1.2. An example of the pictures used for training the artificial neural networks are shown in Figure 6.3

A network with three hidden layers

This network consists of three hidden layers of thirty, ten and two neurons respectively, as in Figure 6.5 and 6.4. As input, it takes the entire window pattern of 20-by-20 pixels and produces a two-dimensional vector output, which classifies the window pattern as 'face' or 'non-face'. Specifically, the output vector equals $[1, 0]$, if the

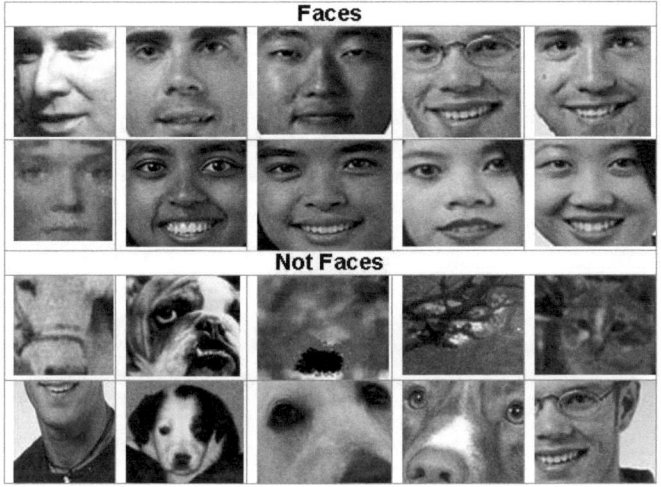

Figure 6.3: Sample images of our Face Detection training set

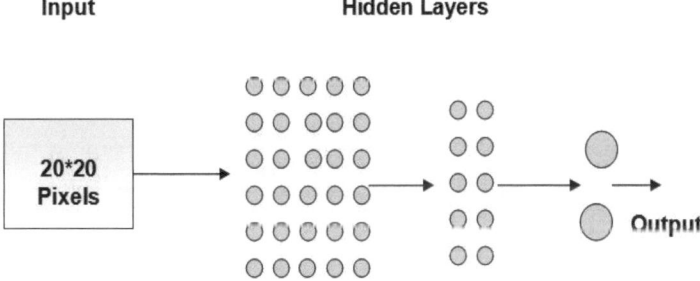

Figure 6.4: Three Hidden Layer Network (Simple Demonstration)

window pattern represents a face, and $[0,1]$, otherwise. This implies that the output vector describes the degree of membership of the network input image in each of the 'face-image' and 'non-face-image' classes.

A network with four hidden layers

This neural network consists of four hidden layers with one, four, four and two neurons, respectively. Its input data consists of the following three types: (1) the entire

Ioanna-Ourania Stathopoulou and George A. Tsihrintzis

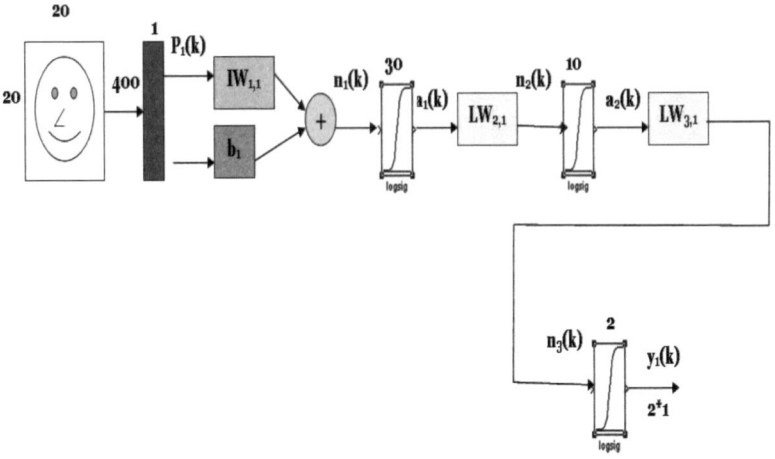

Figure 6.5: Three Hidden Layer Network

window pattern (a 20-by-20 pixel image), (2) four portions of the window pattern, each 10-by-10 pixels and (3) an additional four portions of the window pattern, each 5-by-20 pixels. The three input data types are fed into different hidden layers of the network. Specifically, the first, second, and third input data sets are fed into the first, second and third hidden layer, respectively. The output vector of this network is again a two-dimensional vector, which equals $[1, 0]$, if the input data represent a face, and $[0, 1]$, otherwise. Clearly, the first network consists of fewer hidden layers, but contains a higher total number of neurons and takes less input data than the second network. The network structure is shown in Figures 6.7 and 6.6.

6.1.4 Performance Evaluation

To train these two networks, we used a common training set of 285 images of faces and non-faces, as mentioned before. During the training process, the two networks achieved error rates of 10^{-1} and 10^{-10}, respectively. The neural networks differences in terms of structure, input data and results are described briefly in Table 6.2.

Some results of the two neural networks can be seen in Figure 6.8. The first network, even though it consisted of more neurons than the second one, did not detect faces in the images to a satisfactory degree, as did the second network. On the other hand, the execution speeds of two networks are comparable. Therefore, the second network was found superior in detecting faces in images.

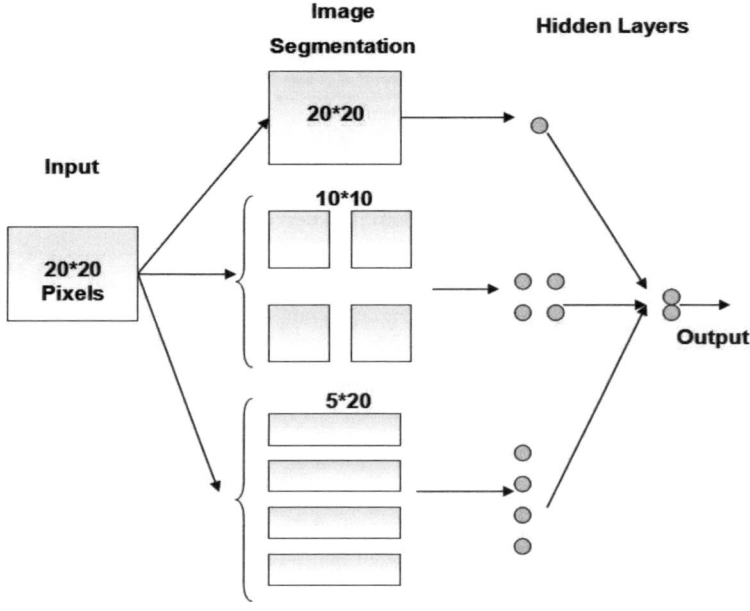

Figure 6 6· Four Hidden Layer Network (Simple demonstration)

Table 6.2: Description of the two neural network classifiers

First Neural Network	Second Neural Network
Neural Network Structure	
3 Hidden Layers	4 Hidden Layers
More Neurons in each layer	Fewer Neurons in each layer
Input Data	
Entire face image data as input	Entire face image data and parts of the face as input
Training Set	
285 face and non face images	285 face and non face images
Error rates	
10^{-1}	10^{-10}

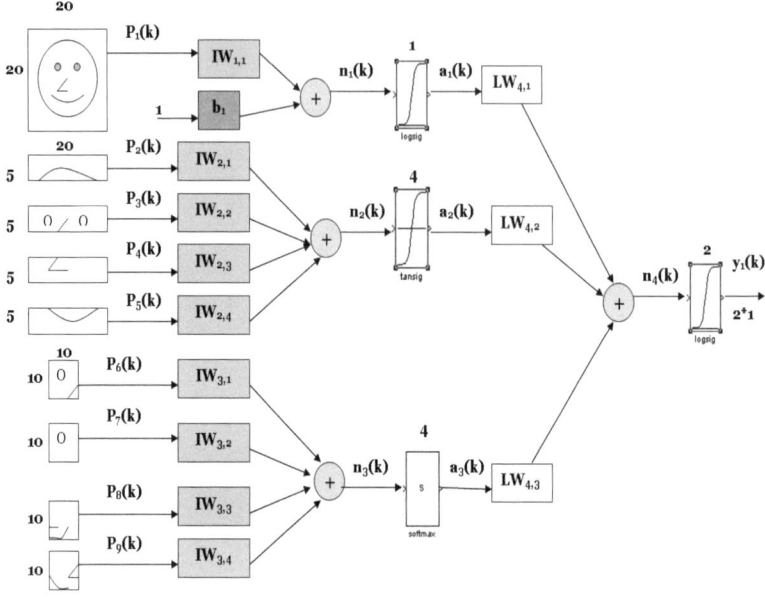

Figure 6.7: Four Hidden Layer Network

To measure the performance of the second network [257, 258, 259, 11, 260] in detecting faces in images, we tested the network in four different sets of images:

1. 120 various images (60 female and 60 male photos) of different sizes and resolutions gathered from the World Wide Web and other sources(e.g scanning old photo images)

2. 50 images (25 female and 25 male photos) from our own facial expression database where people may form some expression

3. 535 face images (205 female and 330 male photos)acquired in the first efforts to construct a facial expression database (low quality images)[259]

4. 50 non human face images (images of pets and animals, complex backgrounds and parts of the face and human)

The first set of images consists of images usually containing more than one faces in complex backgrounds. The faces may be partially occluded, slightly rotated or in side

Face Images			
Input Image	Preprocessed Window Pattern	First ANN's output	Second ANN's output
	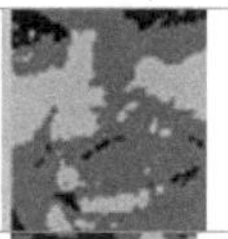	[1 ; 0]	[0.5 ; 0.5]
	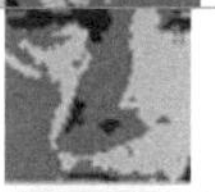	[0.947; 0.063]	[0.5 ; 0.5]
		[1 ; 0]	[0.5 ; 0.5]
		[0.9717;0.0283]	[0.5 ; 0.5]
		[1 ; 0]	[0.6 ;0.4]
Not-Face Images			
Input Image	Preprocessed Window Pattern	First ANN's output	Second ANN's output
		[0 ; 1]	[0.5 ; 0.5]
		[0 ; 1]	[0.5 ,0.5]
		[0 ; 1]	[0.5 ;0.5]

Figure 6.8: The face detection neural networks responses

view. Also there are differences in the size, aspect ratio and resolution among these photos. The second set of face images consists of a random selection of our own facial expression database, so the subjects may be forming one of the seven expressions:

'neutral', 'happy', 'sad', 'surprised', 'disgusted', 'angry' and 'bored-sleepy'. Finally, the third set of images consists of low quality photos acquired with web cameras. This set was constructed during our fist efforts to build a facial expression database, so there is only one face in this photos and the subject may be forming facial expressions and/or images acquired in side view. The dataset included a random selection of images in front and side view and images acquired from subjects forming one of the eight expressions: 'neutral', 'happy', 'sad', 'surprised', 'angry', 'disgusted', 'screaming' and 'bored-sleepy'. The face detection results are summarized in Table 6.3.

Table 6.3: Results of the Face Detection System for the three datasets

Dataset information	# of detected faces	# of undetected faces	Success rates (%)
1st Dataset: Images gathered from WWW and other sources			
Female	51	9	85,00%
Male	58	2	96,67%
Sum	**109**	**11**	**90,83%**
2nd Dataset: Images from our database			
Female	23	2	92,00%
Male	24	1	96,00%
Sum	**47**	**3**	**94,00%**
3rd Dataset: Images from our low quality database			
Female	115	90	56,09%
Male	275	55	83,33%
Sum	**390**	**145**	**72,89%**

The system managed to detect face with respective success rates of 90,83%, 94,00% and 72,89%, for the three sets. Errors (misses) occurred mostly because of overly bright illumination conditions which did not allow the extraction of facial features during k-means clustering. It was also observed that the detection of female faces was more difficult than the detection of male faces, possibly because facial features in female faces are not as tense as those in male faces. The results from these two groups are summarized in Table 6.3. Some typical results of the face detection system are depicted in Figures 6.9, 6.10, 6.11, 6.12, 6.13, and in Table 6.4. Table 6.5 for each of the four sets of images that we use to measure the performance of the Face Detection Subsystem.

In Figures 6.9 and 6.10, we observe the face as detected by our system and placed inside a green box. All images in these Figures correspond to the first test set of images, so they are images gathered from the World Wide Web or old photos scanned and used for testing our face detection system. As this is the case, we may have various faces in an image, where the subjects maybe posing during image shooting, or their faces may be partially occluded, rotated, or blurred due to noise. Specifically, in Subfigure 6.9(a) people are posing during photo shooting, so the resulting photo can be considered to be acquired in a rather controlled environment, as in these cases the photos don't usually contain faces partially occluded or rotated. Moreover the cases of bad quality images or noise because of blurring and/or subjects' movement are scarcely present in this type of images. On the contrary, in Subfigure 6.9(b), the photo is slightly blurred because of the subjects' motion and one of the two faces are slightly rotated. The case of complex backgrounds, many subjects and different face views is shown in Subfigure 6.10(a), where there are many faces of different sizes in the image, some of which are in side view or partially occluded. Finally, in Subfigure 6.10(b) there is an old family photo which was scanned and used to test the neural network classifier. In this case, the photo can be considered of low quality because of the alterations that this photo was subjected to as time passed.

 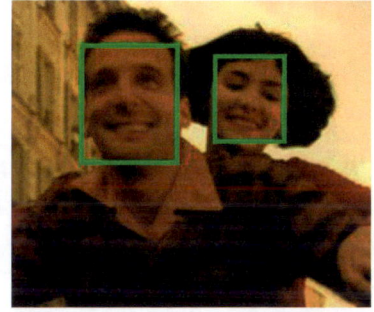

(a) People are posing during photo shoot- (b) Faces are slightly blurred or rotated
ing   because of the subjects' movement

Figure 6.9: Face Detection results for the first set of images (images gathered from the World Wide Web) (a), (b)

As the aim of developing the face detection system was to facilitate and automate the facial expression recognition process, the system should perform well in cases where the subject is forming an expression. In order to check its performance we tested the face detection system using images from our own facial expression database, so, in this case, the subjects are posing during photo shooting and are forming some of the seven facial expressions, which correspond to 'neutral', 'angry', 'happy', 'sad', 'surprised', 'disgusted', or 'bored-sleepy'. Figures 6.11, 6.12 and 6.13 correspond to our facial expression database. Again, we can observe the face detected by our system and placed inside a green box.

Ioanna-Ourania Stathopoulou and George A. Tsihrintzis

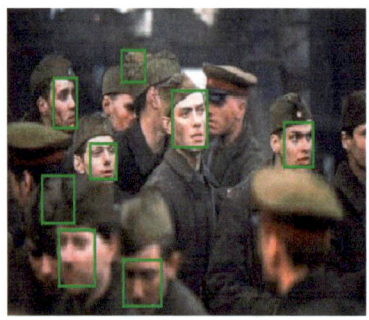
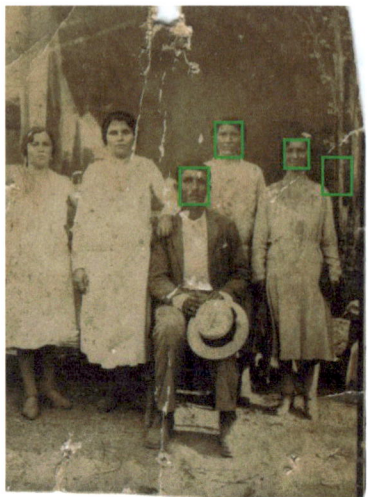

(a) Many faces in complex backgrounds   (b) Scanned old photo

Figure 6.10: Face Detection results for the first set of images (images gathered from the World Wide Web) (a), (b)

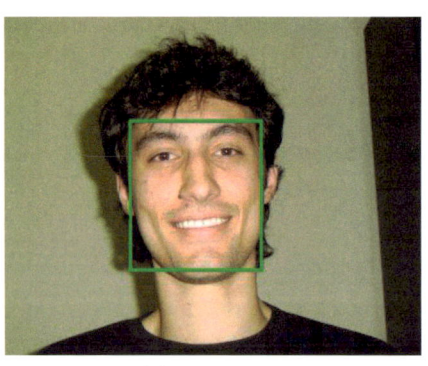
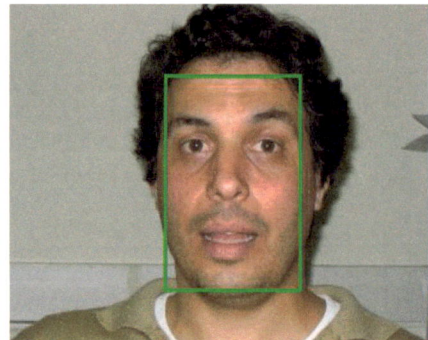

(a) 'Happiness'   (b) 'Surprise'

Figure 6.11: Face Detection results for the second set of images, where the subject is forming an expression (a), (b)

The most challenging task of our face detection system was testing it with 535 face images (205 female and 330 male photos) acquired in the first efforts to construct a facial expression database. As mentioned in Chapter 4, these images are of low quality

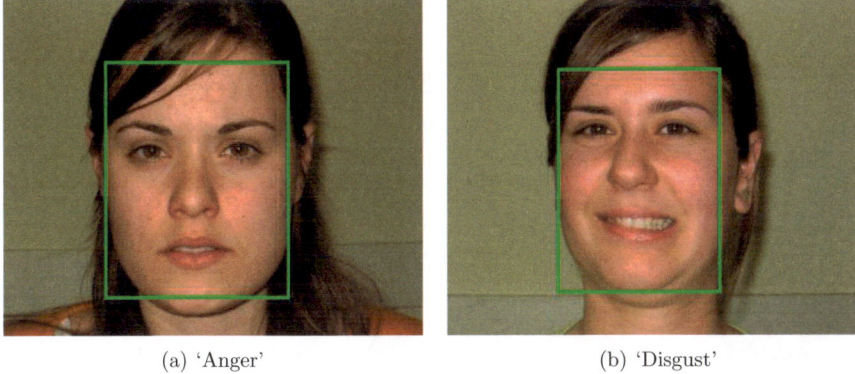

(a) 'Anger'   (b) 'Disgust'

Figure 6.12: Face Detection results for the second set of images, where the subject is forming an expression (a), (b)

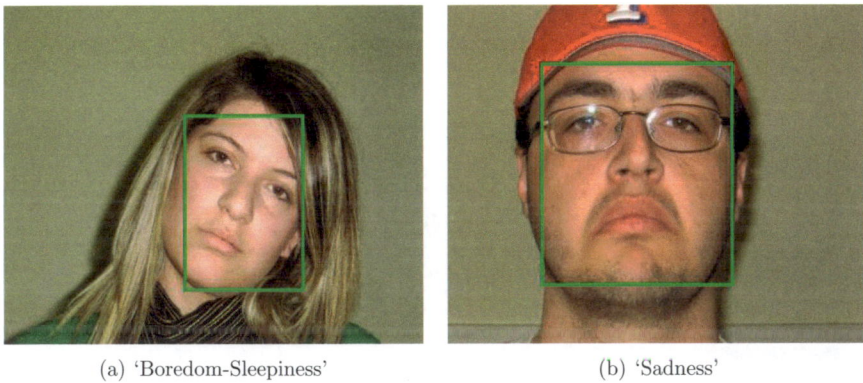

(a) 'Boredom-Sleepiness'   (b) 'Sadness'

Figure 6.13: Face Detection results for the second set of images, where the subject is forming an expression (a), (b)

as they were acquired using simple web cameras. The images were of 320-by-240 pixel resolution, the size of the face varies from 170-by-220 to 70-by-80 pixels and the subjects were forming an expression during photo shooting. Specifically, the subjects maybe forming the 'neutral, 'happy', 'sad', 'surprised' 'bored-sleepy', 'disappointed', 'screaming', 'angry', 'disgusted' and 'talk' expressions. Since we built a three-camera system to acquire the data, we also have faces in front and side view. In Table 6.4, we demonstrate some results from this third set of images. In the first column we depict the image, while in the second column we demonstrate the part of the image which contains a human face. This part was used as input to the Face Detection Subsystem, so it was preprocessed (the result of preprocessing can be seen in third column) and fed to the artificial neural network. The network response is shown in the fourth column.

Table 6.4: Sample images of our facial expression database

Original Image	Window Pattern	Pre-processed image	Network Response
			[1;0]
			[0,836;0,164]
			[0,9531;0,0469]
			[1;0]
			[1;0]
			[0.9865; 0.0135]

Except for the images which contained faces, the final test aimed at checking the system performance in cases where there were no faces. This test consisted of images that could confuse the neural network and lead it to a positive answer. So, in this set we tested our network with 50 images of pets and animals, complex backgrounds and parts of a face or human corpse. In Table 6.5, we demonstrate some results from this fourth set of images. Again, in the first column we depict the image, while in the second column we demonstrate the preprocessed image which is used as an input to the artificial neural network. The network's response is shown in the third column.

Table 6.5: Sample images of the fourth test set - non human faces

Image Details	Original Image	Pre-processed image	Network Response
Animal photo: Cat			[0;1]
Animal photo: Cat			[0;1]
Complex Background			[0;1]
'Face' on planet Mars			[0;1]
Animated 'Face'			[0;1]
'Face' on a pumpkin			[0;1]
'Face' of 'Virgin Mary' on a toast			[0;1]

Finally, in terms of speed, the two networks are essentially comparable. Moreover, the first neural network has more neurons compared to the second, which explains why its speed may decrease, while the second needs more time for the segmentation of a given image into the necessary pieces in order to produce the inputs. However, the delays, in the two cases, are negligible compared to the total time needed to pre-process the image.

Ioanna-Ourania Stathopoulou and George A. Tsihrintzis

6.1.5   Summary and Conclusions

We presented a neural network-based face detection algorithm and system [257, 258, 259, 11, 260]. To achieve higher face detection performance, we built two different neural network architectures and concluded to the use of the second, more complicated neural network architecture. Our system was tested using a training set of 285 face and non-face images of average to good quality, gathered from the World Wide Web. To test its performance, we used four different sets of images, namely: (1) images usually containing more than one faces (maybe partially occluded, slightly rotated or in side view) of various sizes, aspect ratios and resolution in complex backgrounds, (2) random images of our own facial expression database, in which the subjects form one of the seven expressions: 'neutral', 'happy', 'sad', 'surprised', 'disgusted', 'angry' and 'bored-sleepy', (3) low quality images acquired with a web camera and, (4) non face images of animals, human parts and complex backgrounds. Although the neural network had been trained with a set of images of higher (digital camera) quality, it was able to generalize and detected the faces in images at a quite satisfactory rate.

6.2 Introduction to our Facial Expression Recognition System

D EVELOPING a fully automated facial expression recognition system can be considered quite a challenging task as stated in the introduction of this Chapter. Towards building such a system, various tasks needed to be completed first. Specifically, in our first attempts for a facial expression recognition system, we tried to make use of the databases already available over the World Wide Web, as mentioned in Section 3.1, whereas the emotion classes, that our system would be able to recognize, had not yet been determined. These attempts are extensively presented in the following Section 6.3. As our work and study progressed, we settled in developing a facial expression recognition system that could be used for more advanced human-computer interaction techniques. This led us to the identification of the facial expressions corresponding to the 'neutral', 'happy', 'sad', 'surprised', 'angry', 'disgusted' and 'bored-sleepy' as the psychological states that arise very commonly during a typical human-computer interaction session. Moreover, we were able to rationalize and validate the facial features used towards this task, by making use of the questionnaires that had been collected during the empirical studies, presented in Chapter 5. This work is fairly described in Section 6.4.

Ioanna-Ourania Stathopoulou and George A. Tsihrintzis

6.3 First attempts for facial expression recognition

OUR first attempts for facial expression recognition can be identified by the following:

- Use of face databases gathered from World Wide Web: In our first efforts to build a facial expression recognition system, we used the AR Face Database [135] and the Cohn-Kanade AU-Coded Facial Expression Database [139]. As the system evolved and the aforementioned databases could no longer meet our needs, the development of our own facial expression database became mandatory and was finally adopted for our facial expression system.

- Different or fewer emotion classes: The use of the aforementioned databases and the fact that the emotion classes were not yet determined led us to the development of a facial expression recognition system which was adopted to the emotion classes dictated by the respective facial expression database used. As our work and study progressed, we settled in developing a facial expression recognition system that could be used for more advanced human-computer interaction techniques. This led us to the identification of the facial expressions corresponding to the 'neutral', 'happiness', 'sadness', 'surprise', 'anger', 'disgust' and 'boredom-sleepiness' as the psychological states that arise very commonly during a typical human-computer interaction session.

- Simpler / unsophisticated feature extraction algorithm: Another common was the use of a simpler feature extraction algorithm, based on binary images, as described in Section 6.3.1. As the study progressed, we developed our own Eye Detection Algorithm, as described in Section 6.4.2, on which was based our current feature extraction algorithm is based.

The algorithm we have developed [262, 263, 264, 265, 258, 11], as described in the following Subsection 6.3.1, was used for the majority of facial expression databases. Some alterations were made to deal with low quality images [264, 258], as also described in this Subsection. Its performance was tested for various combinations of emotion classes, image databases and/or image qualities. The system performance and some results are shown in Subsection 6.3.4

6.3.1 The Facial Expression Classification Algorithm (1st Attempts)

In detail, our facial expression classification algorithm works as follows:

Ioanna-Ourania Stathopoulou and George A. Tsihrintzis

1. *We detect the front view of the face. The image region defined by the face detection step constitutes the 'window pattern' for our facial expression analysis module, which will be examined to determine the psychological state of the person.*

2. *We preprocess the 'window pattern':*

   (a) *We apply Histogram Equalization techniques to enhance the contrast within the 'window pattern'.*

   (b) *We convert the image to binary and fill any holes in the binary image.*

3. *Feature Extraction: We extract basic corner points of the parts of the face and compute the Euclidean distances between them and certain specific ratios of these distances.*

Feature Extraction Algorithm

The main goal of feature extraction is to convert pixel data into a higher-level representation of shape, motion, color, texture and spatial configuration of the face or its components. This representation is used for subsequent expression categorization. Feature extraction generally reduces the dimensionality of the input space. The reduction procedure retains essential information with high discrimination power and stability. The extracted feature vector consists of the corner points of the eyes, mouth and brows, respectively. The extracted features as well as the distances used to classify the expressions can be seen in Figure 6.14.

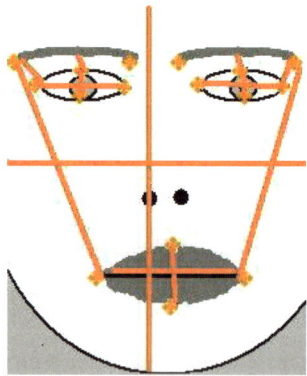

Figure 6.14: The extracted features (orange points) and the calculated distances

Ioanna-Ourania Stathopoulou and George A. Tsihrintzis

Specifically, the feature extraction algorithm works as follows:

1. *We search the binary image of the face and extract each part of the face (eyes, mouth and brows) into a new image of the same size and coordinates as the original image.*

2. *In each image of a part of the face, we locate corner points using relationships between neighboring pixel values. This results in the determination of 16 points which form the feature vector. Typical results of the feature extraction algorithm are seen in Figure 6.15. In the first column, we can observe the 'neutral', 'happy' and 'surprised' facial expressions of a given person and, in the second column, the preprocessed image and the corresponding extracted features for each expression.*

3. *We compute the Euclidean distances between these points, depicted with orange in Figure 6.14, and certain specific ratios of these distances. The results constitute the input vector which is fed into the neural network.*

Image preprocessing for low quality images

In our attempts at developing a most accurate facial expression recognition system, we tested our algorithm on low quality images. Specifically, we used our low quality database of facial expressions, which is further described in Chapter 4, Section 4.1. Most of the pictures acquired by our setup are of poor quality, mainly for three reasons:

- poor analysis of the web cameras (320-by-240 pixels)

- motion-caused blurring, which was the result of the relatively high capture time of the cameras and movements of the subject, and,

- poor lighting conditions when pictures were taken.

On purpose, we did not address any of the above problems by improving the data acquisition hardware, so as to make the image acquisition setup more realistic and closer to the operating conditions of practical human-machine interaction systems. Instead, we attempt to address these difficulties by identifying appropriate image preprocessing algorithms which emphasize facial features, such as the eyes, the mouth and the brows, on which the face detection and facial expression classification algorithms are based. Specifically, the preprocessing algorithms work as follows:

1. *Load the acquired image and covert it to grayscale*

Ioanna-Ourania Stathopoulou and George A. Tsihrintzis

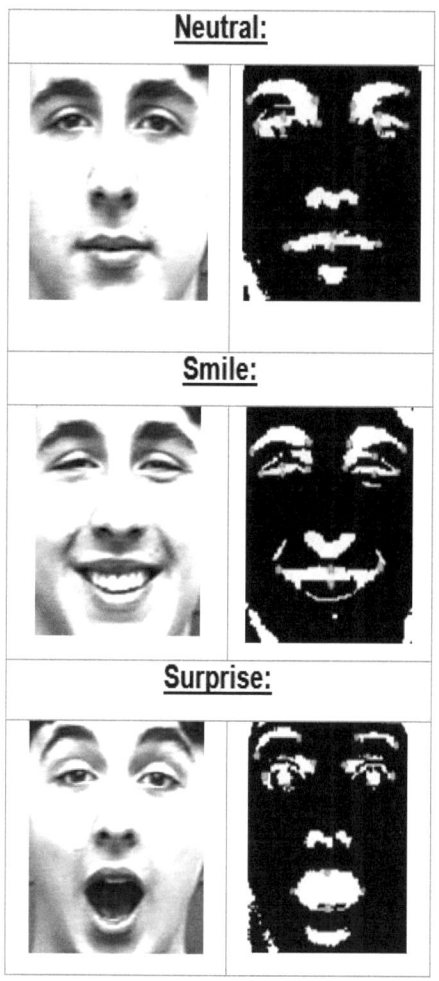

Figure 6.15: Typical results from our feature extraction algorithm

2. *Compute a 3-by-3 unsharp/contrast enhancement filter from the negative of the Laplacian filter with parameter 0.2 and apply it to the input image*

3. *Apply a 3-by-3 Gaussian lowpass filter to the resulting image*

Ioanna-Ourania Stathopoulou and George A. Tsihrintzis

4. *Apply adaptive histogram equalization techniques to enhance the contrast between areas of the image*

5. *Adjust image intensity values, so that 1% of data is saturated at low and high intensities of the input image. This further enhances the contrast in the resulting image.*

6. *Apply a 3-by-3 Gaussian lowpass filter to the resulting image*

7. *Perform two-dimensional median filtering to reduce noise and preserve edges.*

Table 6.6: Demonstration of the preprocessing algorithm for low quality images

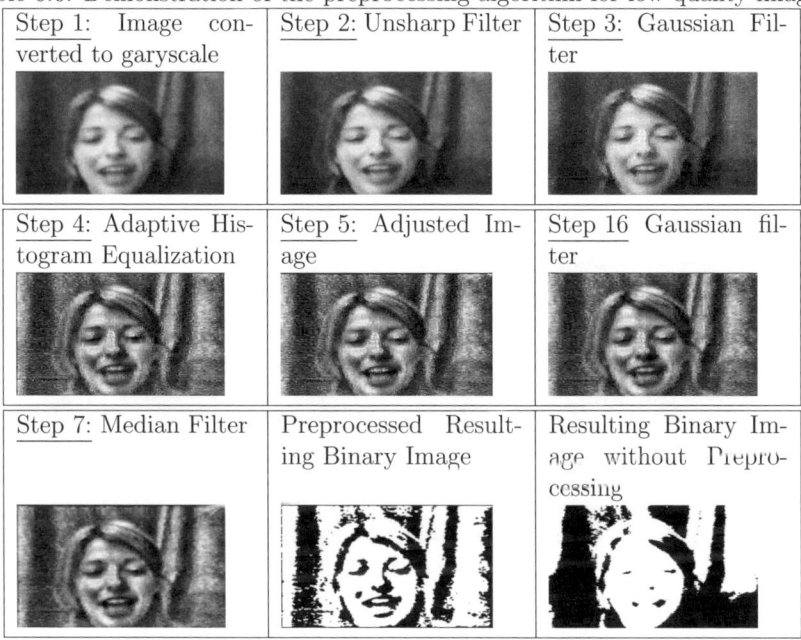

Step 1: Image converted to garyscale	Step 2: Unsharp Filter	Step 3: Gaussian Filter
Step 4: Adaptive Histogram Equalization	Step 5: Adjusted Image	Step 16 Gaussian filter
Step 7: Median Filter	Preprocessed Resulting Binary Image	Resulting Binary Image without Preprocessing

All the steps of the aforementioned algorithm are demonstrated for an example face image in Table 6.6. The resulting image is, then, converted to binary by the facial expression classification algorithm so as to extract features. As the main goal is to be able to discriminate facial features in the resulting binary image, we found that preprocessing was a necessary step to precede the face detection and facial expression classification algorithms. This becomes clear in the example image in Table 6.6, in the second and third column of the last row of which, we show the resulting binary

Ioanna-Ourania Stathopoulou and George A. Tsihrintzis

image with and without preprocessing, respectively. The threshold level for both of these two latter images is 0.4.

6.3.2 Feature Validation (First Attempts)

The location and shape of face parts vary significantly from facial expression to facial expression. During the development of our system, various emotion classes and facial expression databases were used. Specifically, the following systems were developed/tested:

- 2-class system for 'neutral' and 'screaming' expressions [262], using the AR Face Database [135] for training and testing.

- 3-class system for 'neutral', 'happy' and 'surprised' expressions [263], using Cohn-Kanade AU-Coded Facial Expression Database [139] for training and testing.

- 3-class system for 'neutral', 'happy' and 'surprised' expressions [264], using Cohn-Kanade AU-Coded Facial Expression Database [139] for training and our low quality facial expression database for testing.

- 3-class system for 'neutral', 'happy' and 'surprised' expressions [265], using Cohn-Kanade AU-Coded Facial Expression Database [139] for training and our low quality facial expression database for testing for the extension of our system for faces in side view.

- 3-class system for 'neutral', 'happy' and 'surprised' expressions [258], using Cohn-Kanade AU-Coded Facial Expression Database [139] for training and testing using more features.

The features among the aforementioned three main classes ('neutral', 'happy' and 'surprised') contain high discrimination power. The distribution of these classification features for 83 subjects forming each of the three expressions, respectively, is shown in Figures 6.17 and 6.16. Specifically in Figure 6.17, we plot the distribution of the mouth dimension ratio for each of the examined facial expressions. Similarly in Figure 6.16, we plot the distribution of the face dimension ratio relatively to 'neutral' expression.

6.3.3 Neural Network Classifiers (First Attempts)

Based on the requirements set from the databases and the emotion classes we wanted to identify, we built various neural networks. In the case of 2-class system, we built a

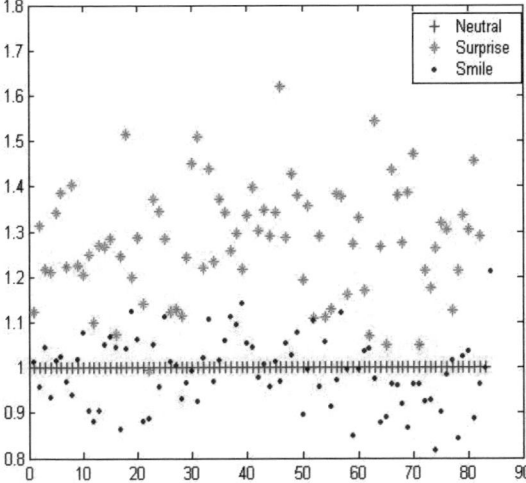

Figure 6.16: Facial Dimension Ratio Distribution

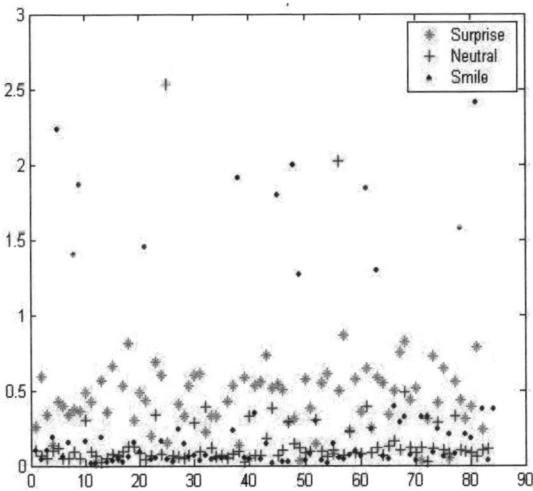

Figure 6.17: Mouth Dimension Ratio Distribution

Ioanna-Ourania Stathopoulou and George A. Tsihrintzis

simple neural network with 2 hidden layers, with 3 and 2 neurons, respectively. The neural network took as input the three main extracted features: (1) left eye ratio, (2) right eye ratio, and (3) mouth ratio. To train the neural network, we used a set of 250 images, 125 images for each expression. These images were contained in the AR Face Database [135] and preprocessed before entered into the neural network. After training with this image set, the neural network achieved an error rate of 0.016. In fact, this error rate was gradually reduced as the number of the images in the training set increased. Given the relatively small size of the training set, this error rate is quite satisfying. According to the requirements set, when the window pattern represented a neutral facial expression, the neural network should produce an output value of 'one' ('1') (or something close to this value). On the other hand, if it represented a screaming face, the output value should be 'zero' ('0'). The output value can be regarded as the degree of membership of the face image in each of the 'neutral' and 'screaming' classes.

In the case of 3-classes system, we built a simple neural network with 2 hidden layers, with 4 and 3 neurons, respectively. The neural network took as input the three main extracted features: (1) left eye ratio, (2) right eye ration, (3) mouth ratio, and (4) face size ratio. To train the neural network, we used a set of 249 images, 83 images for each expression. These images where gathered from the Cohn-Kanade AU-Coded Facial Expression Database [139] and preprocessed before entered into the neural network. After training with this image set, the neural network achieved an error rate varying between 0.01 and 0.016, depending on the neural network architecture and the extracted features fed in the network. Again, this error rate was gradually reduced as the number of images in the training set increased. Given the relatively small size of the training set, this error rate is quite satisfying.

According to the requirements set, when the window pattern represented a 'neutral' facial expression, the neural network should produce an output value of [1;0;0] or so. Similarly, for the 'happy' expression, the output must be [0;1;0] and for the 'surprised', [0;0;1]. The output value can be regarded as the degree of membership of the face image in each of the 'neutral','happy' and 'surprised' classes.

6.3.4 Results from neural network classifiers (First Attempts)

We tested our neural network classifiers in each case mentioned above. Some results are depicted in the following Figures 6.18, 6.19, 6.20 and 6.21.

Specifically, in Figure 6.18, we depict the results for our 2-class system for 'neutral' and 'screaming' expressions [262], using the AR Face Database [135] for training and testing. The system was tested with images of 10 subjects, some of them were already in the training database, as there were two sequences of image shooting of the same subject in the AR Face Database [135]. The result was 20 images, and the neural network showed an accuracy of 100%.

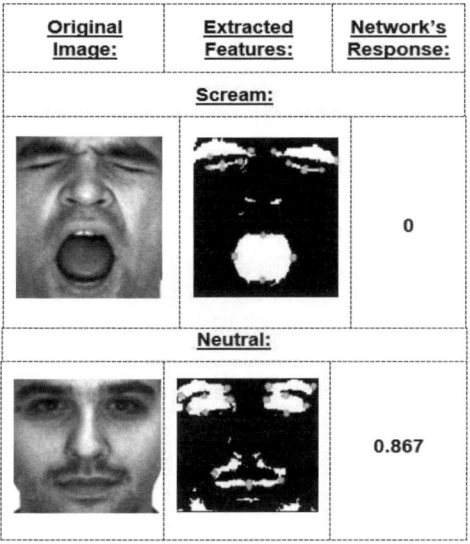

Figure 6.18: Results from our 2-class system

Moreover, in Figure 6.19, we depict the results for our 3-class system for 'neutral', 'happy' and 'surprised' expressions [263], using Cohn-Kanade AU-Coded Facial Expression Database [139] for training and testing. The system was tested with images of 15 subjects. The result was 45 images, and the neural network showed an accuracy of 80%.

In Figure 6.20, we depict the results for our 3-class system for 'neutral', 'happy' and 'surprised' expressions [264], using Cohn-Kanade AU-Coded Facial Expression Database [139] for training and our low quality facial expression database for testing. The system was tested with low quality images of 15 subjects. The result was again 45 images, and the neural network showed an accuracy of 77%.

Finally, the same system was tested for its performance on side view images of low quality. In Figure 6.21, we depict the results for our 3-class system for 'neutral', 'happy' and 'surprised' expressions [265], using Cohn-Kanade AU-Coded Facial Expression Database [139] for training and our low quality facial expression database for testing for the extension of our system for faces in side view. The system was tested with low quality images of the same 15 subjects, as above. The result was again 45 images, and the neural network showed again an accuracy of 77%.

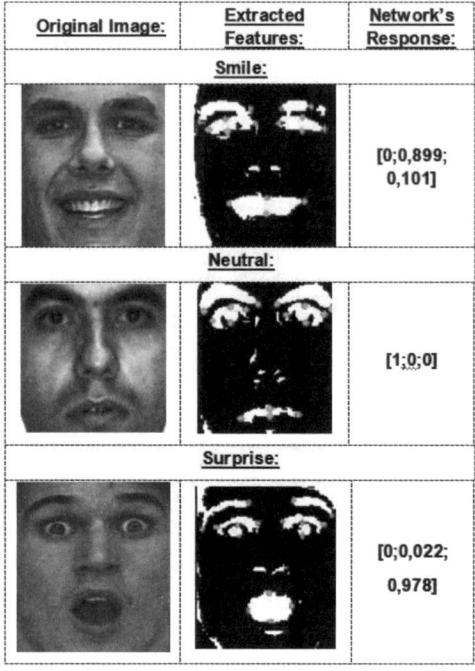

Figure 6.19: Results from our 3-class system with the Cohn-Kanade Database

6.4 Facial expression recognition system

AS our work progressed and with the results available from our empirical studies, described in previous Chapter 5, we considered additional emotion classes in our system [266, 267, 268, 269, 270]. Indeed, based on our studies, facial expressions corresponding to the 'neutral', 'happiness', 'sadness', 'surprise', 'anger', 'disgust' and 'boredom-sleepiness' psychological states arise very commonly during a typical human-computer interaction session, as stated in Chapter 4. Our final facial expression recognition system is identified by the following:

- More facial features are extracted from the image, such as measurements of the texture, head orientation, etc.

- We use our own facial expression database for training and/or testing, as it is more complete in terms of the classes we want to classify.

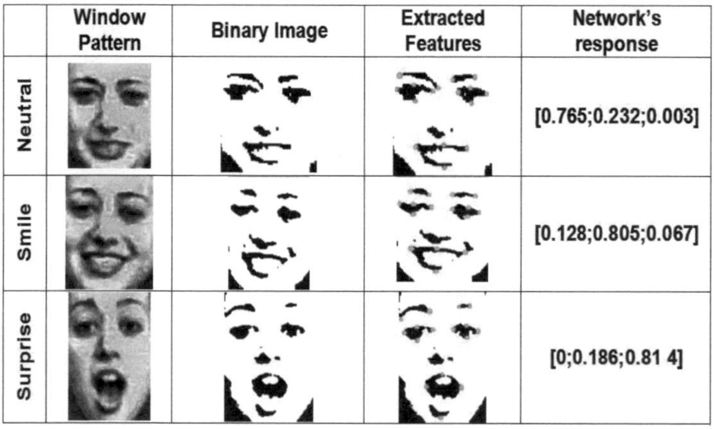

	Window Pattern	Binary Image	Extracted Features	Network's response
Neutral				[0.765;0.232;0.003]
Smile				[0.128;0.805;0.067]
Surprise				[0;0.186;0.81 4]

Figure 6.20: Results from our 3-class system with the Cohn-Kanade Database for training and our low quality database for testing

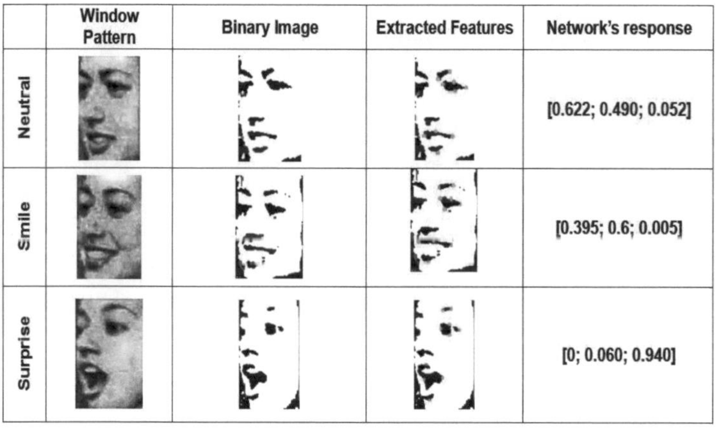

	Window Pattern	Binary Image	Extracted Features	Network's response
Neutral				[0.622; 0.490; 0.052]
Smile				[0.395; 0.6; 0.005]
Surprise				[0; 0.060; 0.940]

Figure 6.21: Results from our 3-class system with the Cohn-Kanade Database for training and our low quality, side view images for testing

- A better, more sophisticated, algorithm to extract the facial features is used, which is based on our eye detection/extraction algorithm, described below.

6.4.1 Feature Selection

The first step in order to compute the needed features, is to identify some important facial points. These facial points are widely used in facial image processing systems and can help us in the computation of the facial features which will be used as input to an artificial neural network. The facial points are summarized in Figure 6.22.

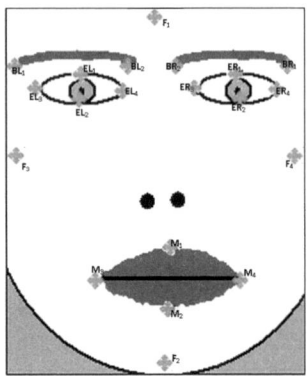

Figure 6.22: The most important facial points which will help us in the extraction of the feature vector for the facial expression recognition task

From the collected dataset, we identified differences between the 'neutral' expression of a model and its deformation into other expressions, as typically high-lighted in Table 6.7.

The changes described in Table 6.7, may show differences among different persons. From our observations we identified the following differences:

- The changes in the texture of the skin from the formation of wrinkles (in cheeks, forehead, cheeks, etc.) depend of the person's skin quality and age. In younger people, wrinkle formation is not so common.

- Usually, 'bored-sleepy' people tend to slightly rotate their head, narrow their eyes and keep their mouth closed (in a away reminiscent of 'sadness'). But there is also a significant number of people who tend to yawn because they feel sleepy

- The vast majority of people, when they are angry, tend to narrow their eyes, but, there is also a number of people who tend to open their eyes wider.

- When someone is disgusted, usually he/she forms an expression as described in Figure 6.7, but, there is also a number of people who turn their head in such cases.

138

Table 6.7: Deformations of the other six expression, compared to 'neutral'

Variations between Facial Expressions:	
Happiness	**Boredom-Sleepiness**
(1)Bigger-broader mouth (2)Slightly narrower eyes (3)Changes in the texture of the cheeks (4)Occasionally, changes in the orientation of brows	(1)Head slightly turned downwards (2)Eyes slightly closed (3)Occasionally, wrinkles formed in the forehead and different direction of the brows (4)Occasionally, mouth opened (subject is yawning)
Surprise	**Sadness**
(1)Longer head (2)Bigger-wider eyes (3)Opened mouth (4)Wrinkles in the forehead (changes in the texture) (5)Changes in the orientation of eyebrows (the eyebrows are raised)	(1)Changes in the direction of the mouth (2) Wrinkles formed on the chin (different texture) (3)Occasionally, wrinkles formed in the forehead and different direction of the brows
Anger	**Disgust**
(1)Wrinkles between the eyebrows (different tex-tures) (2)Smaller (narrower) eyes (3)Wrinkles in the chin (4)The mouth is tight (5)Occasionally, wrinkles over the eyebrows, in the forehead	(1)The distance between the nostrils and the eyes is shortened (2)Wrinkles between the eyebrows and on the nose (3)Wrinkles formed on the chin and the cheeks

Based on the above observations, we can compute the effect of each facial action on the facial points we identified earlier. Also, we can identify the possible facial expression, that each facial action may belong to. Finally, we can identify the facial features that we need to compute. All these, are summarized in Tables 6.8, 6.9 and 6.10.

These observations led us to the identification of the following facial features:

1. **Mouth Ratio:**

$$\frac{||M_1M_2||/||M_3M_4||}{||M_{1Neu}M_{2Neu}||/||M_{3Neu}M_{4Neu}||}$$

2. **Mouth Orientation:** Measurement of the changes of the orientation of the mouth compared to 'neutral' expression

Table 6.8: Facial action and resulting Facial Features

Facial Feature Action	Result to Facial Points	Possible expression - emotion	Identification of the needed facial feature
Broader mouth	$\|M_3M_4\|max$ $\|M_1M_2\|min$	Happiness	Mouth Ratio
Open mouth	$\|M_3M_4\|max$ $\|M_1M_2\|min$	Boredom-Sleepiness (-) Surprise	
The mouth is tight	$\|M_1M_2\|min$	Sadness Anger	
Changes in the direction of the mouth	mouth orientation down	Sadness Boredom - Sleepiness (-) Disgust - Disapproval (-)	Mouth Orientation
	mouth orientation up	Happiness	
Slightly narrower eyes, Eyes slightly Closed	$\|EL_1EL_2\|min$ $\|ER_1ER_2\|min$	Happiness Boredom - Sleepiness Disgust - Disapproval	Eyes Ratio
Bigger, wider eyes	$\|EL_1EL_2\|max$ $\|ER_1ER_2\|max$	Surprise Anger (-)	Eyes Ratio

Table 6.9: Facial action and resulting Facial Features - 2

Facial Feature Action	Result to Facial Points	Possible expression - emotion	Identification of the needed facial feature
Wrinkles in the cheeks	Changes in texture	Happiness Boredom - Sleepiness(-) Sadness(-) Disgust - Disapproval(-)	Texture of the cheeks
Changes in the direction of the eyebrows	brows orientation up	Sadness Boredom - Sleepiness (-) Surprise (-)	Brow Orientation
	brows orientation down	Anger Disgust - Disapproval (-)	
Head slightly turned downwards	head orientation changed	Boredom - Sleepiness Sadness (-)	Head Orientation
Longer head	$\|F_1F_2\|max$	Surprise Boredom - Sleepiness (-)	Head ratio
Broader head	$\|F_3F_4\|max$	Happiness	Head ratio

Ioanna-Ourania Stathopoulou and George A. Tsihrintzis

Table 6.10: Facial action and resulting Facial Features - 3

Facial Feature Action	Result to Facial Points	Possible expression - emotion	Identification of the needed facial feature
Wrinkles on the forehead	Changes in texture	Anger(-)	Texture of the forehead
		Boredom - Sleepiness(-)	
		Sadness(-)	
		Disgust - Disapproval(-)	
Wrinkles on the chin	Changes in texture	Anger(-)	Texture of the chin
		Sadness(-)	
		Disgust - Disapproval(-)	
Wrinkles between the eyebrows	Changes in texture	Anger(-)	Texture of the region between eyebrows
		Disgust - Disapproval(-)	
Wrinkles on the nose	Changes in texture	Disgust - Disapproval(-))	Texture of the nose

3. **Left Eye Ratio:**

$$\frac{||EL_1EL_2||/||EL_3EL_4||}{||EL_{1Neu}EL_{2Neu}||/||EL_{3Neu}EL_{4Neu}||}$$

4. **Right Eye Ratio:**

$$\frac{||ER_1ER_2||/||ER_3ER_4||}{||ER_{1Neu}ER_{2Neu}||/||ER_{3Neu}ER_{4Neu}||}$$

5. **Texture of the left cheek:** Measurement of the changes of the texture of the left cheek compared to 'neutral' expression

6. **Texture of the right cheek:** Measurement of the changes of the texture of the right cheek compared to 'neutral' expression

7. **Left Brow Orientation:** Measurement of the changes of the orientation of the left brow compared to 'neutral' expression

8. **Right Brow Orientation:** Measurement of the changes of the orientation of the right brow compared to 'neutral' expression

9. **Head ratio:**

$$\frac{||F_1F_2||/||F_3F_4||}{||F_{1Neu}F_{2Neu}||/||F_{3Neu}F_{4Neu}||}$$

Ioanna-Ourania Stathopoulou and George A. Tsihrintzis

10. **Texture of the forehead:** Measurement of the changes of the texture of the forehead compared to 'neutral' expression

11. **Texture of the chin:** Measurement of the changes of the texture of the chin compared to 'neutral' expression

12. **Texture of the region between the eyebrows:** Measurement of the changes of the texture of the region between the eyebrows compared to 'neutral' expression

The facial features are summarized in the Figure 6.23.

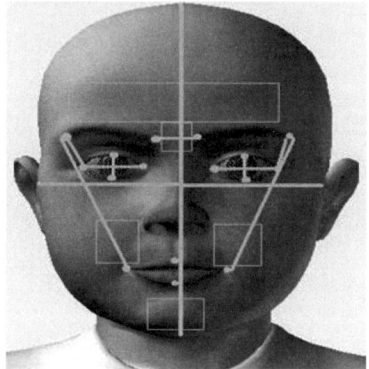

Figure 6.23: The extracted features

6.4.2 Image Preprocessing and Feature Extraction

To convert pixel data into a higher-level representation of shape, motion, color, texture and spatial configuration of the face and its components, we locate and extract the corner points of specific regions of the face, such as the eyes, the mouth and the brows, and compute their variations in size, orientation or texture between the neutral and some other expression. This constitutes the feature extraction process and reduces the dimensionality of the input space significantly, while retaining essential information of high discrimination power and stability. The extracted features, the face regions, and the dimension ratios used to classify the expressions are summarized in Fig. 6.23.

The main algorithm is as follows:

1. Eye Extraction

2. *Based on the location of the eyes, extraction of the other facial features and facial regions.*

3. *Combination of all and computation of feature vector*

Specifically, the basic aim of this process is to extract the needed corner point of the facial features and the respective facial regions. In order to achieve this, we first locate the eyes of the person using a fairly complex algorithm. Based on the location of the eyes, we then extract the rest of the facial feature points which will lead us to the computation of the resulting feature vector. We describe each algorithm separately in the following sections.

The eye extraction algorithm

We apply our eye detection algorithm [266] in the upper 60% of the detected face region. We do not process the lower 40% of the face region to decrease the complexity of the algorithm and the required computational effort. The 60% of the upper detected face is selected based on our studies so as to cover cases of face rotation. For better accuracy, the algorithm computes two different binary images, called 'skin map' and 'clustered image,' respectively, and uses them to detect the eyes. Specifically, the algorithm follows four main steps:

1. *Skin extraction*

2. *K means clustering*

3. *Combination of the resulting images and morphological processing*

4. *Feature extraction*

Skin Extraction

The skin filter is based on the Fleck and Forsyth algorithm [271]. The input color image must be in RGB format with color intensity values ranging from 0 to 255. The algorithm, works as follows:

1. *The RGB image is transformed to log-opponent values I, Rg, and By, given by the Fleck and Forsyth algorithm, as follows:*

   - $I = L(G)$
   - $Rg = L(R) - L(G)$
   - $By = L(B) - (L(G) + L(R))/2$

Ioanna-Ourania Stathopoulou and George A. Tsihrintzis

The L(x) operation is defined as L(x)=105*log(x+1). The log transformation makes the Rg and By values, as well as differences between I values (e.g. texture amplitude), independent of illumination level.

2. *After filtering the Rg and By matrices, a texture amplitude map is used to find regions of low texture information. Usually, the skin is very smooth, so the skin regions are those with little texture.*

3. *In these selected areas, we further select the skin region based on the measures of hue and saturation, so as their color matches that of skin. The acceptable values of hue and saturation, are $110 \leq hue \leq 180$ and $0 \leq saturation \leq 130$, respectively.*

4. *A binary skin map is drawn, where if the pixel in the original image is in the same coordinates as the pixel map is skin, it is represented with 1, or 0 otherwise. The skin map array can be considered as a black and white binary image with skin regions appearing as white. The resulting 'skin map' usually represents the eyes, brows, nostrils, hair and other objects on the face (e.g. glasses), with white regions and the skin with black. Some results after applying the algorithm are shown in Figure 6.24.*

K-means Clustering

On the same 60% of the detected face region, we compute 3 clusters of the image, color each cluster with the corresponding average color, and, finally, convert it to binary. The resulting image is called 'clustered face image' and, as the 'skin map', represents the eyes, brows, nostrils, hair and other objects on the face (e.g. glasses), as white regions and the skin as black. Some results, corresponding to the faces in the skin extraction step, are shown in Figure 6.24.

Morphological Operations-Combining The Two Images

On the two resulting images, we apply morphological operations. Our aim is to remove all other objects and to end up with a binary image of only the eyes, so as to make the eye detection task simpler. The algorithm, works as follows:

1. *We apply a window, which clears the boundary pixels in the input image (usually representing the hair and the nostrils)*

2. *We remove areas whose size is too small. This removes some very small objects on the face (e.g. scars)*

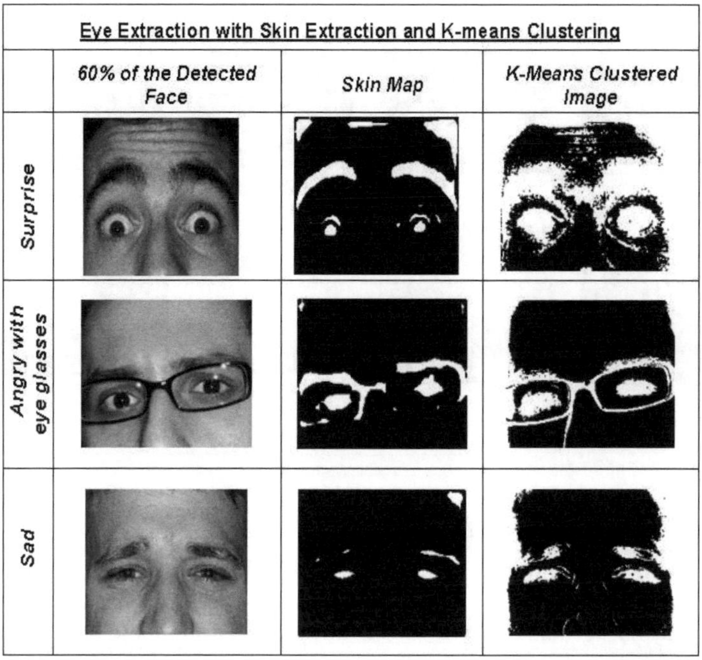

Eye Extraction with Skin Extraction and K-means Clustering		
	60% of the Detected Face	Skin Map	K-Means Clustered Image
Surprise			
Angry with eye glasses			
Sad			

Figure 6.24: Eye Extraction with Skin Extraction and K-means Clustering

3. *We remove the areas whose length is larger than the 1/3 of the total row size. In this step, wide areas, e.g. the skeleton of the glasses are removed.*

4. *Finally, we remove the areas whose length is very small to remove other small objects of the face.*

The image resulting at each step of the aforementioned algorithm is shown in Figure 6.25, in which the input image was the skin map of the second image (i.e., the image of the where the person wearing glasses). The result is an image containing only the two eyes.

The detection is done on the two images. The final location of the eyes is found based on characteristics of the detected areas in the two images, e.g. the relative position of the eyes and their size, in relation to the original image. Each eye is depicted to a binary image, where the features are extracted next.

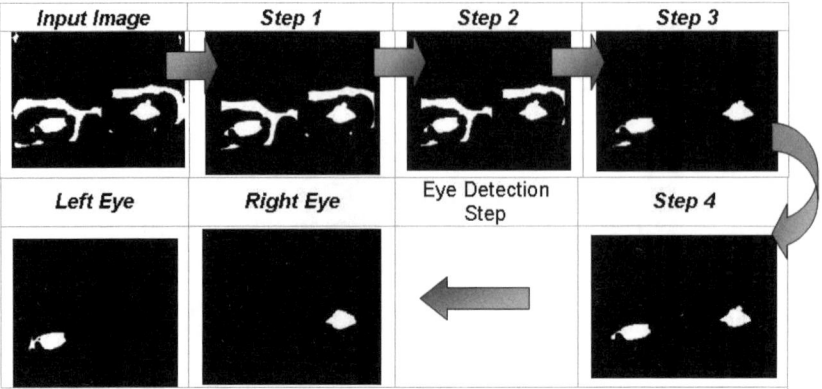

Figure 6.25: Morphological Operations

Feature Extraction After detecting the eyes, we end up with two binary images representing the left and the right eye, respectively. First, we trace the outline of the eye area. Non-zero-valued pixels are assigned to an object and zero-valued pixels constitute the background. The curve is drawn based on these relative values. To compute edge points, first we find the minimum and the maximum coordinates of the computed contour. Then, the center points are computed. Finally, the edge points are computed based on their relationships relatively to the center points and the contour. Finally, the coordinates of the extracted features are drawn in the original (color) image of the original size. The extracted edge points, in the original image, are depicted in Figure 6.26.

Some results of our eye extraction/localization algorithm are shown in Figure 6.27.

6.4.3   The extraction algorithm for the rest of facial features

After successful eye detection and eye feature extraction, the rest of the needed facial portions are detected based on the given location of the eyes Specifically, we apply certain rules in order to locate and extract the rest of the facial features:

- Extraction of the features of the brows: (1) The brows are considered to be a light region above the eyes in the skin map image, after having applied the second step of morphological operations described above, as we can see in Figures 6.24 and 6.25. (2) In order to extract the corner points, we apply the same algorithm as the algorithm used for the extraction of the corner points of the eyes.

Ioanna-Ourania Stathopoulou and George A. Tsihrintzis

Surprise	Angry wearing eye glasses	Sad

Figure 6.26: Extracted Eye Features

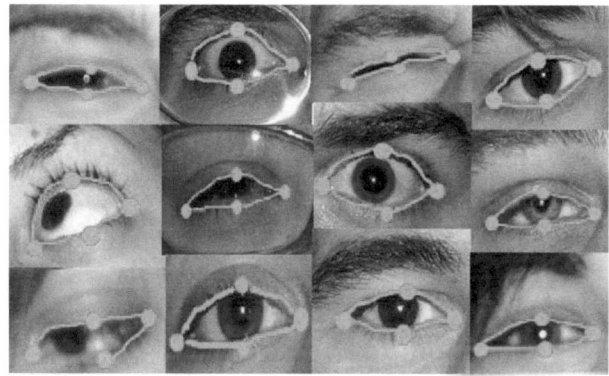

Figure 6.27: Some results of the eye extraction algorithm

- Extraction of the features of the mouth: (1) The location of the mouth is computed in the remaining 40% of the face image. (2) The eyes and the mouth form a 'T' independently of the orientation of the face. The region of the mouth is located based on this rule. (3) After we have detected the location of the mouth, in order to extract the corner points, we apply the same algorithm as the algorithm used for the extraction of the corner points of the eyes.

- Extraction of the region of the chin: (1) The location of the region of the chin is computed in the remaining 40% of the face image. (2) This region starts just after the feature point M_2 of the mouth. (3) Its width is 90% of the width of the mouth and its height 18% of the height of the face.

- Extraction of the region of the cheeks: (1) The location of the region of the cheek is computed in the entire face image. (2) This region starts just after the feature points M_3 and M_4 of the mouth, for each side, respectively. (3) Its width is 18% of the width of the face and its height 18% of the height of the face.

- Extraction of the region between the brows: (1) The location of the region between the brows is computed in the entire face image. (2) This region is between the feature points BL_2 and BR_2. (3) Its width is 10% of the width of the face and its height 10% of the height of the face.

- Extraction of the region of the forehead: (1) The location of the region between the brows is computed in the entire face image. (2) This region is above the brows. (3) Its width is 80% of the width of the face and its height 12% of the height of the face.

6.4.4 Combination of all and computation of feature vector

After successful feature point and region detection, we depict these corner points and facial regions on the original image. We compute the Euclidean distances between these points, depicted with lines in Figure 6.23, and certain specific ratios of these distances. We also compute the orientation of the brows and the mouth. Finally, we compute a measure of the texture for each of the specific regions based on the texture of the corresponding 'neutral' expression. All the above measurements correspond to the features described in Section 'Feature Selection'. The computation of these features leads to the formation of a 12-by-1 feature vector with high discrimination power. This feature vector is fed to an artificial neural network in order to classify the expression.

6.4.5 Quantification of Feature Discrimination Power

The selected features contain high discrimination power and will help us towards the task of facial expression recognition. In the following Figures 6.28, 6.29, 6.30, 6.31, 6.32, 6.33 and 6.34, we demonstrate the probability density for some of the major features for 250 subjects of our Facial Expression Database, which we use in our facial expression recognition system.

Specifically, in Figure 6.28, we demonstrate the probability density for the face size ratio for each of the seven expressions. As we can observe, there is a significant difference in the values for the 'surprise' and 'disgust' emotion (green and magenta line, respectively), compared to the 'happiness' and 'boredom-sleepiness' emotion (red and dark blue line, respectively). This is done because in the former cases people tend to open their mouth and/or eye, so the face ratio become smaller. On the other hand, in the latter cases, the face becomes wider. In the 'anger' and 'sadness' emotion, the values of the face ratio are similar to 'neutral'

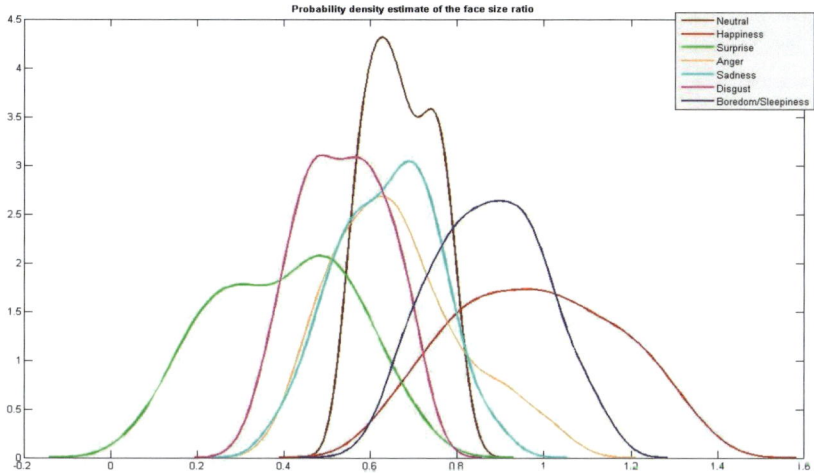

Figure 6.28: Probability Density of the 'Face Size Ratio'

The previous assumption is further illustrated in Figure 6.29, where, again, there is a clear difference between the 'happiness' and the 'surprise' emotion.

In the following Figures 6.30 and 6.31, we observe the probability density estimate for the left and right eye size ratio, respectively. As we can observe, the values follow the same graph for the two eyes. These is because there is no 'expression' in our expression classes that would oblige the subject to treat one of his/her eyes differently from the other (e.g. to blink).

As far as the collected side view images are concerned, our study showed that formation of some expressions involves deformation of a person's head sides and, thus, additional classification features may be derived from side view face images. In fact, features may be more evident in side view rather than front view images for certain expressions. For example, better discrimination between the 'neutral' and 'happy' expression seems to be achieved in front view images, whereas the 'surprised' expression seems to be better identified in side view images. Similarly, the 'sad' and angry' are better discriminated in front rather than in side view images as forehead texture,

Ioanna-Ourania Stathopoulou and George A. Tsihrintzis

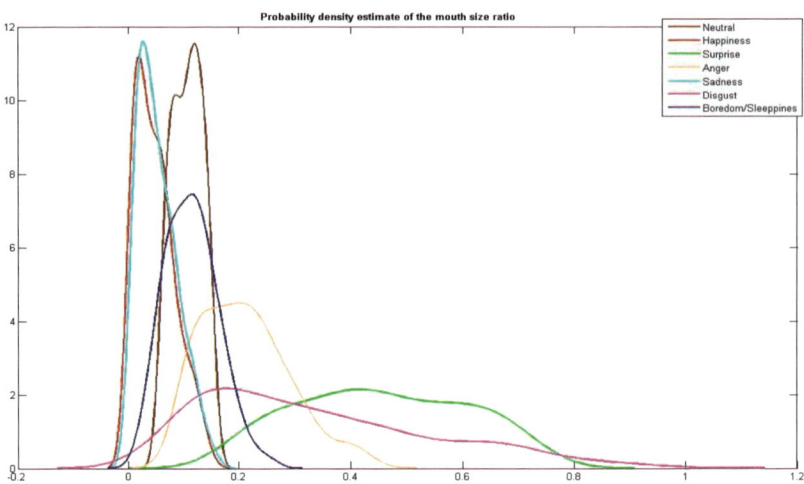

Figure 6.29: Probability Density of the 'Mouth Size Ratio'

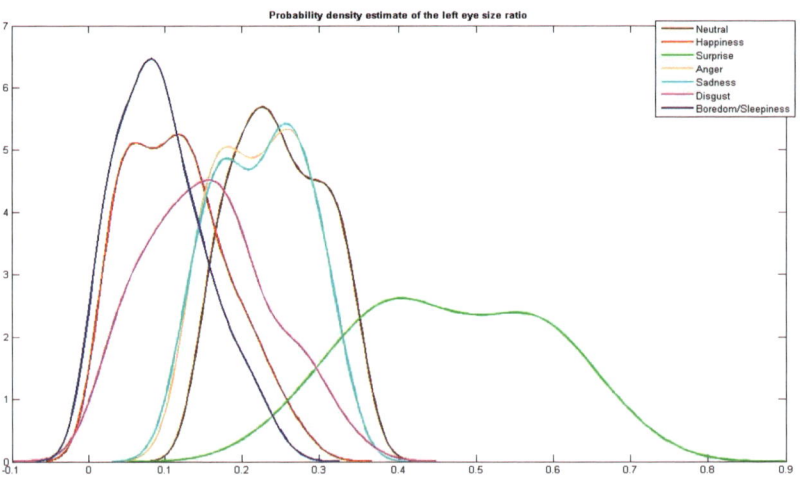

Figure 6.30: Probability Density of the 'Left Eye Size Ratio'

one of the corresponding classification features, is better computed in front rather than side view images. Thus, we conclude that better facial expression classification results can be achieved by using images of several views of a person's face.

Ioanna-Ourania Stathopoulou and George A. Tsihrintzis

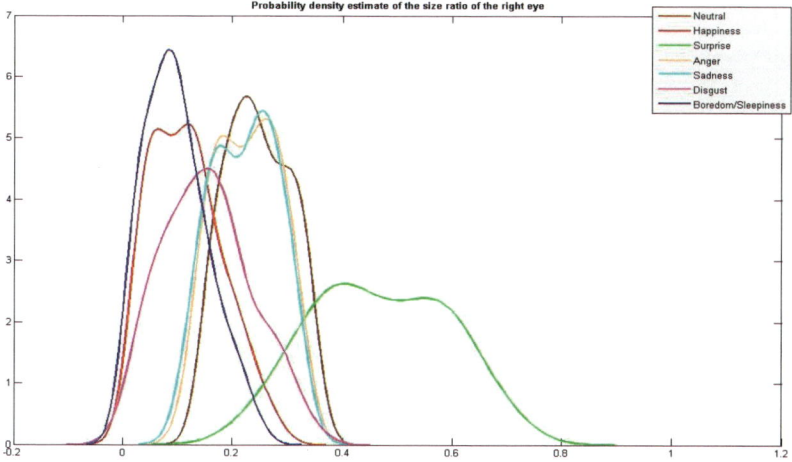

Figure 6.31: Probability Density of the 'Right Eye Size Ratio'

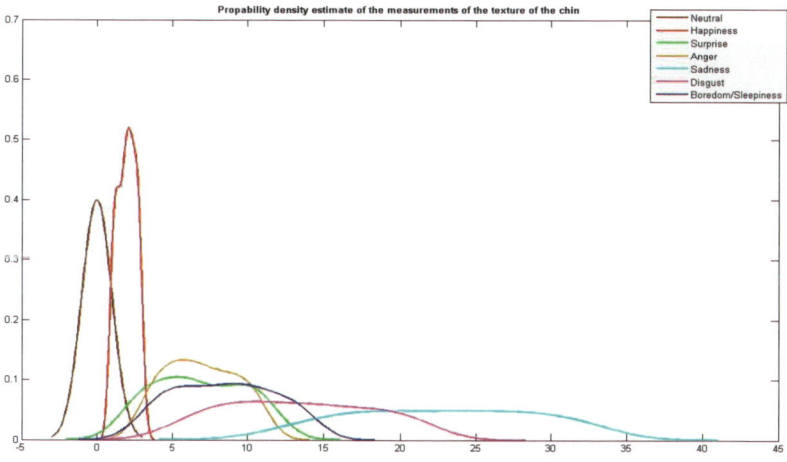

Figure 6.32: Probability Density of the 'Texture of the Region of the Chin'

6.4.6 Classifiers for Facial Expression Classification

Towards building our facial expression recognition system, we developed several classifiers. In our first attempts, we used neural network-based classifiers. Later, we also

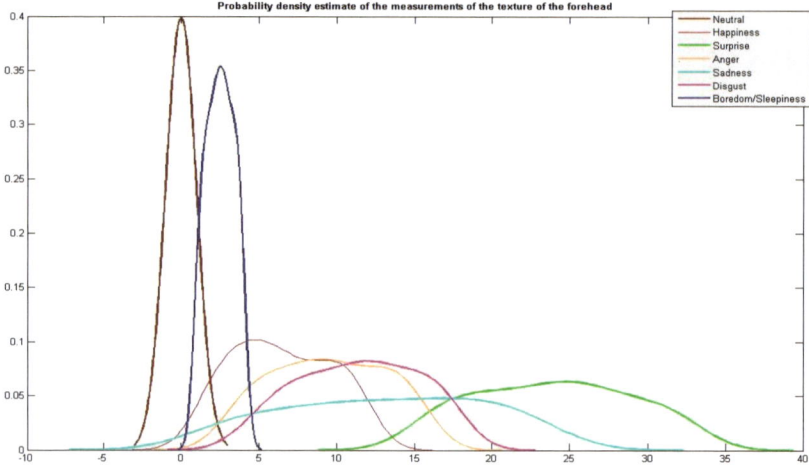

Figure 6.33: Probability Density of the 'Texture of the Region of the Forehead'

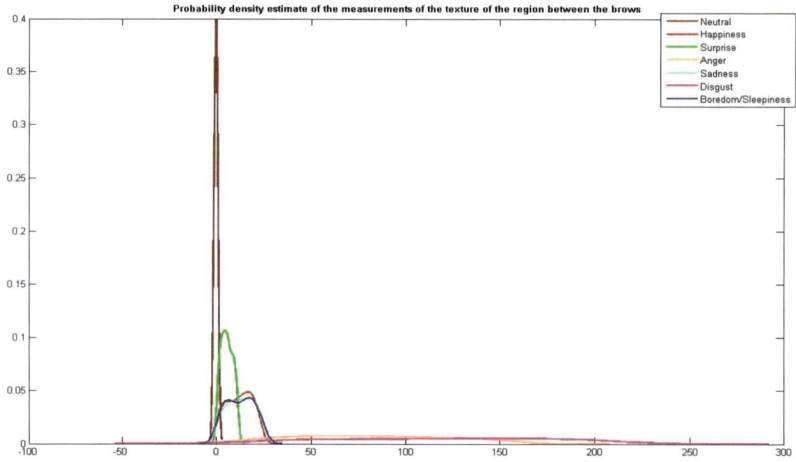

Figure 6.34: Probability Density of the 'Texture of the Region Between the Brows'

tested the performance of facial expression recognition, by developing a more sophisticated classifiers, using the NetLab Tool of Matlab. All the classifiers are described and tested in the following sections.

Ioanna-Ourania Stathopoulou and George A. Tsihrintzis

Neural Network Architecture

In order to classify facial expressions, we developed a two layer artificial neural network which is fed with the following input data: (1) mouth dimension ratio, (2) mouth orientation, (3) left eye dimension ratio, (4) right eye dimension ratio, (5) measurement of the texture of the left cheek, (6) measurement of the texture of the right cheek, (7) left eye brow direction, (8) right eye brow direction, (9) face dimension ratio, (10) measurement of the texture of the forehead, (11) measurement of the texture of the region between the brows, and, (12) measurement of the texture of the chin. The network produces a 7-dimensional output vector which can be regarded as the degree of membership of the face image in each of the 'neutral', 'happiness', 'surprise', 'anger', 'disgust-disapproval', 'sadness' and 'boredom-sleepiness' classes. An illustration of the network architecture can be seen in Figure 6.35. The neural network-based facial expression recognition system, is called **NEU-FACES** [266, 267, 268, 270].

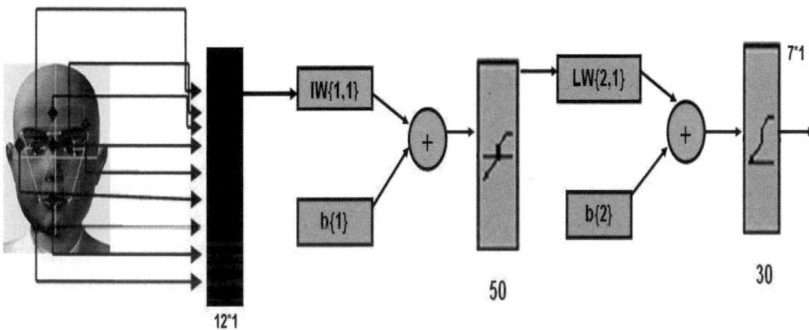

Figure 6.35: The Facial Expression Neural Network Classifier

6.4.7 Classification Performance Assessment

NEU-FACES managed to classify the emotions on a person's face quite satisfactorily. The neural network was trained with a dataset of 230 subjects forming the 7 expression samples from all the emotion classes, i.e., a total of 1610 face images. We tested the classifier with images from 20 subjects forming the 7 facial expressions corresponding to 7 equivalent emotions, a total of 140 images. The results are summarized in Table 6.11. In the first column we demonstrate the emotion classes, while in the following three columns, we show the results of our empirical studies to humans. Specifically, results from the first part of the questionnaire are shown in the

Ioanna-Ourania Stathopoulou and George A. Tsihrintzis

second column, results from the second part are shown in the third column, while the mean success rate is shown in the fourth. In the fifth column, we depict the success rate of our NEU-FACES recognition system for the corresponding emotion.

Table 6.11: Results of the Facial Expression Classification System Compared to Human Classifiers

	Questionare results			NEU-FACES System Results
Emotions	1st Part	2nd Part	Mean Value	
Neutral	39,25%	—-	61,74%	100%
Happiness	68,94%	96,21%	82,57%	90%
Sadness	34,09%	82,58%	58,33%	60%
Disgust - Disapproval	18,74%	13,64%	16,19%	65%
Boredom-Sleepiness	50,76%	78,03%	64,39%	75%
Anger	76,14%	69,7%	72,92%	55%
Surprise	89,77%	95,45%	92,61%	95%

As we can observe, the NEU-FACES achieved higher success rates in most of the emotion compared to the success rates achieved by humans, with exception to the 'anger' emotion, where it achieved a success rate of only 55%. This is due mostly to pretence and to the the difficulty of humans to express such an emotion strongly. The latter is further corroborated by the fact that the majority of the face images depicting 'anger' that were erroneously classified by our system were misclassified as 'neutral'. Generally, the NEU-FACES achieve very good results in positive emotions, such as 'happiness' and 'surprise', where it achieved success rates of 90% and 95%, respectively.

Although the resulting neural network classifier achieved quite good results in classifying the emotions, in certain emotion classes, especially some negative emotions such as 'anger' and 'sadness', the respective success rate was not quite satisfactory. This led us to the development of more sophisticated classifiers which are described in the following Section.

6.4.8 More Sophisticated Classifiers

In order to increase the success rates of our facial expression recognition system further, we developed more sophisticated algorithms [269, 270] and tested their classification success rate. Humans are able to classify facial expressions almost instantly.

Table 6.12: Sample images of our facial expression database

Emotions	Input Image	Extracted Features	Network's Response
Neutral			[0.97;0.02;0;0;0;0.01;0]
Happiness			[0;0.88;0;0;0;0.12;0]
Sadness			[0;0;0.83;0;0.07;0.1;0]
Anger			[0.12;0;0.11;0.77;0;0;0]
Surprise			[0;0;0;0;0.89;0.11;0]
Disgust			[0;0.14;0;0.1;0;0.76;0]
Boredom-Sleepiness			[0;0;0.15;0.13;0;0;0.72]

Specifically, we compared the classification performance of following classifiers in facial expression classification: (1) **R**adial **B**asis **F**unctions (RBF) neural networks, (2) **K**-th **N**earest **N**eighbour (KNN) classifiers (3) **S**upport **V**ector **M**achines (SVM) and (4) **M**ultilayer **P**erceptron (MLP) neural networks. The NetLab toolbox was utilized to construct the RBF network, MLP, network and KNN classifiers, while the SVM classifier was implemented with the OSU-SVM toolbox.

In this task, we concluded to seven features which achieved good results. Namely, the extracted features are:

- Mouth Ratio

- Left Eye Ratio

Table 6.13: Sample images of our facial expression database

Emotions	Input Image	Extracted Features	Network's Response
Neutral			[0.88;0;0.05;0.07;0;0.01;0]
Happiness			[0;1;0;0;0;0;0]
Sadness			[0;0;0.83;0;0;0.17;0]
Anger			[0.14;0;0.12;0.74;0;0;0]
Surprise			[0.04;0;0;0;0.83;0.13;0]
Disgust			[0.01;0;0;0;0.12;0.74;0.13]
Boredom-Sleepiness			[0;0;0;0;0;0.23;0.77]

- Right Eye Ratio

- Head size ratio

- Texture of the forehead: Measurement of the changes of the texture of the forehead compared to 'neutral' expression

- Texture of the chin: Measurement of the changes of the texture of the chin compared to 'neutral' expression

- Texture of the region between the eyebrows: Measurement of the changes of the texture of the region between the eyebrows compared to 'neutral' expression

SVM classifier

The support vector machine (SVM) is a supervised classification system that finds an optimal hyperplane which separates data points that will generalize best to future data. Such a hyperplane is the so called maximum margin hyperplane, which maximizes the distance to the closest points from each class. Let

$$S = \{\mathbf{s}_1, \mathbf{s}_2, \ldots, \mathbf{s}_n\} \tag{6.1}$$

where $\mathbf{s}_j \in \mathbf{R}^\mathbf{d}$ be a set of d-dimensional feature vectors corresponding to the image files of a facial expression database. Any hyperplane separating the two data classes has the form Eq. 6.2

$$f(\mathbf{s}) = \mathbf{w} \cdot \Phi(\mathbf{s}) + b, \tag{6.2}$$

where $f : \mathbf{R}^\mathbf{d} \to [-1, +1]$. The SVM classifier is obtained by solving a quadratic programming problem of the form:

$$\min_{w,b,\xi} \frac{1}{2} \|w\|^2 + C \sum_{i=1}^{2n} \xi_i, \tag{6.3}$$

subject to the constraints

$$y_i(\mathbf{w} \cdot \Phi(\mathbf{s}_i) + b) \geq 1 - \xi_i, \xi_i \geq 0 \forall i \in \{1, \ldots, 2n\}. \tag{6.4}$$

The optimal solution gives rise to a decision function of the following form:

$$f(\mathbf{s}) = \sum_{i=1}^{2n} y_i w_i \Phi(\mathbf{s}_i) \cdot \Phi(\mathbf{s}_j) + b \tag{6.5}$$

A significant characteristic of SVMs is that only a small fraction of the w_i coefficients are non-zero. The corresponding pairs of $\mathbf{s}_i$ entries (known as margin support vectors) and y_i output labels fully define the decision function. Given that the training patterns appear only in dot product terms $\Phi(\mathbf{s}_i) \cdot \Phi(\mathbf{s}_j)$, we can employ a positive definite kernel function $K(\mathbf{s}_i, \mathbf{s}_j) = \Phi(\mathbf{s}_i) \cdot \Phi(\mathbf{s}_j)$ to implicitly map into a higher dimensional space and compute the dot product. Specifically, in our approach we utilize the Gaussian kernel function which is of the form $K(\mathbf{s}_i, \mathbf{s}_j) = \exp\{-\frac{\|\mathbf{s}_i - \mathbf{s}_j\|^2}{2\sigma^2}\}$.

RBF neural network classifier

For our system, we also considered radial basis function (RBF) networks for facial expression classification. RBF networks have the advantages over other classifiers that they use initially unsupervised learning methods to find clusters of facial expressions without presupposed class labels. Then, the RBF network distinguishes facial expression classes using the weights that are learnt during training when the class labels for the samples are included. Also, the RBF network can quickly classify new

Ioanna-Ourania Stathopoulou and George A. Tsihrintzis

facial images of expressions once it has been trained. However, training can require a large amount of time because it traditionally involves finding good parameters for each basis function using gradient descent.

The input layer is determined by the dimensionality d of feature vector of each data point. Thus, the input to our RBF network is a vector $\mathbf{s}_j \in \mathbf{R}^d$.

We will choose M basis functions for our network where each function computes the distance from $\mathbf{s}_i$ to a prototype vector $\mathbf{s}_j$. We use Gaussians for our basis functions: $K(\mathbf{s}_i, \mathbf{s}_j) = \exp\{-\frac{\|\mathbf{s}_i - \mathbf{s}_j\|^2}{2\sigma_j^2}\}$. The parameters $\mathbf{s}_j$ and σ_j for each function are determined using unsupervised or supervised methods. So, the RBF network consisted of fifty basis functions (50 neurons) in the hidden layer.

The number of neurons in the output layer is determined by the number of classes we want to classify in each experiment. The equation for a single output

$$y_k(\mathbf{s}) = \sum_{i=1}^{M} w_{ki} \Phi_i(\mathbf{s}) + b,$$

where $b = w_{k0}$ is the weight of the bias

The network was trained with the Expectation Maximization algorithm for two hundred (200) cycles and its output estimates the degree of membership of the input feature vector in each class. Thus, the value at each output necessarily remains between 0 and 1.

MLP neural network classifier

The Multi-layer Perceptron neural network which was constructed has two feed-forward layers. In this network, the dimensionality of input layer is d, with M hidden units and c output units. The output of the jth hidden unit is given by a weighted linear combination of the d input values:

$$a_j = \sum_{i=1}^{d} w_{ji}^{(1)} \mathbf{s}_i + b^{(1)}, \tag{6.6}$$

where $w_{ji}^{(1)}$ denotes a weight in the first layer going from input i to hidden unit j and $b^{(1)}$ is the bias for the first layer. Similarly, the outputs for the second layer is given in the following form:

$$a_k = \sum_{i=1}^{M} w_{kj}^{(2)} \mathbf{z}_i + b^{(2)}. \tag{6.7}$$

The activation of the kth output unit is obtained by transforming the linear combination using a non-linear activation function, to give:

$$y_k(\mathbf{s}) = \tilde{g}(a_k), \tag{6.8}$$

where g is the activation function.

In other words, an explicit expression for the complete function represented by our network is given in the form:

$$y_k(\mathbf{s}) = \tilde{g}\left(\sum_{i=1}^{M} w_{kj}^{(2)} g\left(\sum_{i=1}^{d} w_{ji}^{(1)} \mathbf{s}_i + b^{(1)}\right) + b^{(2)}\right) \qquad \boxed{6.9}$$

The number of hidden units is five (5). The two-layer network with linear outputs is trained by minimizing a sum-of-squares error function using the scaled conjugate gradient optimizer.

KNN classifier

The KNN classifier was based on the class label prediction of the 10 nearest neighbours.

The NetLab toolbox was utilized in order to construct the RBF network, MLP, network and KNN classifiers, while the SVM classifier was implemented with the OSU-SVM toolbox. More details for the classifiers can be found in [272, 273, 274, 275].

6.4.9 Experimental performance evaluation

Classification results were calculated using 10-fold cross-validation evaluation, where the dataset to be evaluated was iteratively partitioned so that 90% be used for training and 10% be used for testing for each class. This process was iterated with different disjoint partitions and the results were averaged. This ensured that the calculated accuracy was not biased because of the particular partitioning of training and testing.

The results have shown that the SVM classifiers achieved higher results than the other three classifiers. The results presented in Table 6.14 illustrate the SVM classifier as the most appropriate for this task. Also, based on our empirical studies, which were described in Chapter 5, we were able to measure the performance of human observers for the facial expression classification task. As we can observe, all the classifiers perform better than the human classifiers, results are also shown in Table 6.14.

Table 6.14: Human versus computer classifiers

Classifiers	Accuracy for the seven classes	Humans
MLP	88.74%	
RBF	95.37%	64.11%
KNN	96.11%	
SVM	96.97%	

In Table 6.15, we observe the classification accuracy for each of the seven classes depicting the 'neutral', 'happiness', 'surprise', 'anger', 'sadness', 'boredom-sleepiness'

Ioanna-Ourania Stathopoulou and George A. Tsihrintzis

and 'disgust' expression, respectively. The results of the four classifiers are in agreement with the results from the human responses. As we can observe in Table 6.15, the expressions corresponding to 'angry' and 'disgusted' achieved the lower success rates not only from the classifiers but also from the humans.

Table 6.15: Classification rates for each expression

Expressions	MLP	RBF	KNN	SVM	Human responses
Neutral	100%	100%	100%	100%	**62%**
Happy	100%	100%	100%	100%	**83%**
Surprised	99.60%	100%	100%	100%	**93%**
Sad	98.80%	99.20%	99.60%	100%	**58%**
Angry	33.60%	90.40%	98.40%	94.40%	**73%**
Bored-Sleepy	97.20%	99.20%	98.80%	98.40%	**64%**
Disgusted	92.00%	78.80%	76.00%	86.00%	**16%**

Based on these results we consider the SVM classifier as the most appropriate classifier for this problem. Also, as we observe from the results in Table 6.15, the MLP classifier achieved the best classification rate in classifying the 'disgust' expression. In the following Tables 6.16, 6.17, 6.18 and 6.19, we see the confusion matrix for the 250 images for the SVM, RBF, KNN and MLP classifier, respectively.

Table 6.16: Confusion matrix for the SVM classifier

	Neutral	Happy	Surprised	Sad	Angry	Bored/ Sleepy	Disgusted
Neutral	250	0	0	0	0	0	0
Happy	0	250	0	0	0	0	0
Surprised	0	0	250	0	0	0	0
Sad	0	0	0	250	0	0	0
Angry	0	0	0	0	236	0	14
Bored /Sleepy	0	4	0	0	0	246	0
Disgusted	0	0	0	0	35	0	215

The results in Tables 6.16, 6.17, 6.18 and 6.19 show that the misclassification for the 'anger' and 'disgust' expressions are confided to these two expressions. Especially, the MLP classifier, misclassified many images of the 'anger' expression as 'disgust'. The best results for the 'disgust' expression are given from the MLP Classifier, but, in the same time, misclassified many of the 'anger' face images as 'disgust', so it can be trusted in using it. Based on this, we consider the SVM Classifier as most appropriate for this problem because it achieved the best results for the full set of 7 expressions.

Table 6.17: Confusion matrix for the RBF classifier

	Neutral	Happy	Surprised	Sad	Angry	Bored/ Sleepy	Disgusted
Neutral	250	0	0	0	0	0	0
Happy	0	250	0	0	0	0	0
Surprised	0	0	250	0	0	0	0
Sad	0	0	2	248	0	0	0
Angry	0	0	0	0	226	0	24
Bored /Sleepy	0	2	0	0	0	248	0
Disgusted	1	0	1	7	44	0	197

Table 6.18: Confusion matrix for the KNN classifier

	Neutral	Happy	Surprised	Sad	Angry	Bored/ Sleepy	Disgusted
Neutral	250	0	0	0	0	0	0
Happy	0	250	0	0	0	0	0
Surprised	0	0	250	0	0	0	0
Sad	0	0	1	249	0	0	0
Angry	0	0	0	2	246	0	2
Bored/ Sleepy	0	3	0	0	0	247	0
Disgusted	0	0	0	2	58	0	190

Table 6.19: Confusion matrix for the MLP classifier

	Neutral	Happy	Surprised	Sad	Angry	Bored/ Sleepy	Disgusted
Neutral	250	0	0	0	0	0	0
Happy	0	250	0	0	0	0	0
Surprised	0	0	249	1	0	0	0
Sad	0	0	3	247	0	0	0
Angry	0	0	0	5	84	0	161
Bored/ Sleepy	0	7	0	0	0	243	0
Disgusted	0	0	0	3	17	0	230

6.5 Summary - Conclusions

In this Chapter, we described extensively the face detection and facial expression recognition system that we have developed. Face detection is based on a model proposed by P. Sinha. We preprocess the image in order to depict this model and use an artificial neural network, which classifies the image to as 'face' and 'non face'. Towards

Ioanna-Ourania Stathopoulou and George A. Tsihrintzis

this task, we built two different artificial neural networks and decided upon using the second, which demonstrated better performance. To measure the performance of the second network in detecting faces in images, we tested the network in four different set of images: (1) various images of different sizes and resolutions gathered from the World Wide Web and other sources(e.g scanning old photo images), (2) images from our own facial expression database where people may form some expression, (3) face images acquired in the first efforts to construct a facial expression database (low quality images) and, (4) non human face images (images of pets and animals, complex backgrounds and parts of the face and human). The system managed to detect face with 90,83%, 94,00% and 72,89% success rate, for the three first sets, respectively, whereas for the 'non-face' images set the success rate was 100%.

Facial expression recognition can be divided in two sets of attempts. In our first attempts for a facial expression recognition system, we tried to use some of the databases already available over the World Wide Web, as mentioned in Chapter 3, Section 3.1, whereas the emotion classes, that our system would be able to recognize, were not wet been determined. We used a fairly simple feature extraction algorithm which computes specific size ration of some facial portions, such as the eyes, the mouth and the size of the face and, then, feed the computed feature vector to an artificial neural network which classifies the expression. Although the developed system showed some good results and was able to generalize in low quality face images and faces in side view, we soon developed a more sophisticated feature extraction algorithm that we finally adopt. In the newer attempts towards facial expression recognition, we use more facial features are extracted from the image, such as measurements of the texture, head orientation, etc., we use our own facial expression database for training and/or testing, as it is more complete in terms of the classes we want to classify and, a better, more sophisticated, algorithm to extract the facial features is used, which is based on our eye detection/extraction algorithm. After successful eye detection/extraction, the rest of the features are computed based on their relative location with the eyes. The computed feature vector is, again, fed to an artificial neural network which classifies the emotion. The neural network resulted to an average success rate of 77,14% in classifying the expressions. In order to achieve better results, we developed more sophisticated classifiers, using Netlab Toolbox: (1) **R**adial **B**asis **F**unctions neural networks, (2) **K**-th **N**earest **N**eighbour classifiers (3) **S**upport **V**ector **M**achines and (4) **M**ultilayer **P**erceptron neural networks. We trained and tested the classifiers using 10-fold cross validation techniques. Finally, we concluded to the SVM Classifier as the more adequate for this problem, which achieved and accuracy of 96.97%.

7

Human Motion and Gesture Analysis

All human actions have one or more of these seven causes: chance, nature, compulsions, habit, reason, passion and desire.

—Aristotle (384 BC-322 BC)

7.1 Introduction

WITH the progress of computer vision and multimedia technologies, there has been much interest in motion understanding. Human motion analysis is currently one of the most active research fields in computer vision. The aim is to detect, track and identify people, and more generally, to interpret human behaviors, from image sequences involving humans. A significant part of this task consists of capturing large scale body movements, such as movements of the head, arms, torso, and legs. For this reason and because of the similarities (i.e., both involve articulated structures and non-rigid motions, same techniques are used towards both tasks, etc.) gesture analysis can be considered as a part of human motion analysis. D. M. Gavrila [7] identified this research field as *"looking at people"* and presented some of the most important areas that this research can be applied on with promising results, which as summarized in Table 7.1.

Because of its promising applications in various areas, human motion analysis has attracted great interest from computer vision researchers. In this chapter, we will present and compare some of the techniques that have appeared in literature regarding human motion tracking and gesture analysis. Although, as stated before, gesture analysis can be considered as part of human tracking, we will present relevant techniques separately from techniques for human motion tracking and analysis. Finally, we will discuss some techniques in human motion analysis and gesture recognition that aim to emotion recognition, which is the main topic of this book.

Table 7.1: Applications of "Looking at People" [7]

General domain	Specific area
Virtual reality	• Interactive virtual worlds
	• Games
	• Virtual studios
	• Character animation
	• Teleconferencing (e.g., film, advertising, home-use)
"Smart" surveillance systems	• Access control
	• Parking lots
	• Supermarkets, department stores
	• Vending machines, ATMs
	• Traffic
Advanced user interfaces	• Social interfaces
	• Sign-language translation
	• Gesture driven control
	• Signaling in high-noise environments (airports, factories)
Motion analysis	• Content-based indexing of sports video footage
	• Personalized training in golf, tennis, etc.
	• Choreography of dance and ballet
	• Clinical studies of orthopedic patients
Model-based coding	• Very low bit-rate video compression

7.2 Human detection and motion tracking

DETECTING, tracking humans and inferring their pose in videos is arguably one of the most challenging problems in computer vision because of large variations in body shape, appearance, clothing, illumination and background. The problem is further complicated by the non-rigidness of body movement.

The first step when tracking humans and analyzing their motion is to detect the humans on the image plane. Human detection aims at identifying and segmenting regions corresponding to people from the remaining portion of the image. Human detection is significant task in a human motion analysis system, as subsequent processes such as tracking and action recognition are greatly dependent on it. Human motion tracking, on the other hand, involves monitoring each movement of the humans on the image plane by identifying and computing the moving human regions in the image sequences. Generally, human detection is considered a lower-level vision problem than human motion tracking, but sometimes similar techniques and workflows may be used for these two tasks.

Ioanna-Ourania Stathopoulou and George A. Tsihrintzis

Many criteria could be used to classify previous works (some works can be found in [276, 277, 278, 279, 280]), some of these criteria include use or no use of body markers, the use or no use of explicit models, type of models used (e.g., stick figure-based, volumetric, statistical), dimensionality of the tracking space (2-D vs. 3-D), sensor modality (e.g., visible light, infrared, range), sensor multiplicity (monocular vs. stereo), sensor placement (centralized vs. distributed), and sensor mobility (stationary vs. moving). We will categorize relevant approaches on the basis of the following criteria:

Human Detection:

- Global methods

- Part-based methods

- Marker-based approaches

  - Passive markers
  - Active markers

- Markerless approaches

  - Model-based methods
  - Region-based methods
  - Active contour based methods
  - Feature-based methods

The classification of the various techniques for human motion analysis and human detection can be summarized in Figure 7.1.

7.2.1   Marker-based approaches

The techniques in this category usually use optical sensors, e.g. cameras, to analyze the human motion, whereas the human movements are captured by placing markers on the human body. Markers can be defined as special objects that are attached or fixed to the human body, and help to track the movement of its interesting points. Many systems are based on the Moving Light Display (MLD), which was introduced in 1975 by Johansson [281]. Johansson conducted an experiment in which he attached markers to the joints of human subjects in order to track the human movement. This experiment became a milestone in human movement tracking. Marker-based tracking systems are capable of minimising the uncertainty of a subject's movements, due to the unique appearance of markers. This basic theory is still embedded in current

Ioanna-Ourania Stathopoulou and George A. Tsihrintzis

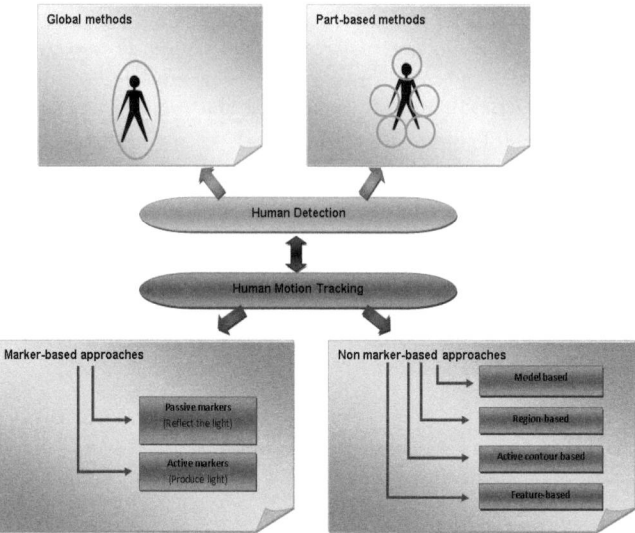

Figure 7.1: Classification in the techniques for human motion tracking and human detection

state-of-the-art motion trackers. These tracking systems can be passive, active or hybrid in style: a passive system uses a number of markers that do not generate any light, but only reflect incoming light. In contrast, markers in an active system can produce light, i.e. infrared, which is then collected by a camera system.

The approaches that use markers to track the human movement are usually designed for commercial use and can be divided into passive or active, depending on whether they use passive or active or hybrid markers. The systems that use passive markers (passive systems), place a number of markers on the human body, which they do not generate any light, but only reflect incoming light. On the other hand, active systems use a number of markers that can produce light, usually infrared light, which is collected by the camera(s).

Passive systems, such as ELITE [282], MaxReflex [283], VICON [284] and Qualisys [285], use a number of cameras that emit a beam of infrared light. The passive markers that are placed onto a subject's body, reflect the infrared light and then their position is captured by the cameras. These systems compute the 3-D position of the target by combining 2-D data from several cameras. The main advantage of such systems is that they do not require that the subjects be linked with wires in order to supply the markers with power supply, as passive markers do not need to generate their own light. However, these systems suffer from disadvantages as well: (1) the simultaneous presence of many markers in the images, requires the use of labeling algorithms to uniquely identify the markers in the image sequences, (2) sometimes the process may fail, if the markers are placed anatomically close to each other, and (3) infrared-based systems only record marker motion, missing information about the environment. This, may lead to erroneous conclusions about the human movement.

Active systems, such as OPTOTRACK [286], COSTEL [287], CODA [288], Polaris (combines passive and active markers) [289] and Kolahi et al. [290], apply a number of light emitting diodes (LEDs)to the human body. The LEDs are connected to a LED control unit which is carried by the subject and activated stroboscopically by a cable or telemetric multiplex signal. Again, based on the emitted light, the markers are recorded by the cameras and the system computes the target position. Major drawbacks in such systems are the mechanical restraints imposed by the LED-wiring attached to the subject, the necessity of a controlled environment and the limitation to the number of markers due to their stroboscopic timing. However, a major advantage of such systems is that they do not need extensive labeling algorithms to unique identify the marker.

Generally, marker-based approaches can achieve high accuracy in human motion analysis, but lack in the compactness due to the use of an amount of markers and to the necessity of controlled environments. Many marker-based systems have achieved high accuracy in human tracking. For example, the CODA [288] system can successfully track a human subject at a 3 m distance, achieving the following position accuracies: $\pm$ 1.5 mm along the transverse axes and $\pm$ 2.5 mm along the longitude axis [291]. Usually, such systems are used in medicine (e.g. for the diagnosis and therapy of orthopedic or neurologic diseases) and in sports (e.g. for the measurement of an athlete's performance).

7.2.2 Markerless approaches

The approaches involving human motion tracking without the use of markers aim at detecting and tracking the movement of human subjects, by processing only the data acquired from cameras, without the use of any markers. The motivation towards this task lies on the fact that human motion analysis can be considered intrusive to the human subjects, when markers are used, especially in active marker-based approaches. Moreover, it is mentioned in [292] and [245] that marker-based vision systems may present he following drawbacks: (1) identification of standard bony landmarks can be unreliable, (2) the soft tissue overlying bony landmarks can move, resulting in noisy data, (3) the marker itself can wobble due to its own inertia, and (4) markers can even come completely adrift.

The research area of markerless human detection has drawn even more attention, mainly because of its applications in human-computer interaction and surveillance systems. Currently, advances in computer vision and the decrease in the prices of computers and cameras make it even easier to develop more advanced surveillance and human computer interaction systems. Although previous approaches have focused intensively in the development of human motion tracking algorithms able to cover a wide variety of scenarios, many problems occur when these algorithms are applied on real life situations. The major challenges in these cases include cluttered background, noise, changes in illumination, occlusion and scale/appearance change of the subjects.

Human detection

For the human detection task, the relevant approaches can be categorized in various ways: (1) in 2-D or 3-D, according to the use or not of stereoscopic input data, (2) attempting detection in static images or in video sequences and, (3) global or part-based methods, according to the techniques used.

Regarding the second categorization, human detection in video sequences usually involves the following two steps: (1) motion segmentation and (2) object classification [293]. Motion segmentation in video sequences involves the detection of regions that correspond to moving objects such as vehicles and people in natural scenes. Detecting moving blobs constitutes the bases for processes that follow detection, such as tracking and activity analysis, because only those changing pixels need to be considered after detection. However, changes in weather, illumination, shadow and repetitive motion from clutter make motion segmentation difficult to achieve quickly and reliably. At present, most segmentation methods use either temporal or spatial information of the images. Since the extracted moving regions from the motion segmentation process may correspond to different moving objects, the object classification step aims at classifying these objects. For example, motion segmentation of the image sequences captured by surveillance cameras in road traffic scenes will probably result in different objects, such as pedestrians, vehicles, and other moving objects such as flying birds, flowing clouds, etc. To track people further and analyze their activities, it is very necessary to correctly distinguish them from other moving objects.

Regarding the third categorization, the proposed techniques can be summarized as following:

- **Global methods:** These approaches [294, 295, 296, 297, 298] use a model (template) of the entire human body to detect a human subject on the image plane. Specifically, usually they use a sliding window which scans the image plane. The window forms the input image which is processed and compared with the given model of the human body. A threshold is used, and when this threshold is surpassed, the human is declared.

Specifically, Oren et al. [294] developed a system which learns from examples and does not rely on any a priori (handcrafted) models or on motion to detect pedestrians in images. The detection technique is based on the idea of the wavelet template that defines the shape of an object in terms of a subset of the wavelet coefficients of its image. The wavelet template is invariant to changes in color and texture and can be used to robustly define a rich and complex class of objects such as humans.

Viola et al. [295, 296] developed a system for pedestrian detection in video sequences based on their AdaBoost algorithm [157]. Their system integrated image intensity information with motion information. They used a detection algorithm that scans two consecutive frames of a video sequence. The detector is trained (using AdaBoost) to take advantage of both motion and appearance information to detect a walking person. The implementation described ran at about 4 frames/second, detected pedestrians at very small scales (as small as 20x15 pixels), and had a very low false positive rate.

Dalal and Triggs [297, 298] studied the question of feature sets for robust visual object recognition. First, they considered existing edge- and gradient-based descriptors and then showed experimentally that grids of Histograms of Oriented Gradient (HOG) descriptors significantly outperform existing feature sets in human detection. A linear SVM is trained on these descriptors. After this, they studied the influence of each stage of the computation with regards to performance. Finally, they came to the conclusion that fine scale gradients, fine orientation binning, relatively coarse spatial binning, and high quality local contrast normalization in overlapping descriptor blocks were important to get good results. They tested their approach on the MIT pedestrian database, first, which showed excellent results. In later studies, they built their own pedestrian database, called INRIA, which contained extremely complicated backgrounds and many changes in the illumination. In these tests, the system demonstrated an accuracy of 89% in detecting humans.

- **Part-based methods:** These approaches are based on the fact that since human movements are non-rigid and arbitrary, boundaries or silhouettes of human body are deformable, leading to difficulties in describing them. Thus, in several approaches [299, 300, 301, 302], parts of the human body (e.g. hands, face etc.) are detected first, and a human body model is assembled next. In these cases, two different methods are used to assemble the human body: (1) top-down approaches, which estimate the whole human position and the part location by modeling the limb likelihood and their relative position jointly [301] and (2) bottom-up detectors are applied on the image to extract candidate parts and then a top-down procedure inferences the configuration and returns a best parts assembly [299, 300, 302]. Most approaches use the canonical tree model for body parts, hence efficiently solving the assembly problem with dynamic programming.

Human tracking

Human tracking is a particularly important task in human motion analysis since it forms the basis for pose estimation and action recognition. In contrast with human detection, human tracking is a higher-level computer vision problem. However, towards both of these two tasks, overlapping techniques may be used such as motion segmentation. Tracking over time typically involves matching objects in consecutive frames using features such as points, lines or blobs. That is to say, tracking may be considered to be equivalent to establishing coherent relations of image features between frames with respect to position, velocity, shape, texture, color, etc.

Object representation   In a tracking scenario, an object can be defined as anything that is of interest for further analysis. Objects, in general, and humans, in particular, can be represented by their shapes and appearances [1]. Based on Yilmaz et al. [1], we have the following representations in terms of shape, which are also depicted in Figure 7.2:

- **Points:** An object is represented by a single point, that is, its centroid (Figure 7.2(a)) [303], or by a set of points (Figure 7.2(b)) [304]. In general, the point representation is suitable for tracking objects that occupy small regions in an image.

- **Primitive geometric shapes:** Object shape is represented by a rectangle or an ellipse (Figure 7.2(c) and Figure 7.2(d), respectively [305]). Object motion for such representations is usually modeled by translation, affine, or projective (homographic) transformation. Though primitive geometric shapes are more suitable for representing simple rigid objects, they are also used for tracking non-rigid objects.

- **Object silhouette and contour:** Contour representation defines the boundary of an object (Figure 7.2(g), Figure 7.2(h). The region inside the contour is called the silhouette of the object (see Figure 7.2(i)). Silhouette and contour representations are suitable for tracking complex nonrigid shapes [306]

- **Articulated shape models:** Articulated objects are composed of body parts that are held together with joints. For example, the human body is an articulated object with torso, legs, hands, head, and feet connected by joints. The relationship between the parts are governed by kinematic motion models, such

Ioanna-Ourania Stathopoulou and George A. Tsihrintzis

as joint angle, for example. In order to represent an articulated object, one can model the constituent parts using cylinders or ellipses as shown in Figure 7.2(e).

- **Skeletal models:** An object skeleton can be extracted by applying a media axis transform to the corresponding silhouette [307]. This model is commonly used as a shape representation for recognizing objects [308]. The skeleton representation can be used to model both articulated and rigid objects (see Figure 7.2(f)).

- **Cardboard models:** The limbs of a person are represented by planar patches. This model is used in human motion recognition [309] (see Figure 7.2(j))

- **3-D models:** This model is used in 3-D human motion recognition (see Figure 7.2(k))

Based on Yilmaz et al. [1], we have the following representations by appearance:

- **Probability densities of object appearance:** The probability density estimates of the object appearance can be either parametric, such as Gaussian [310] and a mixture of Gaussians [311], or non-parametric, such as Parzen windows [312] and histograms [305]. The probability densities of object appearance features (color, texture, etc.) can be computed from the image regions specified by the shape models (interior region of an ellipse or a contour).

- **Templates:** Templates are formed using simple geometric shapes or silhouettes [313]. An advantage of a template is that it carries both spatial and appearance information. Templates, however, only encode the object appearance generated from a single view. Thus, they are only suitable for tracking objects the poses of which do not vary considerably during the course of tracking.

- **Active appearance models:** Active appearance models are generated by simultaneously modeling the object shape and appearance [314]. In general, the object shape is defined by a set of landmarks. Similar to the contour-based representation, the landmarks can reside on the object boundary or, alternatively, they can reside inside the object region. For each landmark, an appearance vector is stored which is in the form of color, texture, or gradient magnitude. Active appearance models require a training phase where both the shape and its associated appearance is learnt from a set of samples using, for instance, the principal component analysis (PCA).

- **Multiview appearance models:** These models encode different views of an object. One approach to represent the different object views is to generate a subspace from the given views. Subspace approaches, for example, Principal Component Analysis (PCA) and Independent Component Analysis (ICA), have been used for both shape and appearance representation [315, 316].

Ioanna-Ourania Stathopoulou and George A. Tsihrintzis

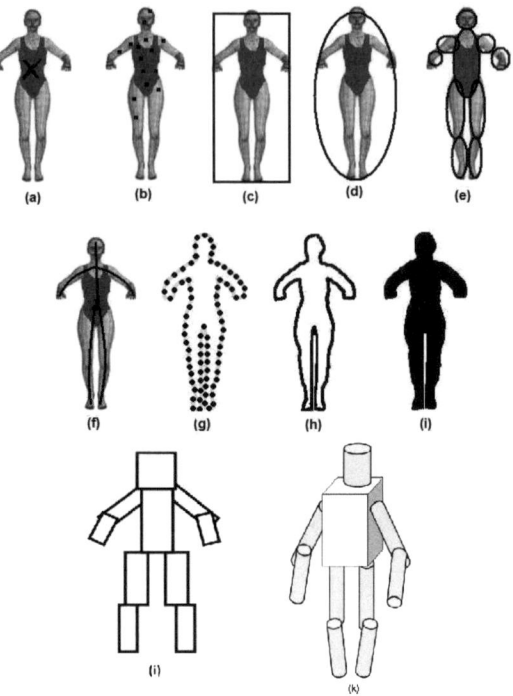

Figure 7.2: Object representations. (a) Centroid, (b) multiple points, (c) rectangular patch, (d) elliptical patch, (e) part-based multiple patches, (f) object skeleton, (g) complete object contour, (h) control points on object contour, (i) object silhouette, (j) cardboard model, (k) 3-D model. [1]

Human tracking techniques Regarding human motion tracking, depending on the techniques used, we can categorize the relevant approaches in various groups. In this monograph, the categorization will be made based on the following:

- **Model-based tracking:** In model-based approaches, an a priori shape model of the human body is assumed. The tracking is achieved by matching projected models with image data. Regarding the model-based tracking process of objects, an interesting survey can be found in [317]. Regarding the models used to represent the human body, the techniques can be categorized to: (1) the stick figure representation, (2) the 2-D contour representation and, (3) the 3-D model representation.

The *stick figure representation* [318, 319, 320, 321, 322, 323, 324, 325, 326, 327, 328, 329, 330, 331] is based on the skeletal structure of the human body where line segments are connected by joints to form a hierarchical structure. Generally, The stick figure model is one of the simplest ways to represent the human body where each part is represented by a stick and the sticks are connected by joints Correspondingly, the stick-figure representation considers a human body as a combination of line segments linked by joints. The stick figure is obtained in various ways, e.g., by means of median axis transform or distance transform. The motion of joints provides a key to motion estimation and recognition of the whole figure. Gavrila and Davis [321] first split the human model into torso-head and limb partitions, and, then, matching is implemented in the partitioned search space. Guo et al. [319] represented the human body structure in the silhouette by a stick figure model which had ten sticks articulated with six joints. Then, in order to track the human they try to find a stick figure with minimal energy in a potential field. Also, in order to reduce the complexity of this matching process, they use prediction and angle constraints of individual joints. Wren et al. [326] developed the Pfinder which employs a multi-class statistical model of color and shape to obtain a 2-D representation of head and hands in a wide range of viewing conditions. Karaulova et al. [325] also used this kind of representation of the human body to build a novel hierarchical model of human dynamics encoded using Hidden Markov models. Their model allowed them to track view-independently the human body in monocular video sequences. Morris and Rehg [329] built a 2D stick figure kinematic model of the body for tracking the motion of the body through single source video. Recent studies by Sidenbladh et al. [331] and Rogez et al. [330] also use the stick figure to construct a low dimensional model of the motion and the further analyze and represent the motion with enhanced information (3-D model of the position and orientation of the body or 2D-shape information, respectively).

On the other hand, *the 2-D contour representation* [332, 333, 334, 309, 335, 336] is basically related to the projection of 3-D human body into the 2-D image contours. In such description, human body segments are analogous to 2-D ribbons or blobs. Niyogi and Adelson [332] observed that walkers generate special signatures in space-time. Based on this observation, they used the spatio-temporal pattern in XYT space to track, analyze and recognize walking figures. They observed an image sequence 'cube' of a fronto-parallel walker. The 'cube' is formed by stacking each of the frames in an image sequence one right after another. They obtained XT-slice of the 'cube' near the walker's ankle and near the walker's head and generated the pattern based on the assumptions that led upon observing them. In order to detect gait, they must find translating blobs in image sequences, and test if the XT-slice of the lower half of the blob

Ioanna-Ourania Stathopoulou and George A. Tsihrintzis

contains a gait signature. Then, they model gait by recovering a set of contours for these XT-slice signatures. A 2-D contour of a a human walking figure constructed and further analyzed in order to recognize the specific human. They tested their approach on 24 different image sequences containing fronto-parallel walkers and obtained 79% recognition rate. Leung and Yang [333] developed a vision system called 'First Sight', which labeled the outline of a moving human body. The system consisted of two main processes: (1) first they extracted the outline of a moving human body from an image sequence and, then, (2) they interpreted the outline and produced a labeled two-dimensional human body stick figure for each frame of the image sequence. IN the second process, in order to develop the model, the used extensive knowledge of the structure, shape, and posture of the human body. They tested their the technique on unedited image sequences with self-occlusions and missing boundary lines with encouraging results. Chang and Huang [334] developed a system to extract the moving ribbons (extremities) by processing the difference between current image frame and reference image frame. By analyzing the moving ribbons on the key frames, they were able to produce the motion parameter curves for each joint on the ribbon. Ju et al. [309] defined a 'cardboard person model' in which a person"s limbs are represented by a set of connected planar patches. The parameterized image motion of these patches was constrained to enforce articulated motion. They used a robust estimation technique in order to find the motion parameters, which provided a rich and concise description of the activity of the human. Pantrigo et al [336] also used a 2-D human body model which consisted of a simple hierarchical set of articulated limbs. The model was easily adaptable to the tracking application requirements. They applied the Path Relinking Particle Filter (PRPF) algorithm [337] to 2-D human pose estimation in different movement tracking activities such as walking and jumping.

Although the 2-D model representation is more robust in terms of computational cost and analysis, it is more sensitive to occlusions and to different camera angles. This led the researchers to build a a more detailed geometric representation of the human body, a 3-D model of the human, by using elliptical cylinders, cones, spheres, etc. [338, 339, 340, 341, 342, 343, 321, 344, 345, 346, 347, 348, 349, 350, 351] Specifically, Rohr [338] constructed a 3-D model of the human body using fourteen cylinders with elliptic cross sections and used it for the recognition of pedestrians. Each cylinder was described by three parameters: one for the length and two for the sizes of the semi-axes and the coordinate system of the whole body was fixed at the center of the torso. First, they detect the moving objects by applying a change detection algorithm on each image point and further applying binary image operations to improve the accuracy. After detecting the human moving, he tries to detect the 3-D position of the human assuming that the person walks parallel to the image plane. Finally, he estimated the 3-D model parameters in consecutive images by applying a Kalman filter. Goddard [340] also used 3-D model representation in order to distinguish three human gaits. Like Rohr [338] he computed the features in the 2-D image plane and tried to fit them in the 3-D model. Wachter and Nagel [347] build a 3-D human model by using right-elliptical cones and described its kinematics by a homogeneous transformation tree. The proposed approach was able to determine the values of a varying number of degrees of freedom (body joints, position and orientation of the person relative to the camera) according to the application and the kind of image sequence, by using an iterated extended Kalman filter (IEKF) and, thus, obtaining important information regarding human motion. Zhao and Nevatia [350] employ a 3-D elliptical human model and segment the human body in crowd situations using a Data-Driven Markov Chain Monte Carlo (DDMCMC) algorithm. Balan and Black [351] proposed a robust and adaptive, appearance model, called RoAM. RoAM is based on the wandering stable lost (WSL) framework and employs an annealed particle filtering algorithm to inference the 3-D body model. More recently, Balan et al. [351] estimated the 3-D human motion from video sequences is quantitatively evaluated using synchronized, multi-camera, calibrated video by applying Bayesian filtering. Specifically, they independently implemented two Bayesian person trackers using two variants of particle filtering and proposed an evaluation measure appropriate for assessing the quality of probabilistic tracking methods. In their research, they evaluated various 3-D motion analysis methods. Their results showed that generally in constrained laboratory environments, previous methods performed quite well, but, in natural settings, multiple cameras and background subtraction are required to achieve reliable tracking

As stated previously, an important advantage of 3-D human models is their ability to handle occlusion and obtain more significant data for action analysis. However, their major drawback of such models is that they require more parameters in order to depict the human body and, thus, they need more computational power and time to analyze this parameters and complete the matching. In such approaches, there must be a balance between these parameters and the equivalent computational time.

- **Region-based tracking:** Region-based tracking methods [352, 353, 354, 326] estimate statistic measurements for each point separately, thereby considering only information from the local neighborhood. The aim is to identify a connected region which can be associated with each moving object in the image plane. The majority of these methods subtract the background in order to

Ioanna-Ourania Stathopoulou and George A. Tsihrintzis

detect and track the motion. For example, Haritaoglu et al. [352] present a real-time visual surveillance system, called W4, in which a statistical model for the background scene is maintained and humans or other objects are tracked by background subtraction. Collins et al. [353] developed a system for autonomous video surveillance and monitoring called VSAM. VSAM uses adaptive background subtraction and three frame differences to track moving objects. Region-based tracking methods work well in scenes containing only a small number of objects. However, they are extremely sensitive to dynamic scene changes due to lighting and extraneous events. Besides, this cannot handle occlusion problems among objects and the 3-D pose of objects cannot be acquired. McKenna et al. [354] proposed an adaptive background subtraction method that combined color and gradient information to effectively cope with shadows and unreliable color cues in motion segmentation. A tracking process was then performed at three levels of abstraction: regions, humans, and groups. Each region that could merge and split had a bounding box. A human was composed of one or more regions grouped together under the condition of geometric structure constraints of the human body. Finally, and a human group consisted of one or more people grouped together. Therefore, using the region tracker and an individual color appearance model, they achieved perfect tracking of multiple humans, even during occlusion.

Generally region-based tracking approach can achieve reliable results. Errors may appear in the presence of long shadows in the image plane. However, this problem may be surpassed by using color information or extracting from the image plane regions without texture (which is usually the case in shadows). Regarding the problem with shadows, a shadow removal algorithm is proposed by [355] which is based on the calculation of the photometric gain and on hysterisis thresholding [356, 357]. Also, in some cases, these approaches do not work very well in cases when the humans are partially occluded by other humans or when human figures are very close to each other. In these case erroneous segmentation of each human figure has been reported.

- **Active contour based tracking:**

Whereas the techniques in model-based tracking have already constructed the model (stick figure, 2-D contour representation or volumetric model) and trying to apply it to the human figure, active-contour-based tracking methods is the opposite process. In active-contour-based tracking methods [358, 359, 360, 361, 362, 363, 364, 365, 366] the outline or the shape of the human body is extracted and represented with bounding contours. Then, they track the human movement by updating these contours dynamically in each frame. Zhong et al. [365] propose a method for object tracking using prototype-based deformable template models and the frame-to-frame deviations of the object shape and the fidelity of the modeled shape to the input image are combined into a criterion. Paragios and Deriche [363] detect and track moving objects in a sequence of images using the front propagation theory and the level-set methodology. Specifically, Paragios and Deriche presented a variational framework for detecting and tracking multiple moving objects in image sequences. A statistical framework, for which the observed inter-frame difference density function was approximated using a mixture model, was used to provide the initial motion detection boundary. Then, the detection and tracking problems were addressed in a common framework that employed a geodesic active contour objective function. Using the level set formulation scheme, complex curves could be detected and tracked while topological changes for the evolving curves were naturally managed. Isard and Blake [360] adopted the stochastic differential equation to describe complex motion model, and combined this approach with deformable templates to cope with human tracking. Recent work of Peterfreund [362] explored a new active contour model based on Kalman filtering for tracking of non-rigid moving targets such as people in spatio-velocity space. The system measurements are employed of gradient-based image potential and optical-flow along the contour. Meanwhile, to improve robustness to clutter and occlusions, an optical-flow-based detection mechanism was proposed. More recently, Buccolieri et al. [366] also used active contours with neural networks for human posture recognition in an automated video surveillance system. Their system consisted of five sequential modules that include the moving target detection process, two levels of segmentation process for interested element localization, features extraction of the object shape and a human posture classification system based on the radial basis functions neural network. Moving objects were detected by using an adaptive background subtraction method with an automatic background adaptation speed parameter and a new fast gradient vector flow snake algorithm. They tested their system for the classification of three different postures such as standing, bending and squatting.

In contrast to the region-based tracking approach, the advantage of having an active contour-based representation is the reduction of computational complexity. But, in order for the active contour based tracking systems to work correctly, a good initial fit of the contours in the human shape is necessary. However, this process is quite difficult, especially for complex articulated objects.

- **Feature-based tracking:**

  Finally, feature-based tracking methods [367, 368, 369, 370, 371, 372, 373, 343, 374, 375, 376, 377, 355, 378] do not treat the human body as a whole object. In order to track the human motion, first, they extract specific features from the human figure. Then, they try to match these features among each image in the sequence and apply clustering techniques to determine which human figure or human part each feature represents. The features which are most commonly used include points, lines, regions or blobs on the human body which will help in the tracking task.

Many approaches use skin extraction techniques or motion detection to extract the features, or a combination of both [375, 378]. Schiele [377] proposed proposed a model-free algorithm which did not use a priori models to detect, track, and segment objects, but built them in the process. Specifically, the algorithm extracted and tracked homogenous regions, which may correspond to objects or object parts and, then models of potential objects by grouping similar moving regions. In [378] a fuzzy feature-based method for online people tracking using an IP PTZ camera is proposed. Their method consists of five steps: (1) target modeling, (2) track initialization, (3) blob extraction, (4) target localization using a fuzzy classifier, and (5) IP PTZ camera control. Skin and motion detection is used to select the most similar target among candidate blobs found in the image. Their results have shown that the proposed method had a good target detection precision (¿89%), low track fragmentation, and the target was almost always localized within 1/6th of the image diagonal from the image center.

Specific points in the human body are the most simple and low-level features that can be used for human motion analysis, such as in [373, 367]. Polana and Nelson [373] used points in the human body in their system which recognized pedestrian behavior with or without occlusion such as walking, running, and passing by another person. Their model-free approach used periodicity information in cyclic motion which is characterized by repeated activity caused by arm swing and foot stepping, etc. They considered an image sequence as a spatiotemporal solid with two spatial dimensions and a time dimension. Repeated activity is indexed by periodic or semi-periodic bumps in the image solid that generate smoothing curves. They referred the curves as 'reference curves', and compare them the test curves in order to recognize activity types. The recognition of pedestrian motion was achieved by choosing the best matching between the reference curves and the test curves.is a good example of point-feature tracking. In addition, Segen and Pingali's tracking system [367] utilized the corner points of moving silhouettes as the features to track and these feature points were matched using a distance measure based on positions and curvatures of points between successive frames.

Generally, the greatest advantage of feature-based approaches is that they work well in the presence of partial occlusion. n the other hand, there are two disadvantages: (1) these methods are unable to recover the 3-D pose of objects and

Ioanna-Ourania Stathopoulou and George A. Tsihrintzis

(2) the feature extraction and processing is usually time consuming. Low-level features, such as points, are easier to extract, in contrary to higher-level features such as lines and blobs.

7.3 Hand Gesture recognition

In recent years, there has been a tremendous effort in research toward novel devices and techniques that improve the naturalness of interaction with computers. Gesture recognition is one most promising attempt in this direction. Generally, gestures are expressive, meaningful body motions involving physical movements of the fingers, hands, arms, etc., with the intent of conveying meaningful information or interacting with the environment. Although gestures include many body parts, this survey will be centered in hand gesture recognition, as hand movements are considered to be the most effective, general-purpose interaction tool because of their ability in communication and manipulation.

7.3.1 The meaning of hand gestures

Recognizing gestures is a complex task which involves many aspects such as motion modeling, motion analysis, pattern recognition and machine learning, and, even psycho-linguistic studies. In this section, we briefly present the meaning of hand gestures, based on the psychologic and psycho-linguistic literature. Based on these studies, there have been several relevant debates and psycho-linguistics suggest various ways to classify a gesture.

First studies were conducted in 1960 by William Stokoe [379], who studied sign language and formed the 'Stokoe notation'. Based on his studies, the gestures can be described by four aspects, namely: hand shape, movement and orientation, location and relative location.

Kendon [380] in 1986, described a philology of gesture and classified gestured int the following categories: (1) gesticulation, (2) language-like gestures, (3) pantomimes, (4) emblems, and (5) sign language. Gesticulation is the term that refers to idiosyncratic and spontaneous movements of hands and arms which accompany speech. Language-like gestures are similar to gesticulation, but grammatically integrated in the utterance. They occur within a sentence as a substitute, usually, of an adjective. Pantomime are gestures without speech used in theater to communicate a story. Emblems are "italianate" gestures (e.g. insults and praises), the meaning of which depends on convention, culture and lexicon. Finally, sign language is a set of gestures and postures for a full-fledged linguistic communication system. Sign languages are characterized by a specific set of vocabulary and grammar.

McNeil [381] classified Kendon's [382] categories further, as follows:

Ioanna-Ourania Stathopoulou and George A. Tsihrintzis

179

gesticulation $\Rightarrow$ language-like gestures $\Rightarrow$ pantomimes $\Rightarrow$ emblems $\Rightarrow$ sign languages.

In this categorization, moving from left to right:

1. speech becomes less obligatory

2. gestures become more language-like (e.g., more systematized)

3. gestures become more conventionalized

Nespoulos and Lecours [383] classify the gestures in terms of universality (arbitrariness) as well as in terms of their use (functionality). In terms of their universality (arbitrariness), we have the following categories: (1) arbitrary gestures, (2) mimetic gestures and (3) deictic gestures. Arbitrary gestures are uncommon gestures, which need to be learnt. Mimetic gestures are more common gestures, which are present within a culture. Deictic gestures are used for pointing to an object or an action. In terms of their use (functionality), we have the following categories:(1) quasi-linguistic expression, (2) co-verbal expression, (3) social interaction, (4) meta-communication, and (5) extra-communication. Gestures for quasi-linguistic expression occur in the absence of any verbal behaviour. In the contrary, gestures for co-verbal expression occur in the presence of verbal behaviour. The gestures for social interaction constitute pragmatic elements of interaction strategies. Gestures in meta-communication involve the expression of the speaker's own verbal behaviour and gestures in extra-communication involve gestures without semiotic value.

Researchers in human-computer interaction classify the gestures on different categories. Quek [384, 385] distinguishes gestures into communicative and manipulative, that is gestures intended for communication and gestures intended for manipulating objects. This distinction is made because it is important when considering vision-based gesture interpretation. Communicative gestures are meant for visual interpretation. No visually obscured part of the hand will carry information necessary to understanding the gesture. Manipulative gestures, on the other hand, are not subject to such constraints. There is ultimately no guarantee that such gestures are visually interpretable. This is not to say that manipulative gestures are unimportant. If, however, one intends for users to manipulate objects in a virtual environment, it may be more appropriate to use implements like glove devices to transduce the hand motion. Another device in human-computer interaction, which can be considered as a manipulative gesture device, is the computer keyboard, as it detects downward finger movements.

Pavlovic et al. [2] adopt and further generalize the taxonomy proposed by Quek [384, 385]. They classify all hand/arm movements into two major classes: gestures and unintentional movements. Unintentional movements are those hand/arm movements that do not convey any gestural information. Gestures themselves can have two modalities: manipulative and communicative. Manipulative gestures are used to convey an act to objects, e.g. object rotation or movement. Communicative gestures, on the other hand, have an inherent communicational purpose. In natural environments, they are usually accompanied by speech. Communicative gestures can be either acts or symbols. Symbols are those gestures that have a linguistic role. They symbolize some referential action when they are used to refer to a word during speech (e.g. circular motion of index finger may be a referent for a wheel) or are used as modalizers of speech (e.g. "Look at that wing!" and a modalizing gesture specifying that the wing is vibrating). Acts, on the other hand, are gestures that are directly related to the interpretation of the movement itself. These movements are classified as mimetic (which imitate some actions) or deictic (pointing acts). Based on Pavlovic et al. [2], the most common gestures which are present and commonly used during human-computer interaction, are symbols and they are usually represented by different static hand postures. The taxonomy of Pavlovic et al. [2] is shown in Figure 7.3.

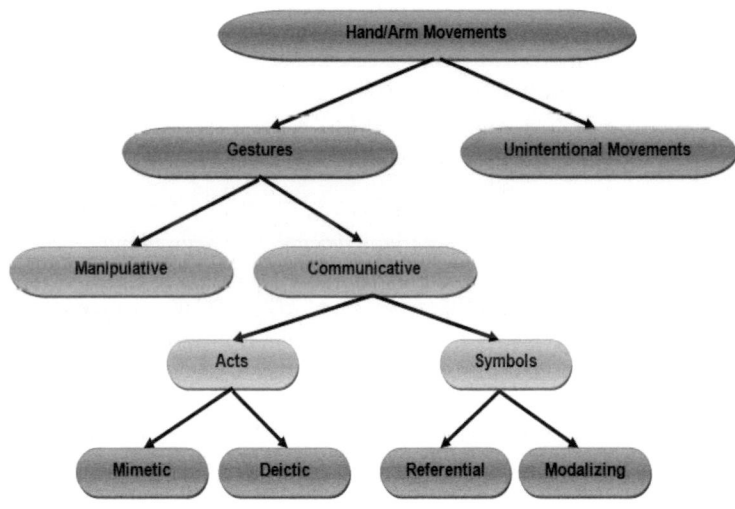

Figure 7.3: Gesture taxonomy for Human-Computer Interaction [2]

Ioanna-Ourania Stathopoulou and George A. Tsihrintzis

7.3.2 Techniques for hand gesture recognition

As static gestures can convey important information, the first works in the literature involve techniques for static hand gesture (posture) recognition. The other major category of approaches towards human gesture recognition, involve dynamic hand gesture recognition. The human hand has a complex anatomical structure consisting of many connected parts and joints. The complex relations between all these parts provide a total of roughly 27 degrees of freedom (DoF) [386].

The hand gesture recognition task requires the understanding of the human hand's anatomical structure in order to determine which kind of postures and gestures are comfortable to make. Although hand postures and gestures are often considered identical, in reality gestures can be considered as a sequence of postures. A hand posture is a static hand pose without involvement of movements (e.g. the 'stop' signal: where someone shows the inner part of his/her hand and holding it in that position). On the other hand, a hand gesture is defined as a dynamic movement referring to a sequence of hand postures connected by continuous motions over a short time span (e.g. the 'no, don't do that' signal: where someone show his/hers index finger and moves it right and left).

After this clarification, the gesture recognition task can be divided in two tasks: (1) static hand gesture (posture) recognition, which can be considered a low-level task and (2) dynamic hand gesture recognition, which can be considered a higher-level task and, actually, requires prior completion of the low-level task.

Static hand gesture (posture) recognition

Researches for static hand gesture (posture) recognition, use a static image as input data and attempt to recognize the gesture depicted on the image plane.

Cui et al. [387] use a self-organizing framework called the SHOSLIF-M for learning and recognizing spatio-temporal events (or patterns) from intensity image sequences. The proposed framework consists of a multiclass, multivariate discriminant analysis to automatically select the most discriminating features (MDF), a space partition tree to achieve a logarithmic retrieval time complexity for a database of n items, and a general interpolation scheme to perform view inference and generalization in the MDF space based on a small number of training samples. The system is tested to recognize 28 different hand signs. The experimental results show that the trained system can achieve a 96% recognition rate for test sequences that have not been used in the training phase

Triesch and Malsburg [388] developed a system for the classification of hand postures against complex backgrounds in grey-level images. The system employed elastic graph matching, which the researchers had already used for the recognition of faces. Hand postures are represented by labeled graphs with an underlying two-dimensional

Ioanna-Ourania Stathopoulou and George A. Tsihrintzis

topology. Attached to the nodes are jets, which are a sort of local image description based on Gabor filters. The system reaches an 86.2% rate of correct classification on their gallery of 239 images of ten postures against complex backgrounds. The system was robust with respect to certain variations in size of hand and shape of posture.

Quek and Zhao [389] presented an inductive learning system that was able to derive a rule base of disjunctive normal form formulate in which each DNF describes a hand pose, and each conjunct within the DNF constitutes a single rule. They used twenty-eight features such as the area of the bounding box, the compactness of the hand and the normalized moments, in order to form the input feature vector for their learning algorithm. From these features, only the reduced feature set needed to be computed at recognition time. They trained their system with 931 instances of 20 different hand poses. The system produced compact rule sets and had a recognition rate of 94%.

Nolker and Ritter [390] detected the 2-D location of fingertips by the Local Linear Mapping (LLN) neural network. These 2-D locations were mapped to 3-D position by the Parametric Self-Organizing Map (PSOM) neural network, as PSOM had the ability to perform an associative completion of fragmentary input. By this means, their approach could recognize hand pose from different views.

Starner and Pentland [391] used Hidden Markov models (HMMs) for the recognition of hand gestures in which are found in sign language. Their HMM-based system recognizes sentence level American Sign Language (ASL) and attains a word accuracy of 99.2% without explicitly modeling the fingers.

In recent years, Athitsos and Sclaroff [392] focus their research on 3-D hand configuration. Their method can generate a ranked list of plausible 3-D hand configurations that best match an input image. Hand pose estimation is formulated as an image database indexing problem, where the closest matches for an input hand image are retrieved from a large database of synthetic hand images. The system can function in the presence of clutter, thanks to two novel clutter-tolerant indexing methods. First, a computationally efficient approximation of the image-to-model chamfer distance is obtained by embedding binary edge images into a high-dimensional Euclidean space. Second, a general-purpose, probabilistic line matching method identifies those line segment correspondences between model and input images that are the least likely to have occurred by chance.

Dynamic hand gesture recognition

Researches for dynamic hand gesture recognition, use video as input data in which movement of the hand is recorded. The video is decomposed into a set of frames, which are preprocessed in order to remove unnecessary data and highlight necessary components. Usually, each frame depicts a hand posture which can be translated into

Ioanna-Ourania Stathopoulou and George A. Tsihrintzis

a letter or word. Dynamic hand gestures are, as mentioned earlier, a sequence of hand postures connected by continuous motions. Thus, a recognizer can be trained against a possible grammar. Just like phrases which are built up from words, hand gestures are built up from postures. For this reason, many researchers in dynamic hand gesture recognition use techniques similar to the techniques used in speech recognition.

Model-based approaches Model-based approaches use 3-D hand models with considerable degrees of freedom (DoF) for gesture recognition. They build a 3-D model of the hand and attempt to fit the projected 3-D model to the observed image features in order to understand the gesture. Thus, in these approaches the aim is to find the right image features in a high-dimensional space. The majority of the model-based approaches follow these steps:

1. **Model construction:** The first step of model-base approaches is to construct a model of the hand, which will be used in order to recognize the posture and understand the gesture. The majority of the approaches use the kinematic hand model, but some approaches also try to model the natural hand motion or the shape of the hand.

   - *Kinematic hand model:* The kinematic hand model [2, 3] is based on the human hand skeleton and tries to mimic the human hand skeleton kinematics. The human hand skeleton consists of 27 bones divided in three groups: carpals (wrist bones - 8), metacarpals (palm bones - 5), and, phalanges (finger bones - 14). The joints connecting the bones exhibit different degrees of freedom (DoF). The skeleton anatomy and the kinetic model are shown in Figure 7.4 [3].

     Joints between the bones are named according to their location on the hand: metacarpophalangeal (MCP) (i.e., joining fingers to the palm), interphalangeal (IP) (i.e., joining finger segments) and carpometacarpal (CMC) (i.e., connecting the metacarpal bones to the wrist). Most of the joints connecting carpals have very limited freedom of movement as well as carpal-metacarpal joints. IP joints have one Degree of Freedom (1 DoF), whereas MCP joints are considered to have two Degrees of Freedom (2 DoFs): abduction/adduction and flexion/extension. The CMC joints of the index and middle fingers are static while the CMC joints of the pinky and the ring finger have limited motion capability reflecting palm folding or curving, which is often discarded yielding a rigid palm. The CMC of the thumb, which is also called trapeziometacarpal (TM), is the most difficult to model.

   - *Model of the natural hand motion:* Some approaches use the model of the natural hand motion. This model aims at capturing the constrains in the

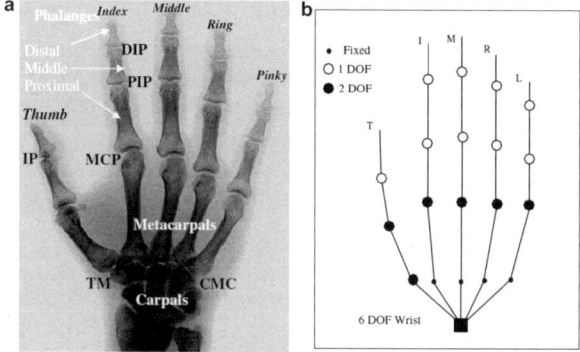

Figure 7.4: Skeletal hand model: (a) Hand anatomy, (b) the kinematic model. [3]

active motion of the hand, that is the motion which is provoked without external forces, that are not applicable in the kinematic model. Towards this task, some attempts use the kinematic model and complement it with static constraints that reflect the range of each parameter and dynamic constraints that reflect the joint angle dependencies [393, 394]. Even though constraints would help reduce the size of the search space, too many or too complicated constraints would also add to computational complexity. The accurate selection of the constraints is a crucial part in the development of the model. As stated previously, the most common constraints derive from constraints of joints within the same finger, constraints of joints between fingers, and the maximum range of finger motions. All these are presented as either equalities or inequalities. However, due to the large variation in finger motion, there are yet more constraints that cannot be explicitly represented by equations and have nothing to do with structural limitations. In order to compute these constraints, the majority of the researchers use learning methods on real motion data which are collected by real users who use gloves [395, 396, 392, 397, 398].

- *Model of the shape of the hand:* Finally, in case where the hand model needs to be projected many times on the input image(s) to obtain features that can be matched against the observed features, for computational efficiency reasons, some approaches use more rough shape models. These models are usually composed of simple geometric shapes such as cylinders, spheres, ellipsoids attached to each link or joint of the hand skeleton [399, 393, 400].

2. **Hand localization/segmentation:** A major step is to detect the hands within

the image plane and extract them from the remaining portion of the image. This task is quite complex and sometimes some restrictions on the background (e.g. uniform dark background) or on the user (e.g. the user should wear long dark sleeves) may be applied. The hand localization / segmentation is usually done by using one of the following techniques:

- *Skin extraction, background substraction:* The hands are extracted from the background by thresholding the image frame based on the HSV skin color space [401, 402, 403]

- *Use of markers or gloves:* Some earlier applications resort to the use of uniquely colored gloves or markers on hands [404, 405]. Although, from the computational point of view, these methods are easier to implement they tend to reduce the naturalness of the interaction, thus they are usually discouraged.

- *Motion analysis:* Newer techniques localize the hands by applying motion analysis techniques (similar to the techniques used for human tracking) and extracting the hands from the static objects of the background.

- *Infrared cameras:* Newer techniques also use infrared cameras that are tuned to human temperature [406, 407]. In these cases, since infrared cameras are adjusted to measure a range of temperatures approximating human body temperature, e.g., typically between $30^{o}C$ and $34^{o}C$, image pixel values corresponding to human skin are higher than other image pixels. Hence, image regions corresponding to human skin can be easily identified by binarizing the input image with a threshold value.

- *Deformable templates:* Some approaches also use deformable templates which describe the hand or the fingers to extract the hand from the image plane [408, 409]

- *Object detection with classification-based techniques:* Finally, some approaches use classifiers which are trained to detect the hand. The use of conventional classifiers would result in large processing times for the hand subregions. Employing boosted cascades of classifiers improve processing speed drastically [157]. Kolch et al. [410] and Ong et al.[411] have introduced some interesting approaches for fast hand detection.

3. **Feature Extraction and Matching:**

After the position and the extent of the hand has been computed, features must be extracted in order to match the model with the localized hand and to compute the model parameters which will result in the recognition of the gesture. Depending on the model used, it is necessary to compute different parameters, but, generally, the extracted features are common regardless of the model.

The features can be classified to the following categories:

- **Fingertips:** Some approaches use the fingertips [405, 412, 413] as the important features that help to fit the model on the hand. However, in these cases, the robustness and accuracy of the results largely depend on the performance of fingertip detection. Usually, fingertip location information is used for the computational of parameters in 3-D model-based approaches, but, also, in 2-D appearance-based models. In order to detect the fingertips, several approaches have appeared in the literature. The most simple and commonly used in earlier approaches is the use of marked gloves or color markers to detect the location of the fingertips ([404, 405]). Then, the location is extracted using histogram-based techniques. Other techniques use fingertip templates [414, 415] or finger templates [416], which are extracted from real images. Other researchers use infrared cameras [406, 407] and, based on their input, detect the various regions of the hand. After localizing the fingers, a circular template is used to extract the corresponding fingertips, resulting in an approach which is more invariant with regards to rotation and more robust to illumination differences. Some fingertip extraction algorithms are based on the characteristic properties of fingertips in the image, e.g. the curvature local maxima on the boundary of the silhouette [417, 418, 403]. These methods usually operate poorly when they have to deal with noisy input data.

- **Contours / Edges:** Besides the extraction of fingertips, other approaches, towards enhancing the robustness, use edge detection and lines to locate the hand [342, 419]. In order to produce the contours and/or the lines, these techniques rely on simple edge detection techniques in color or grayscale images. Alternatively, other techniques compute contours from a given model (silhouette) of the hand. The first group of approaches usually do not work well in cluttered backgrounds. Some approaches combine both methods (edge detection and model matching) [420, 398, 421, 392], in an attempt to increase the robustness.

- **Shapes / Silhouettes:** Some approaches work with the silhouette of the hand (e.g. splines [422]) and 3-D hand model where each finger phalanx is represented using a truncated cylinder [423]. The silhouette image itself contains less information than the full image, which makes this method weak under occlusions. This is a drawback of the method, as occlusions are very common in the real world. However, silhouette extraction may

Ioanna-Ourania Stathopoulou and George A. Tsihrintzis

also be used in further computations of location and extraction of higher-level features (e.g. fingertips or contours).

4. **Hand Tracking:** The final step of model-based gesture recognition consists of the continuous matching of the computed features to the input hand model during each given frame. Erol et al. [3], discriminate the approaches into the following two categories:

- **Single hypothesis tracking:** Single hypothesis tracking involves searching for the best fit at which the matching error is minimized. In order to achieve this best fit, some approaches use explicit matching error minimization techniques (e.g. Gauss-Newton method [424], Stochastic Gradient Descent [425], Nelder Mead Simplex [426], Genetic Algorithms and Simulated Annealing [427], and, Kalman filters [399]). On the other hand, other approaches use physical forces to fit the model [428, 429]. Specifically, they use the matching error to create forces to be applied on the surface of the articulated model. Then, the model parameters are updated by solving the dynamic equations of the kinematic model.

- **Multiple hypothesis tracking:** Multiple hypothesis tracking approaches usually use particle filters, tree-based filters, Bayesian networks, and Kalman filters.

Appearance-based approaches   Besides model-based approaches, some studies use appearance-based approaches to recognize and track hand motion [392, 430, 431, 419, 432]. These studies, first extract features of the hand and attempt to estimate the hand states directly from these image features. The features used in these approaches are similar to the ones used in the model-based approaches, examined earlier. A nonlinear mapping is learnt from a large amount of training images. These approaches can quickly estimate the hand configuration once the mapping is learnt. However, it is difficult to determine the structure of the mapping function and the set of optimal training data.

7.4 Emotion Recognition Systems from Body Movements and Gestures

Although there are a lot of researches on human tracking, human motion analysis and gesture analysis, there are a relatively small number of researches regarding emotion recognition from body movements and gestures. The majority of these approaches

Ioanna-Ourania Stathopoulou and George A. Tsihrintzis

have appeared over the last decade and aim at facilitating human-computer inter-action by allowing computers the ability to recognize their user's emotional state. Based on the input data, we can categorize relevant approaches as follows:

- **Emotion recognition systems from body movements and/or hand/arm gestures:** These systems try to recognize the emotional state of a person from the movements or the posture of the body as well as the movements of the hands or arms [433, 434, 435, 436, 437, 438, 439]. Specifically, Bianchi-Berthouze and Kleinsmith [433] addressed the issue of adding the capability to robots to rec-ognize the affective state of the human by interpreting their gestural cues. To achieve that, they used an associative neural network called *categorizing and learning module* (CALM) [440], which incorporates brain-like structural and functional constraints such as modularity and organization with excitatory and inhibitory connections. To evaluate their proposed framework, they collected emotional gestures with a VICON motion capture system. Twelve subjects of different gender, race and age were asked to perform as actors for the experi-ment. Dressed in a suit with 34 markers located on the joints and segments of his/her body, each subject performed an in-place freely decided emotional ges-ture. The total set consisted of 138 gestures depicting the following emotions: 'anger', 'happiness' and 'sadness'. The CALM network achieved a performance of 95,7% in classifying the emotions.

Bernhardt and Robinson [434] developed a computational model for describing and detecting affective content in everyday body movements. In their approach, they divided complex motions into a set of automatically derived motion primi-tives and, then, analyzed each primitive in terms of dynamic features which were shown to encode affective information. They also developed an algorithm to de-rive unbiased motion features adapted to personal movement idiosyncrasies, for persons already in the database. In order to classify the emotional states, they developed a SVM-based classifier and tested by applying Leave-One-Subject-Out cross-validation (LOSO-CV) tests. The system achieved 50% and 81% classification rates for biased and unbiased features, respectively.

Camurri et al. [435, 436] explored the classification of expressive gesture in human full-body movement and in particular in dance performances. Their system consisted of four layers. In the first layer, they analyzed the video and movement (techniques for background subtraction, motion detection, motion tracking etc.). In the second layer, they computed the low-level features by applying computer vision techniques on the incoming images and computing statistical measures. In the third layer, they computed mid-level features and maps, e.g. gesture segmentation and representation of gestures as trajectories in semantic spaces (e.g., Laban's Effort space, energy-articulation space). In the final (fourth) layer, they classified the movement in four emotional classes, namely: 'anger', 'fear', 'joy' and 'grief'. For the classification step, they first used statistical techniques by computing a one-way ANOVA for each motion cue [435]. Later, they developed decision tree models for better results [436]. They developed five decision tree models, which achieved different performance among the various emotional states. They compared the system performance towards the classification accuracy of human spectators. Human spectators managed to classify the emotion with 56% accuracy, while the system achieved a 40% accuracy.

More recently, Castellano et al. [437] presented an approach for the recognition of acted emotional states from the body movements and gesture expressivity. Their approach was based on the fact that distinct emotions are often associated with different qualities of body movement. In order to classify the emotion, they used non-propositional movement qualities (e.g. amplitude, speed and fluidity of movement) to infer emotions, rather than trying to recognize different gesture shapes expressing specific emotions [441]. Their data set included 240 gestures which were collected when they asked ten participants (six male and four female) to project eight emotional states ('anger', 'despair', 'interest', 'pleasure', 'sadness', 'irritation', 'joy' and 'pride') equally distributed in the valence arousal space. To extract the silhouette and the hands of the subjects, they used the EyesWeb platform [442]. They computed five different expressive motion cues: quantity of motion and contraction index of the body, velocity, acceleration and fluidity of the hand"s barycentre, using the EyesWeb Expressive Gesture Processing Library. They analyzed the emotional behaviour based on both direct classification of time series and a model that provides indicators describing the dynamics of expressive motion cues. For the first task, they built a nearest neighbour based on DTW distance (1NN-DTW) classifier. They evaluated their system over two perspectives: (1) train and evaluation of performance using only the personal set of gestures (i.e. training one classifier per subject), and (2) train and evaluation of performance using the universal set (i.e. an inter-subject enabled classifier using the universal set of gestures). Both classifiers were evaluated in the classification task of four (namely, 'anger', 'joy', 'pleasure' and 'sadness') and all the eight emotional states. Their system was not able to discriminate successfully between the eight emotions, but achieved an accuracy of 61% for the four emotions.

Burgoon et al. [438] considered contextual cues, as well as analyzing cues from multiple body regions to lay the foundation for automatic identification of emotion from video. Their approach did not aim at classifying the body movements in discrete emotion classes, rather than identifying the person's emotional state in terms of positive/negative valence (pleasant/unpleasant) and high/low arousal/intensity. They first tracked the head and hands once an individual had been identified. In order to achieve this, they used a blob analysis developed by the Computational Bio-medicine Imaging and Modeling Center at Rutgers University [443], which is based on color analysis, eigenspace-based shape segmentation and Kalman filters to track head and hand positions throughout the video segment. General metrics, such as position, size, and angles were computed for each blob and utilized when generating meaningful features. For blob analysis, Time Delay Neural Networks (TDNN) and Recurrent Neural Networks (RNN) were tested in the task of classifying individual gestures and RNN were found more adequate.

Kapur et al. [439] classified full-body skeletal movements data obtained with a technology based on the VICON motion capturing system to classify four emotional states, namely: 'sadness', 'joy', 'anger' and 'fear'. VICON uses a series of 6 cameras to capture lightweight markers placed on various points of the body in 3-D space and digitizes movement into x, y, and z displacement data. They videotaped the movements of five subjects depicting the four emotions that they were asked to portray. They developed and tested five different classifiers: (1) a logistic regression, (2) a Naive-Bayes with a single multidimensional Gaussian distribution modeling each class, (3) a Decision Tree classifier based on the C4.5 algorithm, (4) a multi-layer perceptron back-propagation artificial neural network, and (5) a support vector machine trained using Sequential Minimal Optimization (SMO). Experimental results with different classifiers showed that automatic classification of this data ranged from 84% to 92% depending on how it was calculated. They also compared the system performance towards the classification accuracy of human spectators, who managed to classify the emotion with 93% accuracy.

All these approaches are summarized in Table 7.3, based on the requirement set in Table 7.2.

- **Multimodal emotion recognition systems:** These systems incorporate two or more input data in order to recognize the emotional state. The modalities usually include body movements and/or hand gestures with facial expressions [444, 445]

  Balomenos et al. [444] developed an intelligent rule-based system for emotion classification into the six basic emotions, by using facial and hand movement information. Facial analysis included a number of processing steps which attempted to detect or track the face, to locate characteristic facial regions such as eyes, mouth and nose on it, to extract and follow the movement of facial features, such as characteristic points in these regions, or model facial gestures

Ioanna-Ourania Stathopoulou and George A. Tsihrintzis

Table 7.2: Requirements/Test for the emotion recognition systems from body movements and gestures

1	Type of movements (Can be 'stylized', when the subjects the emotion instead of feeling it, or, alternatively, 'non-stylized' or other)
2	Type of classifier
3	Use of markers
4	Number of emotion classes
5	Names of emotion classes
6	Classification rate

Table 7.3: Review of the emotion recognition systems from body movements and gestures, based on the requirements in Table 7.2

Reference	1	2	3	4	5	6
Bianchi-Berthouze [433]	non-stylized	CALM ANN	Yes	3	'angry', 'happy', 'sad'	95,7%
Bernhardt [434]	non-stylized	SVM	No	4	'neutral', 'angry', 'happy', 'sad'	50%, 81%
Camurri [435, 436]	dancing moves	ANOVA, Decision trees	No	4	'angry', 'fear', 'joy', 'grief'	40%
Castellano [437]	stylized	INN-DTW	No	4	'anger', 'joy', 'pleasure', 'sadness'	61%
Burgoon [438]	non-stylized	TDNN, RNN	No	-	No emotional classes	n.a.
Kapur [439]	stylized	Perceptron, SVM	Yes	4	'anger', 'sad', 'joy', 'fear'	84% - 92%

using anatomic information about the faces. Hand gesture analysis included tracking the person's hands by creating moving skin color areas which were tracked between subsequent frames. They tracked the centroid of those skin masks in order to estimate the user's movements. To facilitate the tracking process, they used a-priori knowledge related to the expected characteristics of the input image: the head is in the middle area of upper half of the frame and the hand segments near the respective lower corners. They trained a Hidden Markov Model (HMM) Classifier to classify among the following gesture classes: hand clapping - high frequency, hand clapping - low frequency, lift of the hand - low speed, lift of the hand - high speed, hands over the head - gesture, hands over the head - posture and italianate gestures. For the multimodal emotion classification task, the correlated these classes to the six emotional states. Specifically:

- *'Joy'*: hand clapping - high frequency
- *'Sadness'*: hands over the head - posture
- *'Anger'*: lift of the hand - high speed, italianate gestures
- *'Fear'*: hands over the head - gesture, italianate gestures
- *'Disgust'*: lift of the hand - low speed, hand clapping-low frequency
- *'Surprise'*: hands over the head - gesture

The two subsystems were combined as a weighted sum, where the weights were 0.75 and 0.25 for the facial expression recognition modality and the affective gesture recognition modality, respectively.

Gunes et al. [445] also fused facial expression and body gesture information for bimodal emotion recognition. Their system was tested for the six following emotional classes: 'anxiety', 'anger', 'disgust', 'fear', 'happiness' and 'uncertainty'. They also built their own bimodal database (FABO) that consisted of recordings of facial expressions alone and combined face and body expressions [446]. To form the training and testing set, they processed 54 sequences of frames in total, 27 for face and 27 for body from four subjects and selected the more expressive. Half of the frame were used for training and the other half for testing purposes. Their facial analysis subsystem was based on the FACS coding system, specifically, they identified the following for each emotion class:

- *'Anxiety'*: Lip bite; stretching of the mouth; eyes turn up/down/left/right; lip wipe
- *'Happiness'*: Corners of lips are drawn back and up; mouth may or may not be parted with teeth exposed or not; cheeks are raised; lower eyelid shows wrinkles below it, and may be raised but not tense; wrinkles around the outer corners of the eyes

- *'Anger':* Brows lowered and drawn together; lines appear between brows; lower lid is tensed and may or may not be raised; upper lid is tense and may or may not be lowered due to brows action; lips are either pressed firmly together with corners straight or down or open

- *'Fear':* Brows raised and drawn together; forehead wrinkles drawn to the center; upper eyelid is raised and lower eyelid is drawn up; mouth is open; lips are slightly tense or stretched and drawn back

- *'Disgust':* Upper lip is raised; lower lip is raised and pushed up to upper lip or it is lowered; nose is wrinkled; cheeks are raised; brows are lowered; tongue out

- *'Uncertainty':* Lid drop; inner brow raised; outer brow raised; chin raised; jaw sideways; corners of the lips are drawn downwards

They trained a BayesNet classifier which achieved an average performance of 76.40%.

For their body analysis subsystem, they identified the following for each emotion class:

- *'Anxiety':* Hands close to the table surface; fingers moving; fingers tapping on the table

- *'Happiness':* Body extended; hands kept high; hands made into fists and kept high

- *'Anger':* Body extended; hands on the waist; hands made into fists and kept low, close to the table surface

- *'Fear':* Body contracted; body backing; hands high up, trying to cover bodily parts

- *'Disgust':* Body backing; left/right hand touching the neck or face

- *'Uncertainty':* Shoulder shrug; palms up

They also used a BayesNet classifier which achieved an average performance of 89.90%. For the fusion of the two modalities, the applied two different methods:

- *Feature-level fusion:* They fused all the features from the two modalities into a bigger vector matrix. Best-first search method was used with ten-fold cross validation to obtain a decisive reduction in the features' number and fed to a BayesNet classifier. The average classification rate was 94.03% for subjects already in the database.

– *Decision-level fusion:* In this case, the final classification was based on the fusion of the outputs the different modalities. They tested various approaches, including the sum rule, product rule and the use of using weights. Sum rule provided the best fusion result with average recognition accuracy of 91.1%.

Finally, el Kaliouby and Robinson [447] proposed a vision-based computational model to infer acted mental states from head movements and facial expressions. Their system was evaluated on videos that were posed by lay people in a relatively uncontrolled recording environment for six mental states: agreeing, concentrating, disagreeing, interested, thinking and unsure. They used a use Dynamic Bayesian Networks (DBNs) to model the unfolding of mental states over time and each display was represented as a Hidden Markov Model (HMM) of a sequence of head/facial actions, recognized non-intrusively, in real time. Head actions were described by the magnitude and direction of 3 Euler angles, while facial actions were extracted using motion, shape and colour analysis of the lips, mouth and eyebrows. The writers had trained and tested their system on videos from the Mind-Reading DVD (MR) [448], a guide to emotions developed for Autism Spectrum Disorders and achieve an average accuracy of 77.4%. They further tested the generalization of their system by collecting videos at the IEEE International Conference on Computer Vision and Pattern Recognition (CVPR 2004). The classification rate was highest for disagreeing (85.7%) and lowest for thinking (26.7%).

Generally, in the area of affective computing, there is a lack of researches on emotion recognition from body movements and hand/arm gestures, compared to the number of researches on human motion analysis and/or hand gesture analysis. Although there have been some psychological studies regarding emotion and nonverbal communication in expressive movements [77, 78, 79], these studies were based on acted, stylized basic emotions. But, in affective computing the spontaneity of the emotions is very important and must be taken into account. Moreover, there is a lack of a widely accepted model which can represent human movements with regards to the experienced emotion, for example, like the Facial Action Coding System (FACS) [449] which is considered the basis in the development of facial expression analysis systems. Maybe this is why that the majority of the approaches in emotion recognition from body movements and hand/arm gestures try to develop their own model by observing the persons' movements when they experiencing an emotion. Despite all the difficulties, the results are very promising, especially for the development of multimodal affective systems, and further research is necessary.

Ioanna-Ourania Stathopoulou and George A. Tsihrintzis

8

Conclusions and Future Work

All truths are easy to understand once they are discovered; the point is to discover them.

—Galileo Galilei (1564–1642)

8.1 Summary and Conclusions

D EVELOPING a fully automated facial expression system is a quite significant and challenging task. Automated face detection and expression classification in images is a prerequisite in the development of novel human-computer interaction modalities. However, the development of integrated, fully operational such detection/classification systems is known to be non-trivial, a fact that was corroborated by our own statistical results regarding expression classification by humans. Towards building such systems, in this theses, we made the following studies:

1. First of all, we studied the emotion perception from the scientific point of view. Biologists and doctors, have identified some parts of the face that are considered important for human emotion expression and understanding. These include: (1) **the frontal cortex**, (2) **the superior temporal sulcus**, and (3) **the amygdala**. This fact is strengthened the opinion that the emotions are affected by the 'evolution' and, thus, are similar in all cultures. On the other hand, there is a strong disagreement among psychologists about emotion perception. Some studies, mainly conducted by Paul Ekman [25, 20, 26, 27, 28, 29, 30, 31, 32, 33, 34, 35, 36, 37, 38, 39, 40], identified some emotions called **'basic emotions'**, to be similar among different cultures. These emotions ar, namely: **'anger'**, **'disgust'**, **'fear'**, **'happiness'**, **'sadness'** and **'surprise'**. Besides the 'basic emotions', studies have shown that there are also cultural variations in the way in which humans express emotion. These studies have shown that the emotions can be varied: (1) in terms of the expression of emotion, but also (2) in terms of the intensity of the expressed emotion. This fact has further been demonstrated

by our own empirical studies on humans. Also, Russell [450, 82, 85, 86, 87, 84, 88] argues that emotion in general (and facial expression of emotion in particular) can be best characterized in terms of a multidimensional affect space, rather than in terms of discrete emotion categories. More specifically, Russell claims that two dimensions, namely 'pleasure' and 'arousal', are sufficient to characterize facial affect space.

2. The next study involved understanding emotion perception from the human point of view. Towards this task, we conducted two empirical studies. The first study, as described in Section 5.1, was simpler than the second and aimed at setting an error goal for our system. We used images from facial expression databases gathered from World Wide Web [135, 139] and asked people to map the emotion based on the subject's expression. Our second empirical study, which is described in in Section 5.1, was more complicated and aimed not only at an error goal, but also, at understanding the mechanisms of facial expression recognition by humans. In this study, we used our own facial expression database [9]. The results showed us that the cultural exposure increases the chances of correct recognition of facial expressions indicating cultural dependence in the ways people express themselves. This is demonstrated by the significant difference between the error rates of the first questionnaire, where we used images on non-Greek subjects, and the second questionnaire, where we used images from our own facial expression database. Specifically, for the majority of the expressions the success rates were extremely comparable for the second questionnaire, as they achieved a difference from 13% to 46%, compared to the first questionnaire. Exceptions were observed for the 'neutral' and the 'disgust' emotion. Moreover, we were able to identify the emotions that are present during a typical human-computer interaction, so facial expressions corresponding to the **'neutral', 'happiness', 'sadness', 'surprise', 'anger', 'disgust' and 'boredom-sleepiness'** psychological states arise very commonly during human-computer interaction.

3. We also studied previous attempts towards the development of: (1) a facial expression database, (2) a face detection system and (3) a facial expression recognition system. We set the requirements for an ideal result for each of the aforementioned three occasions, respectively. Our study concluded to the fact that there are some interesting attempts but there is none that can cover all the requirements. Moreover, the majority of the methods usually address the problem of facial expression classification to the 'basic emotion' classes, which they do not include the 'boredom-sleepiness' emotion. Finally, as there is a culturally specificity on emotion perception, the development of a facial expression recognition system for Greek people is extremely important.

Ioanna-Ourania Stathopoulou and George A. Tsihrintzis

4. Our study also showed that led us to the assumption that we must create our own facial expression database. This fact, led us to the creation of two different databases, namely:

(1) The database of low quality images: this database consists of many subjects, depicting many expressions, but the image quality is quite low as we used web cameras to acquire the data and,

(2) The database of high quality images: this database consists again of many subjects, depicting the expressions recognized by our system, and the image quality is quite high as we we used digital cameras to acquire the data

5. Finally, we created our own face detection and facial expression recognition system. Face detection is based on a model of the human face proposed by P. Sinha. We preprocess the image in order to depict this model and use an artificial neural network, which classifies the image to 'face' and 'non-face'. Towards this task, we built two different artificial neural networks and decided upon using the second, which demonstrated better results. To measure the performance of the second network in detecting faces in images, we tested the network in four different set of images: (1) various images of different sizes and resolutions gathered from the World Wide Web and other sources(e.g scanning old photo images), (2) images from our own facial expression database where people may form some expression, (3) face images acquired in the first efforts to construct a facial expression database (low quality images) and, (4) non-human face images (e.g., images of pets and animals, complex backgrounds and parts of the face and human). The system managed to detect face with 90,83%, 94,00% and 72,89% success rate, for the three first sets, respectively, whereas for the 'non-face' images set the success rate was 100%.

6. Facial expression recognition can be divided to two sets of attempts. In our first attempts for a facial expression recognition system, we tried to use some of the databases already available over the World Wide Web, as mentioned in Section 3.1, whereas the emotion classes, that our system would be able to recognize, were not wet been determined. We used a fairly simple feature extraction algorithm which computes specific size ration of some facial portions, such as the eyes, the mouth and the size of the face and, then, feed the computed feature vector to an artificial neural network which classifies the expression. Although the developed system showed some good results and was able to generalize in low quality face images and faces in side view, we soon developed a more sophisticated feature extraction algorithm that we finally adopt. In the newer attempts towards facial expression recognition, we use more facial features are extracted from the image, such as measurements of the texture, head orientation, etc., we

Ioanna-Ourania Stathopoulou and George A. Tsihrintzis

use our own facial expression database for training and/or testing, as it is more complete in terms of the classes we want to classify and, a better, more sophisticated, algorithm to extract the facial features is used, which is based on our eye detection/extraction algorithm. After successful eye detection/extraction, the rest of the features are computed based on their relative location with the eyes. The computed feature vector is, again, fed to an artificial neural network which classifies the emotion. The neural network resulted to an average success rate of 77,14% in classifying the expressions. In order to achieve better results, we developed more sophisticated classifiers, using Netlab Toolbox: (1) **R**adial **B**asis **F**unctions neural networks, (2) **K**-th **N**earest **N**eighbour classifiers (3) **S**upport **V**ector **M**achines and (4) **M**ultilayer **P**erceptron neural networks. We trained and tested the classifiers using 10-fold cross validation techniques. Finally, we concluded to the SVM Classifier as the more adequate for this problem, which achieved and accuracy of 96.97%.

8.2 Current and Future Work

8.2.1 Towards a multimodal emotion recognition system

Recently, the recognition of emotions of users while they interact with software applications has been acknowledged as an important research topic. How people feel may play an important role on their cognitive processes as well [89]. Thus the whole issue of human-computer interaction has to take into account users' feelings. Picard [90] points out that one of the major challenges in affective computers is to try to improve the accuracy of recognizing people's emotions. Improving the accuracy on emotion recognition may imply the combination of many modalities in user interfaces. Indeed, human emotions are usually expressed in many ways. For example, as we articulate speech we usually move the head and exhibit various facial emotions [451]. Ideally evidence from many modes of interaction should be combined by a computer system so that it can generate as valid hypotheses as possible about users' emotions. This view has been supported by many researchers in the field of human-computer interaction [452, 97, 90]. However, progress in emotion recognition based on multiple modalities has been quite slow. Although several approaches have been proposed to recognize human emotions based on facial expressions or speech, relatively limited work has been done to fuse these two and other modalities to improve the accuracy and robustness of the emotion recognition system [453].

In view of the above, it is our aim to improve the accuracy of visual-facial emotion recognition by combining other modalities, namely keyboard stroke pattern information and audio-lingual information. Currently, a system that combines two modalities, namely the keyboard and the voice, has been already constructed and is described briefly in [454]. As we described in Chapter 5, towards building a facial expression recognition system, we conducted a fairly intensive empirical study. Towards combining the three modalities, we had to determine the extent to which these three different modalities can provide emotion recognition from the perspective of a human observer. Moreover, we had to specify the strengths and weaknesses of each modality.

In this way, we could determine the weights of the criteria that correspond to the respective modalities from the perspective of a human observer. Hence, for the purposes of our research we conducted empirical studies concerning emotion recognition based on two modalities: the audio-lingual, keyboard stroke patterns and the visual-facial. The above empirical studies constitute an important milestone for our research and yield important results. Not only do they provide the basis towards the combination of modalities into the affective user modeling component of our tri-modal system, but they also give evidence for other researchers to use since, currently, there are not many results from such empirical studies in the literature. Indeed, after an extensive search of the literature, we found that there is a shortage of empirical evidence concerning the strengths and weaknesses of these modalities. The most relevant research work is that of De Silva et al. [96] who performed an empirical study and reported results on human subjects' ability to recognize emotions. However, De Silva et al. focus on the audio signals of voice concentrating on the pitch and volume of voice rather than lingual keywords that convey affective information. On the other hand, in our research we have included the lingual aspect of users' spoken words on top of the pitch and volume of voice and have compared the audio-lingual results with the results from the other two modes so that we can see which modality conveys more information for human observers. Our work has been conducted for six emotions, namely 'happiness', 'sadness', 'surprise', 'anger' and 'disgust' as well as the emotionless state which we refer to as 'neutral'. The multimodal system is shown in Figure 8.1.

Currently, we have studied the possibility of combining the three modalities, based on the following empirical studies:

- Audio-lingual information and Visual-facial information [455, 456]

- Keyboard stroke pattern information and Visual-facial information [457, 458]

- Audio-lingual information, Keyboard stroke pattern information and Visual-facial information [459, 460]

Some of the results from combining the three modalities, based on their empirical studies, are shown in Figure 8.2 [460].

Finally, we are currently developing the combination of these modalities in terms of the unimodal systems results. But, all these are beyond the scopes of this thesei and will be presented in future works.

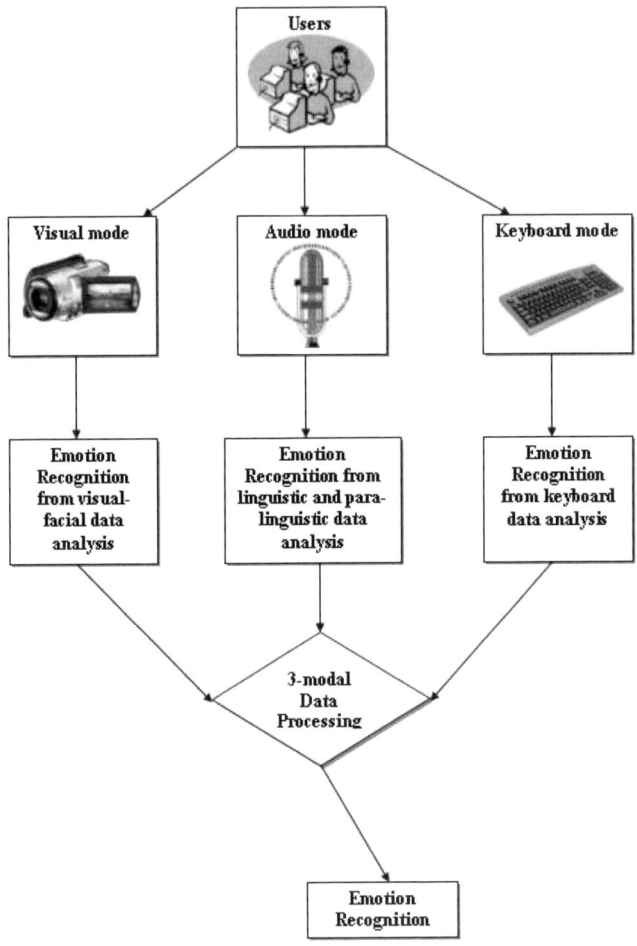

Figure 8.1: The architecture of our multimodal emotion recognition system

8.2.2 Towards extending the visual-facial expression recognition

In the future, we will extend this work in the following three directions: (1) We will improve our system by using wider training sets so as to cover a wider range of poses

Ioanna-Ourania Stathopoulou and George A. Tsihrintzis

Visual-facial modality		Keyboard-stroke pattern and audio-lingual information		
Facial Expression	(%)	(%) for keyboard-stroke patterns	(%) for audio-lingual	Mean value
Neutral				
	61,74%	65%	18%	41,50%
Surprise				
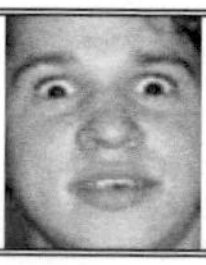	92,61%	5%	62%	33,50%
Anger				
	72,92%	74%	79%	76,50%
Happiness				
	82,57%	60%	46%	53%
Sadness				
	58,33%	57%	48%	52,50%
Disgust				
	16,19%	4%	57%	30,50%

Figure 8.2: Some results from combining the three modalities

and cases of low quality of images. (2) We will investigate the need for classifying into more than the currently available facial expressions, so as to obtain more accurate estimates of a computer user's psychological state. In turn, this may require the extraction and tracing of additional facial points and corresponding features. (3) We plan to apply our system for the expansion of human-computer interaction techniques,

Ioanna-Ourania Stathopoulou and George A. Tsihrintzis

such as those that arise in mobile telephony, in which the quality of the input images is too low for existing systems to operate reliably. Finally, we will also investigate the possibility of using other type of image or input data in order to classify the emotion, such as stereoscopic images, thermal images and video sequences.

Ioanna-Ourania Stathopoulou and George A. Tsihrintzis

Bibliography

[1] A. Yilmaz, O. Javed, and M. Shah, "Object tracking: A survey," *ACM Computing Surveys (CSUR)*, vol. 38, no. 4, 2006.

[2] V. I. Pavlovic, R. Sharma, and T. S. Huang, "Visual interpretation of hand gestures for human-computer interaction: A review," *IEEE Trans. on Pattern Analysis and Machine Intelligence*, vol. 19, no. 7, pp. 677–695, 1997.

[3] A. Erol, G. Bebis, M. Nicolescu, R. D. Boyle, and X. Twombly, "Vision-based hand pose estimation: A review," *Comput. Vis. Image Underst.*, vol. 108, no. 1-2, pp. 52–73, 2007.

[4] D. Neth, P. A. M. Martinez, P. B. Clymer, and P. J. Todd, "Facial configuration and the perception of facial expression dissertation," *Arbor Ciencia Pensamiento Y Cultura*, 2007.

[5] D. McNair, M. Lorr, and L. Droppleman, *Manual of the Profile of Mood States*. San Diego, CA: Educational and Industrial Testing Services, 1981.

[6] M. Pantic and L. Rothkrantz, "Automatic analysis of facial expressions: The state of the art," *IEEE Transactions on Pattern Analysis and Machine Intelligence*, vol. 22, no. 12, pp. 1424–1445, December 2000.

[7] D. M. Gavrila, "The visual analysis of human movement: a survey," *Computer Vision and Image Understanding*, vol. 73, no. 1, pp. 82–98, 1999.

[8] P. Barkhuysen, E. Krahmer, and M. Swerts, "Problem detection in human-machine interactions based on facial expressions of users," *Speech Communication*, vol. 45, pp. 343–359, 2005.

[9] I.-O. Stathopoulou and G. A. Tsihrintzis, "Facial Expression Classification: Specifying Requirements for an Automated System," in *Proceedings of the 10th International Conference on Knowledge-Based & Intelligent Information & Engineering Systems, LNAI: Vol. 4252*. Berlin, Heidelberg: Springer-Verlag, October 2006, pp. 1128–1135.

[10] I.-O. Stathopoulou and G. A. Tsihrintzis, "Towards automated inferencing of Emotional State from face Images," in *2nd International Conference on Software and Data Technologies*, Barcelona, Spain, July, 5-8 2007.

[11] I.-O. Stathopoulou and G. A. Tsihrintzis, *Automated Processing and Classification of Face Images for Human - Computer Interaction Applications*, ser. Studies in Computational Intelligence. Springer Berlin / Heidelberg, 2008, vol.

104, ch. Intelligent Interactive Systems in Knowledge-Based Environments, pp. 107–136.

[12] I.-O. Stathopoulou and G. A. Tsihrintzis, "An empirical study of facial expression classification by human observers," in preparation.

[13] A. P. Association, *Diagnostic and Statistical Manual of Mental Disorders*, 4th ed. American Psychiatric Association, 1984.

[14] E. Shouse, "Feeling, emotion, affect," *Media and Culture (M/C) Journal*, vol. 8, no. 6, December 2005.

[15] G. Deleuze, "Lecture transcripts on spinoza's concept of affect," January 1978.

[16] B. Massumi, *Parables for the Virtual: Movement, Affect, Sensation*, S. Fish and F. Jameson, Eds. Duke University Press (June 2002), 2002.

[17] G. Deleuze and F. Guattari, *A Thousand Plateaus: Capitalism and Schizophrenia*. University of Minnesota Press, December 1987.

[18] S. Iverson, I. Kupfermann, and E. R. Kandel, *Principles of Neuroscience*. New York: McGraw-Hill, 2000, ch. Emotional states and feelings, pp. 1209–1226.

[19] M. B. Arnold, *The Nature of Emotion*. Baltimore: Penguin, 1968.

[20] P. Ekman, *In J. Cole (Ed.),Nebraska Symposium on Motivation*. Lincoln: University of Nebraska Press, 1972, vol. 19, ch. Universals and cultural differences in facial expressions of emotion.

[21] W. B. Cannon, "The James-Lange theory of emotion: a critical examination and an alternative theory," *American Journal of Psychology*, vol. 39, pp. 106–124, 1927.

[22] J. Panksepp, *Affective Neuroscience: The Foundations of Human and Animal Emotions*. New York: Oxford University Press, 1998.

[23] A. R. Damasio, *Descartes' Error: Emotion, Reason, and the Human Brain*. Harper Perennial, 1995.

[24] C. Darwin, "The expression of the emotions in man and animal," *London: J. Murray. de Haan, M., Humphreys, K. & Johnson, M.H*, vol. 1872, pp. 200–212.

[25] P. Ekman, *Cross-cultural studies of facial expression*. London: Academic Press Inc., 1973, ch. Darwin and Facial Expression, pp. 169–222.

[26] P. Ekman, "Universal Facial Expressions in Emotion," *Studia Psychologica*, vol. 15, no. 2, pp. 140–147, 1973.

[27] P. Ekman and W. Friesen, *Unmasking the face: A Guide to Recognizing Emotions from Facial Expressions.* Englewood Cliffs, NJ: Prentice Hall, 1975.

[28] P. Ekman and W. Friesen, *Manual for the Facial Action Coding System.* Palo Alto: Consulting Psychologists Press, 1977.

[29] P. Ekman and W. Friesen, *The Facial Action Coding System: A Technique for the Measurement of Facial Movement*, P. Ekman and H. Oster, Eds. San Diego: Consulting Psychology Press, 1978.

[30] P. Ekman and H. Oster, "Facial Expressions of Emotion," *Annual Review of Psychology*, vol. 30, pp. 527–554, 1979.

[31] P. Ekman and W. Friesen, "A new pan-cultural facial expression of emotion," *Motivation and Emotion*, vol. 10, no. 2, pp. 159–268, 1986.

[32] P. Ekman, W. Friesen, and S. Ancoli, "Facial Signs of Emotional Experience," *Journal of Personality and Social Psychology*, vol. 39, no. 6, pp. 1125–1134, 1980.

[33] P. Ekman, W. Friesen, M. Osullivan, and K. Scerer, "Relative Importance of Face, Body, and Speech in Judgements of Personality and Affect," *Journal of Personality and Social Psychology*, vol. 38, no. 2, pp. 270–277, 1980.

[34] P. Ekman, R. J. Davidson, and W. V. Friesen, "The duchenne smile: emotional expression and brain physiology ii. journal of personality and," *Social Psychology*, vol. 58, pp. 342–353, 1990.

[35] P. Ekman, "Are - there basic emotions?" *Psychological Review*, vol. 99, no. 3, pp. 550–553, July 1992.

[36] P. Ekman, "Facial Expression of Emotion - New Findings, New Questions," *Psychological Science*, vol. 3, no. 1, pp. 34–38, January 1992.

[37] P. Ekman, "Facial Expression and Emotion," *American Psychologist*, vol. 48, no. 4, pp. 384–392, April 1993.

[38] E. Rosenberg and P. Ekman, "Conceptual and methodological issues in the judgment of facial expressions of emotion," *Motivation and Emotion*, vol. 19, no. 2, pp. 111–138, June 1995.

[39] P. Ekman, *Basic Emotions.* Dalgleish, T. and Power, M, 1999.

Ioanna-Ourania Stathopoulou and George A. Tsihrintzis

[40] D. Matsumoto and P. Ekman, "The relationship among expressions, labels, and descriptions of contempt," *Journal of Personality ans Social Psychology*, vol. 87, no. 4, pp. 529–540, October 2004.

[41] R. C. Solomon, "Back to basics: On the very idea of "basic emotions"," *Journal for the Theory of Social Behaviour*, vol. 32, pp. 115–158, 2002.

[42] G. B. Duchenne de Boulogne, *The Mechanism of Human Facial Expression*, ser. Studies in Emotion and Social Interaction, R. A. Cuthbertson, Ed. Cambridge University Press, July 1990.

[43] A. Ortony and T. Turner, "What's basic about basic emotions?" *Psychological Review*, vol. 97, no. 3, pp. 315–331, 1990.

[44] J. Russell, "Negative results on a reported facial expression of contempt," *Motivation and Emotion*, vol. 13, no. 3, pp. 281–291, 1991.

[45] J. Haidt and D. Keltner, "Culture and facial expression: Open-ended methods find more expressions and a gradient of recognition," *Cognition and Emotion*, vol. 13, no. 3, pp. 225–266, 1999.

[46] J. E. LeDoux, *The Emotional Brain*, Simon and Schuster, Eds. New York: Simon and Schuster, 1998.

[47] D. Matsumoto and P. Ekman, "American-japanese cultural differences in judgements of emotional expressions of different intensities," *Motivation and Emotion*, vol. 13, no. 2, pp. 143–157, January 2005.

[48] C. Izard, "Innate and universal facial expressions: evidence from developmental and cross-cultural research," *Psychological Bulletin*, vol. 115, pp. 288–299, 1994.

[49] H. Elfenbein and N. Ambady, "On the universality and cultural specificity of emotion recognition: a meta-analysis," *Psychological Bulletin*, vol. 128, no. 2, pp. 205–235, 2002.

[50] P. E. Griffiths, *What Emotions Really Are: The Problem of Psychological Categories*, ser. Science and Its Conceptual Foundations. University Of Chicago Press, August 1998.

[51] K. Nakamura, R. Kawashima, K. Ito, M. Sugiura, T. Kata, A. Nakamurea, K. Hatano, S. Nagumo, K. Kubota, H. Fukuda, and S. Kojima, "Activation of the right inferior frontal cortex during assessment of facial emotion," *Journal of Neurophysiology*, vol. 82, pp. 1610–1614, 1999.

[52] C. J. Harmer, K. V. Thilo, J. C. Rothwell, and G. M. Goodwin, "Transcranial magnetic stimulation of medial-frontal cortex impairs the processing of angry facial expressions," *Nature Neuroscience*, vol. 4, pp. 17–18, 2001.

[53] V. Gallese, C. Keysers, and G. Rizzolatti, "A unifying view of the basis of social cognition," *Trends in Cognitive Sciences*, vol. 8, pp. 396–403, 2004.

[54] M. Jabbi, J. Bastiaansen, and C. Keysers, "A common anterior insula representation of disgust observation, experience and imagination shows divergent functional connectivity pathways," *PLoS ONE*, vol. 3, no. 8, pp. 29–39, August 2008.

[55] J. S. Morris, A. Ohman, and R. J. Dolan, "Conscious and unconscious emotional learning in the human amygdala," *Nature*, vol. 393, pp. 467–480, 1998.

[56] J. S. Morris, B. Degelder, L. Weiskrantz, and R. J. Dolan, "Differential extrageniculostriate and amygdala responses to presentation of emotional faces in a cortically blind field," *Brain*, vol. 124, pp. 1241–1252, 2001.

[57] P. J. Whalen, S. L. Rauch, N. L. Etcoff, S. C. Mcinerney, M. B. Lee, and M. A. Jenike, "Masked presentations of emotional facial expressions modulate amygdala activity without explicit knowledge," *The Journal of Neurosciences*, vol. 18, pp. 411–418, 1998.

[58] P. Vuilleumier, J. L. Armony, J. Driver, and R. J. Dolan, "Distinct spatial frequency sensitivities for processing faces and emotional expressions," *Nature Neuroscience*, vol. 6, pp. 624–631, 2003.

[59] R. Saxe and N. Kanwisher, "People thinking about thinking people," *NeuroImage*, vol. 19, pp. 1835–1842, 2003.

[60] G. Hein and R. T. Knight, "Superior temporal sulcus—it's my area: Or is it?" *J. Cognitive Neuroscience*, vol. 20, no. 12, pp. 2125–2136, 2008.

[61] E. Redcay, "The superior temporal sulcus performs a common function for social and speech perception: implications for the emergence of autism," *Neuroscience and Biobehavioral Reviews*, vol. 32, no. 1, pp. 123–142, 2008.

[62] M. Zilbovicius, I. Meresse, N. Chabane, F. Brunelle, Y. Samson, and N. Boddaert, "Autism, the superior temporal sulcus and social perception," vol. 29, no. 7, pp. 359–366, 2006.

[63] K. S. Labar, M. J. Crupain, J. T. Voyvodic, and G. Mccarthy, "Dynamic perception of facial affect and identity in the human brain," *Cerebral Cortex*, vol. 13, pp. 1023–1033, 2003.

Ioanna-Ourania Stathopoulou and George A. Tsihrintzis

[64] P. Graf and D. Schachter, "Implicit and explicit memory for new associations in normal and amnesic subjects," *Journal of Experimental Psychology: Learning, Memory and Cognitio*, vol. 11, pp. 501–518, 1985.

[65] L. Feldman Barrett, P. M. Niedenthal, and P. Winkielman, *Emotion and Consciousness*, 1st ed., L. Feldman Barrett, P. M. Niedenthal, and P. Winkielman, Eds. The Guilford Press, 2005.

[66] H. Critchley, E. Daly, M. Phillips, M. Brammer, E. Bullmore, S. Williams, T. Van Amelsvoort, D. Robertson, A. David, and D. Murphy, "Explicit and implicit neural mechanisms for processing of social information from facial expressions: a functional magnetic resonance imaging study," *Human Brain Mapping*, vol. 9, no. 2, pp. 93–105, February 2000.

[67] A. R. Hariri, V. S. Mattay, A. Tessitore, F. Fera, and D. R. Weinberger, "Neocortical modulation of the amygdala response to fearful stimuli," *Biological Psychiatry*, vol. 53, no. 6, pp. 494 – 501, 2003. [Online]. Available: http://www.sciencedirect.com/science/article/B6T4S-4845GNN-6/2/af825f9f083d5ab2c3afc1c4979b4205

[68] J. S. Winston, J. O'Doherty, and R. J. Dolan, "Common and distinct neural responses during direct and incidental processing of multiple facial emotions," *NeuroImage*, vol. 20, pp. 84–97, 2003.

[69] M. L. Keightley, G. Winocur, S. J. Graham, H. S. Mayberg, S. J. Hevenor, and C. L. Grady, "An fmri study investigating cognitive modulation of brain regions associated with emotional processing of visual stimuli," *Neuropsychologia*, vol. 41, no. 5, pp. 585 – 596, 2003.

[70] J. Scheuerecker, T. Frodl, N. Koutsouleris, T. Zetzsche, M. Wiesmann, A. Kleemann, H. Bruckmann, G. Schmitt, H.-J. Mfller, and E. Meisenzahl, "Cerebral differences in explicit and implicit emotional processing – an fmri study," *Neuropsychobiology*, vol. 56, pp. 32–39, 2007.

[71] M. L. Gorno-Tempini, S. Pradelli, M. Serafini, G. Pagnoni, P. Baraldi, C. Porro, R. Nicoletti, C. Umita, and P. Nichelli, "Explicit and incidental facial expression processing: an fmri study," *NeuroImage*, vol. 14, pp. 465–473, 2001.

[72] R. C. Gur, L. Schroeder, T. Turner, C. McGrath, R. M. Chan, B. I. Turetsky, D. Alsop, J. Maldjian, and R. E. Gur, "Brain activation during facial emotion processing," *NeuroImage*, vol. 16, no. 3, Part 1, pp. 651 – 662, 2002. [Online]. Available: http://www.sciencedirect.com/science/article/B6WNP-46HDMPV-9/2/fb8fc5d411223944e4962b74f0658090

[73] "Character and handwriting," *Psychological Bulletin*, vol. 16, no. 1, pp. 28 – 31, 1919. [Online]. Available: http://www.sciencedirect.com/science/article/ B6WY5-4NVH9FX-9/2/e725a25b634705e575b8ceb896e0319d

[74] H. Wang, H. Prendinger, and T. Igarashi, "Communicating emotions in online chat using physiological sensors and animated text," in *CHI '04: CHI '04 extended abstracts on Human factors in computing systems*. New York, NY, USA: ACM, 2004, pp. 1171–1174. [Online]. Available: http://dx.doi.org/10.1145/985921.986016

[75] C. Bartneck, "Emmuu - an embodied emotional character for the ambient intelligent home," Ph.D. dissertation, Eindhoven University of Technology, Eindhoven, 2002.

[76] P. Ekman, *Handbook of Cognition and Emotion*. Sussex, U.K.: John Wiley & Sons, Ltd, 1999.

[77] M. De Meijer, "The contribution of general features of body movement to the attribution of emotions," *Journal of Nonverbal Behaviour*, vol. 13, no. 4, pp. 247–268, 1989.

[78] H. G. Wallbott, "Bodily expression of emotion," *European Journal of Social Psychology*, vol. 28, no. 6, pp. 879–896, December 1998.

[79] A. Shaarani and D. Romano, "Basic emotions from body movements," in *Proc of CCID 2006:The First International Symposium on Culture, Creativity and Interaction Design. HCI 2006 Workshops, The 20th BCS HCI Group conference*, Queen Mary, University of London, UK, 2006.

[80] J. A. Russell, "A circumplex model of affect. journal of personality and," *Social Psychology*, vol. 39, pp. 1161–1178, 1980.

[81] J. A. Russell and M. Bullock, "Multidimensional scaling of emotional facial expressions: similarity from preschoolers to adults. journal of personality and," *Social Psychology*, vol. 48, pp. 1290–1298, 1985.

[82] J. Russell, "Is there Universal Recognition of Emotion from Facial Expression - A Review of the Cross-Cultural Studies," *Psychological Bulletin*, vol. 115, no. 1, pp. 102–141, January 1994.

[83] J. A. Russell and J. M. Fernandez-Dols, *The Psychology Of Facial Expression*. Cambridge University Press, 1997.

Ioanna-Ourania Stathopoulou and George A. Tsihrintzis

[84] J. Russell, "Core affect and the psychological construction of emotion," *Psychological Review*, vol. 110, no. 1, pp. 145–172, January 2003.

[85] J. Russel, "Facial Expressions of Emotion - What Lies Beyond Minimal Universability," *Psychological Bulletin*, vol. 118, no. 3, pp. 379–391, November 1995.

[86] J. Carroll and J. Russell, "Do facial expressions signal specific emotions? Judging emotion from the face in context," *Journal of Personality and Social Psychology*, vol. 70, no. 2, pp. 205–218, February 1996.

[87] J. Russell and L. Barrett, "Core affect, prototypical emotional episodes, and other things called Emotion: Dissecting the elephant," *Journal of Personality and Social Psychology*, vol. 76, no. 5, pp. 805–819, May 1999.

[88] J. Russell, J. Bachorowski, and J. Fernandez-Dols, "Facial and vocal expressions of emotion," *Annual Review of Psychology*, vol. 54, pp. 329–349, 2003.

[89] D. Goleman, *Emotional Intelligence*. New York, USA: Bantam Books, 1995.

[90] R. Picard, "Affective computing: challenges," *International Journal of Human-Computer Studies*, vol. 59, no. 1-2, pp. 55–64, July 2003.

[91] D. Goren and H. Wilson, "Quantifying facial expression recognition across viewing conditions," *Vision Research*, vol. 46, no. 8-9, pp. 1253–1262, April 2006.

[92] C. Nass and B. Reeves, "Combining, Distinguishing, and Generating Theories in Communication - A domains of Analysis Framework," *Communication Research*, vol. 18, no. 2, pp. 240–261, April 1991.

[93] B. Reeves and C. Nass, *The Media Equation: How People Treat Computers, Television, and New Media Like Real People and Places*. Cambridge University Press and CSLI, New York., 1998.

[94] T. Ganel, Y. Goshen-Gottstein, and M. Goodale, "Interactions between the processing of gaze direction and facial expression," *Vision Research*, vol. 45, pp. 1191–1200, 2005.

[95] R. Picard, "Affective computing for future agents," *Cooperative Information Agents IV*, vol. 1860, p. 14, 2000.

[96] L. De Silva, T. Miyasato, and R. Nakatsu, "Facial Emotion Recognition Using Multimodal Information," in *Proceedings of IEEE Int. Conf. on Information, Communications and Signal Processing - ICICS*, Singapore, Thailand, September 1997.

[97] M. Pantic and L. J. M. Rothkrantz, "Toward an affect-sensitive multimodal human-computer interaction," *Proceedings of the IEEE*, vol. 91, no. 9, pp. 1370–1390, September 2003.

[98] U. Hess, S. Blairy, and R. E. Kleck, "The intensity of emotional facial expressions and decoding accuracy," *Journal of Nonverbal Behavior*, vol. 21, pp. 241–257, 1997.

[99] U. Hess, R. B. Adams, and R. E. Kleck, "Facial appearance, gender and emotion expression," *Emotion*, vol. 4, pp. 378–388, 2004.

[100] L. R. Brody and J. A. Hall, *Handbook of emotions*, 2nd ed. New York: Guilford Press, 2000, ch. Gender, emotion, and expression, pp. 447–460.

[101] A. H. Fischer, "Sex differences in emotionality: Fact or stereotype?" *Feminism & Psychology*, vol. 3, pp. 303–318, 1993.

[102] S. S. Haugh, C. D. Hoffman, and G. Cowan, "The eye of the very young beholder: Sex typing of infants by young children," *Child Development*, vol. 51, pp. 598–600, 1980.

[103] L. Gaelick, G. V. Bodenhausen, and R. S. Wyer, "Emotional communication in close relationships," *Journal of Personality and Social Psychology*, vol. 49, pp. 1246–1265, 1985.

[104] A. Mignault and A. Chaudhuri, "The many faces of a neutral face: head tilt and perception of dominance and emotion," *Journal of Nonverbal Behavior*, vol. 27, pp. 111–132, 2003.

[105] N. B. Humphrey, *Growing points in ethology*. Cambridge: Cambridge University Press, 1976, ch. The social function of intellect, pp. 303–317.

[106] L. Cosmides, J. Tooby, and J. Barkow, *The adapted mind*. New York: Oxford University Press, 1992, ch. Evolutionary psychology and conceptual integration, pp. 3–18.

[107] R. W. Byrne, *Social intelligence and interaction*. New York: Cambridge University Press, 1995, ch. The ape legacy: the evolution of Machiavellian intelligence and anticipatory interactive planning, pp. 37–52.

[108] K. L. Schmidt and J. F. Cohn, "Human facial expressions as adaptations: Evolutionary questions in facial expression research," *American Journal of Physical Anthropology* , *S33*, pp. 3–24, 2001.

Ioanna-Ourania Stathopoulou and George A. Tsihrintzis

[109] R. Hassin and Y. Trope, "Facing faces: Studies on the cognitive aspects of physiognomy," *Journal of Personality and Social Psychology*, vol. 78, pp. 837–852, 2000.

[110] A. Todorov, C. P. Said, A. D. Engell, and N. N. Oosterhof, "Understanding evaluation of faces on social dimensions," *Trends in Cognitive Sciences*, vol. 12, no. 12, pp. 455–460, 2008.

[111] L. A. Zebrowitz and J. M. Montepare, "Social psychological face perception: Why appearance matters," *Social and Personality Psychology Compass*, vol. 2, pp. 1497–1517, 2008.

[112] M. Bar, M. Neta, and H. Linz, "Very first impressions," *Emotion*, vol. 6, pp. 269–278, 2006.

[113] J. Willis and A. Todorov, "First impressions: Making up your mind after 100 ms exposure to a face," *sychological Science*, vol. 17, pp. 592–598, 2006.

[114] A. Todorov, M. Pakrashi, and N. N. Oosterhof, "Evaluating faces on trustworthiness after minimal time exposure," *Social Cognition*, vol. 27, pp. 813–833, 2009.

[115] I. V. Blair, C. M. Judd, and K. M. Chapleau, "The influence of afrocentric facial features in criminal sentencing," *Psychological Science*, vol. 15, pp. 674–679, 2004.

[116] J. L. Eberhardt, P. G. Davies, V. J. Purdie-Vaughns, and S. L. Johnson, "Looking deathworthy: Perceived stereotypicality of black defendants predicts capital-sentencing outcomes," *Psychological Science*, vol. 17, pp. 383–386, 2006.

[117] A. C. Little, R. P. Burriss, B. C. Jones, and S. C. Roberts, "Facial appearance affects voting decisions," *Evolution and Human Behavior*, vol. 28, pp. 18–27, 2007.

[118] K. Dion, E. Berscheid, and E. Waltser, "What is beautiful is good. journal of personality and," *Social Psychology*, vol. 24, pp. 207–213, 1972.

[119] G. R. Adams and T. L. Huston, "Social perception of middle-aged persons varying in physical attractiveness," *Developmental Psychology*, vol. 11, pp. 657–658, 1975.

[120] J. E. Scheib, S. W. Gangestad, and R. Thornhill, "Facial attractiveness, symmetry and cues of good genes," in *Proceedings of the Royal Society of London B*, vol. 266, 1999, pp. 1913–1927.

[121] T. Valentine, S. Darling, and M. Donnelly, "Why are average faces attractive? the effect of view and averageness on the attractiveness of female faces," *Psychonomic Bulletin & Review*, vol. 11, pp. 482–487, 2004.

[122] M. S. Gazzaniga and C. S. Smylie, "Hemispheric mechanisms controlling voluntary and spontaneous facial expressions," *Journal of Cognitive Neuroscience*, vol. 2, pp. 239–245, 1990.

[123] W. E. Rinn, "The neuropsychology of facial expression: A review of the neurological and psychological mechanisms for producing facial expressions," *Psychological Bulettin*, vol. 95, pp. 52–77, 1984.

[124] G. Rhodes, L. A. Zebrowitz, A. Clark, S. M. Kalick, A. Hightower, and M. R, "Do facial averageness and symmetry signal health?" *Evolution and Human Behavior*, vol. 22, pp. 31–46, 2001.

[125] I. S. Penton-Voak and D. I. Perrett, "Female preference for male faces changes cyclically - further evidence," *Evolution and Human Behavior*, vol. 21, pp. 39–48, 2000.

[126] S. V. Paunonen, K. Ewan, J. Earthy, S. Lefave, and H. Goldberg, "Facial features as personality cues," *Journal of Personality*, vol. 67, pp. 555–583, 1999.

[127] M. Csikszentmihalyi, *Flow: The Psychology of Optimal Experience*. New York, USA: Harper Perennial, 1994.

[128] J. Klein, R. Picard, and J. Riseberg, "Support for Human Emotional Needs in Human-Computer Interaction," in *Proceedings ofCHI'97 Workshop on Human Needs and Social Responsibility*, 1997.

[129] J. Mayer and P. Salovey, "The Intelligence Of Emotional Intelligence," *Intelligence*, vol. 17, no. 4, pp. 433–442, October-December 1993.

[130] J. Mayer, M. Dipaolo, and P. Salovey, "Perceiving Affective Content in Ambitious Visual-Stimuli - A Component Of Emotional Intelligence," *Journal Of Personality Assessment*, vol. 54, no. 3-4, pp. 772–781, 1990.

[131] J. Mayer, P. Salovey, and D. Caruso, "Emotional intelligence: Theory, findings, and implications," *Psychological Inquiry*, vol. 15, no. 3, pp. 197–215, 2004.

[132] H. Marsh and R. Shavelson, "Self-concept: Its multifaceted, hierarchical structure," *Educational Psychologist*, vol. 20, no. FAL, pp. 107–204, 1985.

[133] A. Ortony, G. L. Clore, and A. Collins, *The Cognitive Structure of Emotions*. New York, USA: Cambridge University Press, 1988.

[134] M. Rosenberg, *Conceiving the Self.* New York, USA: Basic Books Inc, 1979.

[135] A. Martinez and R. Benavente, "The AR face database," University of Wisconsin - Madison Computer Sciences Department, Tech. Rep. CVC Technical Report Num.24, June 1998.

[136] M. J. Lyons, J. Budynek, and S. Akamatsu, "Automatic classification of single facial images," *IEEE Trans. on Pattern Analysis and Machine Intelligence,* vol. 21, no. 12, pp. 1357–1362, 1999.

[137] M. Lyons, S. Akamatsu, M. Kamachi, and J. Gyoba, "Coding facial expressions with gabor wavelets," in *FG '98: Proceedings of the 3rd. International Conference on Face & Gesture Recognition.* Washington, DC, USA: IEEE Computer Society, 1998, p. 200.

[138] A. Georghiades, P. Belhumeur, and D. Kriegman, "From few to many: Illumination cone models for face recognition under variable lighting and pose," *IEEE Trans. Pattern Anal. Mach. Intelligence,* vol. 23, no. 6, pp. 643–660, 2001.

[139] T. Kanade, Y. Tian, and J. F. Cohn, "Comprehensive database for facial expression analysis," in *FG '00: Proceedings of the Fourth IEEE International Conference on Automatic Face and Gesture Recognition 2000.* Washington, DC, USA: IEEE Computer Society, 2000, p. 46.

[140] M. Pantic, M. Valstar, R. Rademaker, and L. Maat, "Web-based database for facial expression analysis," in *IEEE Int'l Conf. on Multimedia and Expo 2005,* June 2005, pp. 317–321. [Online]. Available: http://pubs.doc.ic.ac.uk/Pantic-ICME05-2/

[141] A. Colmenarez and T. Huang, "Face detection with information-based maximum discrimination," in *CVPR '97: Proceedings of the 1997 IEEE Computer Society Conference on Computer Vision and Pattern Recognition (CVPR '97).* Washington, DC, USA: IEEE Computer Society, 1997.

[142] G. Yang and T. Huang, "Human face detection in a complex background," *Pattern Recognition,* vol. 27, no. 1, pp. 53–63, 1994.

[143] S. Lee, Y. Ham, and R. Park, "Recognition of human front faces using knowledge-based feature extraction and neuro-fuzzy algorithm," *Pattern Recognition,* vol. 29, no. 11, pp. 1863–1876, 1996.

[144] T. K. Leung, M. C. Burl, and P. Perona, "Finding faces in cluttered scenes using random labeled graph matching," in *ICCV '95: Proceedings of the Fifth*

International Conference on Computer Vision. Washington, DC, USA: IEEE Computer Society, 1995.

[145] H. A. Rowley, S. Baluja, and T. Kanade, "Rotation invariant neural network-based face detection," in *CVPR '98: Proceedings of the IEEE Computer Society Conference on Computer Vision and Pattern Recognition (CVPR'98).* Washington, DC, USA: IEEE Computer Society, 1998.

[146] H. A. Rowley, S. Baluja, and T. Kanade, "Neural network-based face detection," *IEEE Transactions On Pattern Analysis and Machine intelligence,* vol. 20, pp. 23–38, 1998.

[147] M.-H. Yang and N. Ahuja, *Face Detection and Gesture Recognition for Human-Computer Interaction.* Norwell, MA, USA: Kluwer Academic Publishers, 2001.

[148] P. Juell and R. Marsh, "A hierarchical neural network for human face detection," *Pattern Recognition,* vol. 29, no. 5, pp. 781–787, 1996.

[149] C. Lin and K. Fan, "Triangle-based approach to the detection of human face," *Pattern Recognition,* vol. 34, no. 5, pp. 1271–1284, 2001.

[150] K.-K. Sung and T. Poggio, "Example-based learning for view-based human face detection," *IEEE Trans. Pattern Anal. Mach. Intell.,* vol. 20, no. 1, pp. 39–51, 1998.

[151] L.-L. Huang and A Shimizu, "A multi-expert approach for robust face detection," *Pattern Recogn.,* vol. 39, no. 9, pp. 1695–1703, 2006.

[152] M. Castrillón, O. Déniz, C. Guerra, and M. Hernández, "Encara2: Real-time detection of multiple faces at different resolutions in video streams," *Journal of Visual Communication and Image Representation,* vol. 18, no. 2, pp. 130–140, 2007.

[153] S. Phimoltares, C. Lursinsap, and K. Chamnongthai, "Face detection and facial feature localization without considering the appearance of image context," *Image Vision Comput.,* vol. 25, no. 5, pp. 741–753, 2007.

[154] S. Kadoury and M. D. Levine, "Face detection in gray scale images using locally linear embeddings," *Computer Vision and Image Understanding,* vol. 105, no. 1, pp. 1–20, 2007.

[155] C. Kotropoulos and I. Pitas, "Rule-based face detection in frontal views," in *ICASSP '97: Proceedings of the 1997 IEEE International Conference on Acoustics, Speech, and Signal Processing (ICASSP '97) - Volume 4.* Washington, DC, USA: IEEE Computer Society, 1997.

Ioanna-Ourania Stathopoulou and George A. Tsihrintzis

[156] C. P. Papageorgiou, M. Oren, and T. Poggio, "A general framework for object detection," in *Computer Vision, 1998. Sixth International Conference on*, 1998, pp. 555–562. [Online]. Available: http://dx.doi.org/10.1109/ICCV.1998.710772

[157] P. Viola and M. Jones, "Rapid object detection using a boosted cascade of simple features," *Computer Vision and Pattern Recognition, IEEE Computer Society Conference on*, vol. 1, pp. 511–518, April 2001. [Online]. Available: http://dx.doi.org/10.1109/CVPR.2001.990517

[158] M. Jones and P. Viola, "Fast multi-view face detection," Mitsubishi Electric Research Laboratories, Tech. Rep., 2003.

[159] C. Liu, "A bayesian discriminating features method for face detection," *IEEE Transactions on Pattern Analysis and Machine Intelligence*, vol. 25, pp. 725–740, 2003.

[160] H. Schneiderman and T. Kanade, "A statistical approach to 3d object detection applied to faces and cars," in *CMU-RI-TR*, 2000, pp. 0–6.

[161] S. Z. Li and Z. Zhang, "Floatboost learning and statistical face detection," *IEEE Transactions on Pattern Analysis and Machine Intelligence*, vol. 26, pp. 1–12, 2004.

[162] C. Huang, H. Ai, Y. Li, and S. Lao, "Vector boosting for rotation invariant multi-view face detection," in *ICCV '05: Proceedings of the Tenth IEEE International Conference on Computer Vision (ICCV'05) Volume 1*. Washington, DC, USA: IEEE Computer Society, 2005, pp. 446–453.

[163] B. Wu, H. Ai, C. Huang, and S. Lao, "Fast rotation invariant multi-view face detection based on real adaboost," in *Automatic Face and Gesture Recognition, 2004. Proceedings. Sixth IEEE International Conference on*, 2004, pp. 79–84. [Online]. Available: http://ieeexplore.ieee.org/xpls/abs_all.jsp?arnumber=1301512

[164] M.-H. Yang, D. J. Kriegman, and N. Ahuja, "Detecting faces in images: A survey," *IEEE Transactions on Pattern Analysis and Machine Intelligence*, vol. 24, pp. 34–58, 2002.

[165] E. Hjelmas and B. Lowu, "Face detection: a survey," *Comput. Vision Image Understand.*, vol. 83, no. 3, pp. 236–274, 2001.

[166] Y. Dai and Y. Nakano, "Face-texture model based on sgld and its application in face detection in a color scene," *Pattern Recognition*, vol. 29, pp. 1007–1017, 1996.

[167] A. Tankus, "Face detection by direct convexity estimation," *Pattern Recognition Letters*, vol. 18, pp. 913–922, 1997.

[168] E. Saber and A. M. Tekalp, "Frontal-view face detection and facial feature extraction using color, shape and symmetry based cost functions," *Pattern Recognition Letters*, pp. 669–680, 1998.

[169] S.-H. Jeng, H. Y. Liao, C. C. Han, M. Y. Chern, and Y. T. Liu, "Facial feature detection using geometrical face model: An efficient approach," *Pattern Recognition*, vol. 31, no. 3, pp. 273–282, March 1998. [Online]. Available: http://dx.doi.org/10.1016/S0031-3203(97)00048-4

[170] J.-G. Wang and E. Sung, "Frontal-view face detection and facial feature extraction using color and morphological operations," *Pattern Recognition Letters*, vol. 20, pp. 1053–1068, 1999.

[171] G. Wei and I. K. Sethi, "Face detection for image annotation," *Pattern Recognition Letters*, vol. 20, pp. 1313–1321, 1999.

[172] C.-C. Han, H.-Y. M. Liao, G.-J. Yu, and L.-H. Chen, "Fast face detection via morphology-based pre-processing," *Pattern Recognition*, vol. 33, pp. 1701–1712, 2000.

[173] J. Wang and T. Tan, "A new face detection method based on shape information," *Pattern Recognition Letters*, vol. 21, pp. 463–471, 2000.

[174] C. Chen, C.-W. Hsu, and T.-L. Lin, "Image prediction using face detection and triangulation," *Pattern Recognition Letters*, vol. 22, pp. 1347 1357, 2001.

[175] H. Yao and W. Gao, "Face detection and location based on skin chrominance and lip chrominance transformation from color images," *Electronic Engineering*, vol. 34, pp. 1555–1564, 2001.

[176] Y. Wang and B. Yuan, "A novel approach for human face detection from color images under complex background," *Pattern Recognition*, vol. 34, pp. 1983–1992, 2001.

[177] O. Ayinde and Y.-H. Yang, "Region-based face detection," *Pattern Recognition*, vol. 35, pp. 2095 – 2107, 2002.

[178] J. Zhou, D. Zhang, and C. y. Wu, "Orientation analysis for rotated human face detection," *Image and Vision Computing*, vol. 20, 2002.

Ioanna-Ourania Stathopoulou and George A. Tsihrintzis

[179] L. Hock Koh, S. Ranganath, and Y. V. Venkatesh, "An integrated automatic face detection and recognition system," *Pattern Recognition*, vol. 35, pp. 1259–1273, 2002.

[180] I.-S. Hsieh, K.-C. Fan, and C. Lin, "A statistic approach to the detection of human faces in color nature scene," *Pattern Recognition*, vol. 35, pp. 1583–1596, 2002.

[181] L.-l. Huang, A. Shimizu, Y. Hagihara, and H. Kobatake, "Face detection from cluttered images using a polynomial neural network," *Test*, vol. 51, pp. 197 – 211, 2003.

[182] J. Wu and Z.-H. Zhou, "Efficient face candidates selector for face detection," *Pattern Recognition*, vol. 36, pp. 1175 – 1186, 2003.

[183] K.-W. Wong, K.-M. Lam, and W.-C. Siu, "A robust scheme for live detection of human faces in color images," *Signal Processing*, vol. 18, pp. 103–114, 2003.

[184] K.-W. Wong, K.-M. Lam, and W.-C. Siu, "An efficient algorithm for human face detection and facial feature extraction under different conditions," *Pattern Recognition*, vol. 34, pp. 1993–2004, 2004.

[185] H. Bae and S. Kim, "Real-time face detection and recognition using hybrid-information extracted from face space and facial features," *Image and Vision Computing*, vol. 23, pp. 1181–1191, 2005.

[186] C. Kubleck and A. Ernst, "Face detection and tracking in video sequences using the modifed census transformation," *International Journal of Computer Vision*, vol. 24, pp. 564–572, 2006.

[187] P. Shih and C. Liu, "Face detection using discriminating feature analysis and support vector machine," *Pattern Recognition*, vol. 39, pp. 260 – 276, 2006.

[188] T. Kondo and H. Yan, "Automatic human face detection and recognition under non-uniform illumination," *Pattern Recognition*, vol. 32, 2006.

[189] P. Wang and Q. Ji, "Multi-view face and eye detection using discriminant features," *Computer Vision and Image Understanding*, vol. 105, pp. 99–111, 2007.

[190] C. Lin, "Face detection in complicated backgrounds and di erent illumination conditions by using ycbcr color space and neural network," *Pattern Recognition Letters*, vol. 28, pp. 2190–2200, 2007.

[191] J. Meynet, V. Popovici, and J.-P. Thiran, "Face detection with boosted gaussian features," *Pattern Recognition*, vol. 40, pp. 2283 – 2291, 2007.

[192] C.-F. Juang and S.-J. Shiu, "Using self-organizing fuzzy network with support vector learning for face detection in color images," *Electrical Engineering*, vol. 71, pp. 3409–3420, 2008.

[193] M. S. Bartlett, J. C. Hager, P. Ekman, and T. J. Sejnowski, "Measuring facial expressions by computer image analysis," *Psychophysiology*, vol. 36, pp. 253–263, 1999.

[194] M. S. Bartlett, G. Littlewort, I. Fasel, and J. R. Movellan, "Real time face detection and facial expression recognition: Development and application to human computer interaction," in *CVPR 2003: Proceedings of the 2003 IEEE Computer Society Conference on Computer Vision and Pattern Recognition (CVPR 2003), Workshop for HCI*, 2003, pp. 139–157.

[195] G. D. Kearney and S. Mckenzie, "Machine interpretation of emotion: Design of memory based expert system for interpreting facial expressions in terms of signaled emotions (janus)," *Cognitive Science*, vol. 17, pp. 589–622, 1993.

[196] J. Cohn and T. Kanade, "Use of automated facial image analysis for measurement of emotion expression," in *The handbook of emotion elicitation and assessment. Oxford University Press Series in Affective Science*, J. A. Coan and J. B. Allen, Eds., 2006, (In Press).

[197] A. Goneid and R. El Kaliouby, "Facial feature analysis of spontaneous facial expression," in *Proceedings of the 10th International AI Applications Conference*, 2002.

[198] J. Lien, T. Kanade, J. Cohn, and C. Li, "Detection, tracking and classification of action units in facial expression," *Journal of Robotics and Autonomous Systems*, vol. 31, no. 3, pp. 131–146, 2000.

[199] I. Cohen, N. Sebe, L. Chen, A. Garg, and T. S. Huang, "Facial expression recognition from video sequences: Temporal and static modeling," in *Computer Vision and Image Understanding*, 2003, pp. 160–187.

[200] D. Terzopoulos and K. Waters, "Analysis and synthesis of facial image sequences using physical and anatomical models," *IEEE Trans. Pattern Anal. Mach. Intell.*, vol. 15, no. 6, pp. 569–579, 1993.

[201] I. A. Essa and A. P. Pentland, "Coding, analysis, interpretation, and recognition of facial expressions," *IEEE Trans. on Pattern Analysis and Machine Intelligence*, vol. 19, no. 7, pp. 757–763, 1997.

[202] Z. Zhang, M. Lyons, M. Schuster, and S. Akamatsu, "Comparison between geometry-based and gabor-wavelets-based facial expression recognition using multi-layer perceptron," in *FG '98: Proceedings of the 3rd. International Conference on Face & Gesture Recognition*. Washington, DC, USA: IEEE Computer Society, 1998.

[203] W. Zhao, R. Chellappa, P. J. Phillips, and A. Rosenfeld, "Face recognition: A literature survey," *ACM Comput. Surv.*, vol. 35, no. 4, pp. 399–458, 2003.

[204] M. J. Black and Y. Yacoob, "Tracking and recognizing rigid and non-rigid facial motions using local parametric models of image motion," in *In ICCV*, 1995, pp. 374–381.

[205] M. N. Dailey, G. W. Cottrell, and R. Adolphs, "A six-unit network is all you need to discover happiness," in *In TwentySecond Annual Conference of the Cognitive Science Society*. Erlbaum, 2000, pp. 101–106.

[206] M. Rosenblum, Y. Yacoob, and L. Davis, "Human expression recognition from motion using a radial basis function network architecture," *IEEE Transactions on Neural Networks*, vol. 7, no. 5, pp. 1121–1138, 1996.

[207] I. Kotsia, I. Buciu, and I. Pitas, "An analysis of facial expression recognition under partial facial image occlusion," *Image Vision Comput.*, vol. 26, no. 7, pp. 1052–1067, 2008.

[208] B. Hernández, G. Olague, R. Hammoud, L. Trujillo, and E. Romero, "Visual learning of texture descriptors for facial expression recognition in thermal imagery," *Comput. Vis. Image Underst.*, vol. 106, no. 2-3, pp. 258–269, 2007.

[209] Z. Hammal, L. Couvreur, A. Caplier, and M. Rombaut, "Facial expression classification: An approach based on the fusion of facial deformations using the transferable belief model," *Int. J. Approx. Reasoning*, vol. 46, no. 3, pp. 542–567, 2007.

[210] D. H. Kim, S. U. Jung, and M. J. Chung, "Extension of cascaded simple feature based face detection to facial expression recognition," *Pattern Recogn. Lett.*, vol. 29, no. 11, pp. 1621–1631, 2008.

[211] D. Liang, J. Yang, Z. Zheng, and Y. Chang, "A facial expression recognition system based on supervised locally linear embedding," *Pattern Recogn. Lett.*, vol. 26, no. 15, pp. 2374–2389, 2005.

[212] T. Xiang, M. K. H. Leung, and S. Y. Cho, "Expression recognition using fuzzy spatio-temporal modeling," *Pattern Recognition*, vol. 41, no. 1, pp. 204–216, 2008.

[213] M. Pantic and L. Rothkrantz, "Expert system for automatic analysis of Facial Expression," *Image and Vision Computing Journal*, vol. 18, no. 11, pp. 881–905, July 2000. [Online]. Available: http://pubs.doc.ic.ac.uk/Pantic-IVCJ00/

[214] C.-L. Huang and Y.-M. Huang, "Facial expression recognition using model-based feature extraction and action parameters classification," *Journal of Visual Communication and Image Representation*, vol. 8, no. 3, pp. 278–290, 1997.

[215] G. W. Cottrell and J. Metcalfe, *EMPATH: Face, Emotion, Gender Recognition Using Holons*, 1991, vol. ed, pp. 564–571.

[216] A. Rahardja, A. Sowmya, and W. H. Wilson, "A neural network approach to component versus holistic recognition of facial expressions in images," *SPIE, Intelligent Robots and Computer Vision X: Algorithms and Techniques*, vol. 1607, pp. 62–70, 1991.

[217] K. Matsuno, C. W. Lee, and S. Tsuji, "Recognition of facial expression with potential net," in *Proc. Asian Conf. Computer Vision*, 1993, pp. 504–507.

[218] K. Mase, "Recognition of facial expression from optical flow," *IEICE Trans.*, vol. 74, pp. 3474–3483, 1991.

[219] Y. Moses, D. Reynard, and A. Blake, "Determining facial expressions in real time," in *Proc. Int'l Conf. Automatic Face and GestureRecognition*, vol. pp, 1995, pp. 332–337.

[220] M. Rosenblum, Y. Yacoob, and L. Davis, "Human emotion recognition from motion using a radial basis function network architecture," in *Proc. IEEE Workshop on Motion of Non-Rigid and Articulated Objects*, vol. pp, 1994, pp. 43–49.

[221] Y. Yacoob and L. Davis, "Recognizing facial expressions by spatio-temporal analysis," *Proc. Int'l Conf. Pattern Recognition*, vol. 1, pp. 747–749, 1994.

[222] H. Kobayashi and F. Hara, "Recognition of six basic facial expressions and their strength by neural network," in *Proc. Int'l Workshop Robot and Human Comm.*, 1992, pp. 381–386.

[223] H. Ushida, T. Takagi, and T. Yamaguchi, "Recognition of facial expressions using conceptual fuzzy sets," *Proc. Conf. Fuzzy Systems*, vol. 1, pp. 594–599, 1993.

[224] P. Vanger, R. Honlinger, and H. Haken, "Applications of synergetics in decoding facial expression of eemotion," in *Proc. Int'l Conf. Automatic Face and Gesture Recognition*, vol. pp, 1995, pp. 24–29.

[225] G. J. Edwards, T. F. Cootes, and C. J. Taylor, "Face recognition using active appearance models," in *ECCV '98: Proceedings of the 5th European Conference on Computer Vision-Volume II*. London, UK: Springer-Verlag, 1998, pp. 581–595.

[226] H. Hong, H. Neven, and C. Von Der Malsburg, "Online facial expression recognition based on personalized galleries," in *FG '98: Proceedings of the 3rd. International Conference on Face & Gesture Recognition*. Washington, DC, USA: IEEE Computer Society, 1998.

[227] C. L. Huang and Y. M. Huang, "Facial expression recognition using model-based feature extraction and action parameters classification," *Journal of Visual Communication and Image Representation*, vol. 8, no. 3, pp. 278–290, 1997. [Online]. Available: http://dx.doi.org/10.1006/jvci.1997.0359

[228] C. Padgett and G. W. Cottrell, "Representing face images for emotion classification," in *Proc. Conf. Advances in Neural Information Processing Systems*, vol. pp, 1996, pp. 894–900.

[229] M. Yoneyama, Y. Iwano, A. Ohtake, and K. Shirai, "Facial expressions recognition using discrete hopfield neural networks," *Proc. Int'l Conf. Information Processing*, vol. 3, pp. 117–120, 1997.

[230] F. Hara and H. Kobayashi, "State of the art in component development for interactive communication with humans," *Advanced Robotics*, vol. 11, pp. 585–604, 1997.

[231] J. Zhao and G. Kearney, "Classifying facial emotions by backpropagation neural networks with fuzzy inputs," *Proc. Conf. Neural Information Processing*, vol. 1, pp. 454–457, 1996.

[232] M. J. Black and Y. Yacoob, "Recognizing facial expressions in image sequences using local parameterized models of image motion," *Int'l J. Computer Vision*, vol. 25, pp. 23–48, 1997.

[233] S. Kimura and M. Yachida, "Facial expression recognition and its degree estimation," in *Proc. Computer Vision and Pattern Recognition*, 1997, pp. 295–300.

[234] T. Otsuka and J. Ohya, "Spotting segments displaying facial expression from image sequences using hmm," in *Proc. Int'l Conf. Automatic Face and Gesture Recognition*, vol. pp, 1998, pp. 442–447.

[235] M. Wang, Y. Iwai, and M. Yachida, "Expression recognition from time-sequential facial images by use of expression change model," in *Proc. Int'l Conf. Automatic Face and Gesture Recognition*, 1998, pp. 324–329.

[236] J. F. Cohn, A. J. Zlochower, J. J. Lien, and T. Kanade, "Feature-point tracking by optical flow discriminates subtle differences in facial expression," in *Proc. Int'l Conf. Automatic Face and Gesture Recognition*, vol. pp, 1998, pp. 396–401.

[237] G. J. Edwards, A. Lanitis, C. Taylor, and T. F. Cootes, "Statistical models of face images - improving specificity," in *In British Machine Vision Conference*, 1996, pp. 765–774.

[238] T. F. Cootes, C. J. Taylor, D. H. Cooper, and J. Graham, "Active shape models—their training and application," *Comput. Vis. Image Underst.*, vol. 61, no. 1, pp. 38–59, 1995.

[239] M. Lades, J. C. Vorbr'oggen, J. Buhmann, J. Lange, C. V. D. Malsburg, R. P. W'ortz, and W. Konen, "Distortion invariant object recognition in the dynamic link architecture," *IEEE Trans. on Computers*, vol. 42, pp. 300–311, 1993.

[240] M. Turk and A. Pentland, "Eigenfaces for recognition," *J Cognitive Neuroscience*, vol. 3, pp. 71–86, 1991.

[241] T. Otsuka and J. Ohya, "Recognition of facial expressions using hmm with continuous output probabilities," in *Proc. Int'l Workshop Robot and Human Comm.*, vol. pp, 1996, pp. 323–328.

[242] B. Moghaddam and A. Pentland, "Face recognition using view-based and modular eigenspaces," in *In Automatic Systems for the Identification and Inspection of Humans, SPIE*, 1994, pp. 12–21.

[243] E. P. Simoncelli, "Distributed representation and analysis of visual motion," Ph.D. dissertation, Cambridge, MA, USA, 1993.

[244] J. Wang and E. Adelson, "Layered representation for motion analysis," June 1993, pp. 361–366.

[245] X. Zhou, X. Huang, and Y. Wang, "Real-time facial expression recognition in the interactive game based on embedded hidden markov model," in *CGIV '04: Proceedings of the International Conference on Computer Graphics, Imaging and Visualization.* Washington, DC, USA: IEEE Computer Society, 2004, pp. 144–148.

[246] M. Pardas, A. Bonafonte, and J. Landabaso, "Emotion recognition based on mpeg-4 facial animation parameters," vol. 4, 2002, pp. 3624–3627.

[247] Y. Wang, H. Ai, B. Wu, and C. Huang, "Real time facial expression recognition with adaboost," in *ICPR '04: Proceedings of the Pattern Recognition, 17th International Conference on (ICPR'04) Volume 3.* Washington, DC, USA: IEEE Computer Society, 2004, pp. 926–929.

[248] L. Ma and K. Khorasani, "Facial expression recognition using constructive feedforward neural networks," *Systems, Man, and Cybernetics, Part B: Cybernetics, IEEE Transactions on,* vol. 34, no. 3, pp. 1588–1595, June 2004.

[249] H. Tao and T. S. Huang, "Connected vibrations: A modal analysis approach to non-rigid motion tracking," in *CVPR '98: Proceedings of the 1998 IEEE Computer Society Conference on Computer Vision and Pattern Recognition (CVPR '98),* 1998, pp. 735–740.

[250] T. Wang, H. Ai, and G. Huang, "A two-stage approach to automatic face alignment," in *Third International Symposium on Multispectral Image Processing and Pattern Recognition,* H. Lu and T. Zhang, Eds., vol. 5286, no. 1. SPIE, 2003, pp. 558–563. [Online]. Available: http://link.aip.org/link/?PSI/5286/558/1

[251] A. V. Nefian and H. H. Monson, "Face recognition using an embedded hmm," in *IEEE Conference on Audio and Video-based Biometric Person Authentication,* 1999.

[252] N. Karayiannis and J. Bezdek, "An integrated approach to fuzzy learning vector quantization and fuzzy c-means clustering," *Fuzzy Systems, IEEE Transactions on,* vol. 5, no. 4, pp. 622–628, November 1997.

[253] T. Kobayashi, Y. Ogawa, K. Kato, and K. Yamamoto, "Learning system of human facial expression for a family robot," May 2004, pp. 481–486.

[254] B. Abboud and F. Davoine, "Appearance factorization based facial expression recognition and synthesis," vol. 4, August 2004, pp. 163–166.

226

[255] M. Yuki, W. W. Maddux, and T. Masuda, "Are the windows to the soul the same in the east and west? cultural differences in using the eyes and mouth as cues to recognize emotions in japan and the united states," *Journal of Experimental Social Psychology*, vol. 43, pp. 301–311, 2007.

[256] H. Elfenbein and N. Ambady, "When familiarity breeds accuracy: cultural exposure and facial emotion recognition." *Journal of Personality and Social Psychology*, vol. 85, no. 2, pp. 276–290, 2003.

[257] I.-O. Stathopoulou and G. A. Tsihrintzis, "A new neural network-based method for face detection in images and applications in bioinformatics," in *6th International Workshop on Mathematical Methods in Scattering Theory and Biomedical Technology*, Tsepelovo, Greece, September, 15-18 2003.

[258] I.-O. Stathopoulou and G. A. Tsihrintzis, "Detection and Expression Classification Systems for Face Images (FADECS)," in *Proceedings of the IEEE Workshop on Signal Processing Systems (SiPS"05)*, Athens, Greece, November 2005.

[259] I.-O. Stathopoulou and G. A. Tsihrintzis, "A neural network-based system for face detection in low quality web camera images," in *International Conference on Signal Processing and Multimedia Applicattions*, Barcelona, Spain, July, 28-31 2007.

[260] I.-O. Stathopoulou and G. A. Tsihrintzis, "Appearance - based face detection with artificial neural networks," *Journal of Intelligent Decision Technologies, IOS Press*, 2009, to appear.

[261] C. Fowlkes, S. Belongie, and J. Malik, "Efficient spatiotemporal grouping using the nystrom method," in *CVPR 2001: Proceedings of the 2001 IEEE Computer Society Conference on Computer Vision and Pattern Recognition (CVPR 2001)*, vol. 1, pp. 231–238, 2001.

[262] I.-O. Stathopoulou and G. A. Tsihrintzis, "A neural network-based facial analysis system," in *Proceedings of the 5th International Workshop on Image Analysis for Multimedia Interactive Services*, Lisboa, Portugal, April 2004.

[263] I.-O. Stathopoulou and G. A. Tsihrintzis, "An Improved Neural Network-Based Face Detection and Facial Expression Classification System," in *IEEE International Conference on Systems, Man, and Cybernetics*, The Hague, Netherlands, October 2004.

[264] I.-O. Stathopoulou and G. A. Tsihrintzis, "Pre-processing and expression classification in low quality face images," in *Proceedings of 5th EURASIP Conference*

on Speech and Image Processing, Multimedia Communications and Services, July 2005.

[265] I.-O. Stathopoulou and G. A. Tsihrintzis, "Evaluation of the Discrimination Power of Features Extracted from 2-D and 3-D Facial Images for Facial Expression Analysis," in *Proceedings of the 13th European Signal Processing Conference*, Antalya, Turkey, September 2005.

[266] I.-O. Stathopoulou and G. A. Tsihrintzis, "An Accurate Method for eye detection and feature extraction in face color images," in *Proceedings of the 13th International Conference on Signals, Systems, and Image Processing*, Budapest, Hungary, September 2006.

[267] I.-O. Stathopoulou and G. A. Tsihrintzis, "Neu-faces: A neural network-based face image analysis system," in *ICANNGA '07: Proceedings of the 8th international conference on Adaptive and Natural Computing Algorithms, Part II, LNCS: Vol. 4432*. Berlin, Heidelberg: Springer-Verlag, 2007, pp. 449–456.

[268] I.-O. Stathopoulou and G. A. Tsihrintzis, "Comparative performance evaluation of artificial neural network-based vs. human facial expression classifiers for facial expression recognition," in *KES-IMSS 2008: 1st International Symposium on Intelligent Interactive Multimedia Systems and Services, SCI: Vol. 142*. Berlin, Heidelberg: Springer-Verlag, 2008, pp. 55–65.

[269] A. S. Lampropoulos, I.-O. Stathopoulou, and G. A. Tsihrintzis, "Comparative performance evaluation of classifiers for facial expression recognition," in *KES-IMSS 2009: 2nd International Symposium on Intelligent Interactive Multimedia Systems and Services*, 2009, to appear.

[270] I.-O. Stathopoulou and G. A. Tsihrintzis, "A face detection and visual-facial emotion recognition system," in preparation.

[271] D. A. Forsyth and M. Fleck, "Finding naked people," in *In European Conference on Computer Vision*. Springer-Verlag, 1996, pp. 593–602.

[272] C. M. Bishop, *Neural Networks for Pattern Recognition*, 1st ed. Oxford University Press, 1995.

[273] S. Haykin, *Neural Networks*, 2nd ed. Prentice Hall, 1999.

[274] R. O. Duda, P. E. Hart, and D. G. Strock, *Pattern Classification*, 2nd ed. John Wiley, 2000.

[275] S. Theodoridis and K. Koutroumbas, *Pattern Recognition*, 1st ed. Academic Press, 1998.

[276] G. A. Tsihrintzis and L. C. Jain, Eds., *Multimedia Services in Intelligent Environments - Advanced Tools and Methodologies*, ser. Studies in Computational Intelligence, vol. 120. Springer Berlin / Heidelberg, 2008.

[277] G. A. Tsihrintzis, M. Virvou, and L. C. Jain, Eds., *Multimedia Services in Intelligent Environments - Software Development Challenges and Solutions*, ser. Smart Innovation, Systems and Technologies, vol. 2. Springer Berlin / Heidelberg, 2010.

[278] G. A. Tsihrintzis and L. C. Jain, Eds., *Multimedia Services in Intelligent Environments - Integrated Systems*, ser. Smart Innovation, Systems and Technologies, vol. 3. Springer Berlin / Heidelberg, 2010.

[279] L. C. Jain, M. Sato-Ilic, M. Virvou, G. A. Tsihrintzis, V. Balas, and C. Abeynayake, Eds., *Computational Intelligence Paradigms*, ser. Studies in Computational Intelligence, vol. 137. Springer Berlin / Heidelberg, 2008.

[280] G. Tsihrintzis, M. Virvou, R. Howlett, and L. Jain, Eds., *New Directions in Intelligent Interactive Multimedia*, ser. Studies in Computational Intelligence, vol. 142. Springer Berlin / Heidelberg, 2008.

[281] G. Johansson, "Visual motion perception," *Scientific American*, vol. 232, pp. 76–88, 1975.

[282] G. Ferrigno and A. Pedotti, "Elite: A digital dedicated hardware system for movement analysis via real-time tv signal processing," *IEEE Transactions on Biomedical Engineering*, vol. 32, 1985.

[283] T. Josefsson, E. Nordh, and P. Eriksson, "A flexible high-precision video system for digital recording of motor acts through lightweight reflex markers," *Computer Methods and Programs in Biomedicine*, vol. 49, 1996.

[284] "http://www.vicon.com/."

[285] "http://www.qualisys.se/."

[286] J. Krist, M. Melluish, L. Kehl, and D. Crouch, "Technical description of the optotrack 3D motion measurement system," *in: Gangbildanalyse, Mecke Druck und Verlag, Duderstad*, 1990.

[287] V. Macellari, "Costel: A computer peripheral remote sensing device for 3-dimentional monitoring of human motion," *Journal of Medical and Biological Engineering and Computer*, vol. 21, 1983.

[288] "http://www.charndyn.com/."

[289] "http://www.ndigital.com/polaris.php."

[290] A. Kolahi, M. Hoviattalab, T. Rezaeian, M. Alizadeh, M. Bostan, and H. Mokhtarzadeh, "Design of a marker-based human motion tracking system," *Biomedical Signal Processing and Control*, vol. 2, no. 1, pp. 59 – 67, 2007. [Online]. Available: http://www.sciencedirect.com/science/article/B7XMN-4NBXVXB-1/2/8bc0dc0b98e883f6d3b80d80ed3cf217

[291] H. Zhou and H. Hu, "Human motion tracking for rehabilitation–a survey," *Biomedical Signal Processing and Control*, vol. 3, no. 1, pp. 1 – 18, 2008. [Online]. Available: http://www.sciencedirect.com/science/article/B7XMN-4R1FJ79-1/2/80c14cbb43d772542dacd0557b331f98

[292] "http://www.polyu.edu.hk/cga/faq/."

[293] L. Wang, W. Hu, and T. Tan, "Recent developments in human motion analysis," *Pattern Recognition*, vol. 36, pp. 585–601, 2003.

[294] M. Oren, C. Papageorgiou, P. Sinha, E. Osuna, and T. Poggio, "Pedestrian detection using wavelet templates," in *Computer Vision and Pattern Recognition*, 1997, pp. 193–199.

[295] P. Viola and M. Jones, "Robust real-time object detection," *International Journal of Computer Vision*, 2002. [Online]. Available: http://citeseerx.ist.psu.edu/viewdoc/summary?doi=10.1.1.110.4868

[296] P. Viola, M. J. Jones, and D. Snow, "Detecting pedestrians using patterns of motion and appearance," *in: ICCV*, vol. 2, pp. 734–741, 2003.

[297] N. Dalal and B. Triggs, "Histograms of oriented gradients for human detection," in *Proceedings of International Conference on Computer Vision and Pattern Recognition*, C. Schmid, S. Soatto, and C. Tomasi, Eds., vol. 2, 2005, pp. 886–893.

[298] N. Dalal, B. Triggs, and C. Schmid, "Human detection using oriented histograms of flow and appearance," *in: European Conference on Computer Vision*, 2006.

[299] K. Mikolajczyk, C. Schmid, and A. Zisserman, "Human detection based on a probabilistic assembly of robust part detectors," *in: ECCV*, vol. 1, pp. 69–81, 2004.

[300] G. Mori, X. Ren, A. Efros, and J. Malik, "Recovering human body con gurations: combining segmentation and recognition," *in: CVPR 2004: Proceedings of the 2004 IEEE Computer Society Conference on Computer Vision and Pattern Recognition (CVPR 2004)*, vol. 2, pp. 326–333, 2004.

[301] D. Ramanan, D. A. Forsyth, and A. Zisserman, "Tracking people by learning their appearance," *IEEE Trans. on Pattern Analysis and Machine Intelligence*, vol. 29, pp. 65–81, 2007.

[302] X. Ren, A. C. Berg, and J. Malik, "Recovering human body configurations using pairwise constraints between parts," in *ICCV '05: Proceedings of the Tenth IEEE International Conference on Computer Vision (ICCV'05) Volume 1*. Washington, DC, USA: IEEE Computer Society, 2005, pp. 824–831.

[303] C. J. Veenman, M. J. T. Reinders, and E. Backer, "Resolving motion correspondence for densely moving points," *IEEE Trans. on Pattern Analysis and Machine Intelligence*, vol. 23, no. 1, pp. 54–72, 2001.

[304] D. Serby, E. Koller-Meier, and L. V. Gool, "Probabilistic object tracking using multiple features," in *ICPR '04: Proceedings of the 17th International Conference on Pattern Recognition (ICPR'04)*, vol. 2. Washington, DC, USA: IEEE Computer Society, 2004, pp. 184–187.

[305] D. Comaniciu, V. Ramesh, and P. Meer, "Kernel-based object tracking," *IEEE Trans. Pattern Anal. Mach. Intell.*, vol. 25, no. 5, pp. 564–575, 2003.

[306] A. Yilmaz, "Target tracking in airborne forward looking infrared imagery," *Image and Vision Computing*, vol. 21, no. 7, pp. 623–635, July 2003. [Online]. Available: http://dx.doi.org/10.1016/S0262-8856(03)00059-3

[307] D. Ballard and C. Brown, *Computer Vision*. Prentice-Hall, 1982.

[308] A. Ali and J. K. Aggarwal, "Segmentation and recognition of continuous human activity," August 2002, pp. 28–35. [Online]. Available: http://dx.doi.org/10.1109/EVENT.2001.938863

[309] S. Ju, M. Black, and Y. Yaccob, "Cardboard people: a parameterized model of articulated image motion," *Proc. of IEEE Intl. Conf. on Automatic Face and gesture Recognition*, pp. 38–44, 1996.

[310] S. C. Zhu and A. Yuille, "Region competition: Unifying snakes, region growing, and bayes/MDL for multiband image segmentation," *IEEE Trans. on Pattern Analysis and Machine Intelligence*, vol. 18, no. 9, pp. 884–900, 1996.

[311] N. Paragios and R. Deriche, "Geodesic active regions and level set methods for supervised texture segmentation," *Int. Journal on Computer Vision*, vol. 46, no. 3, pp. 223–247, 2002.

[312] A. Elgammal, R. Duraiswami, D. Harwood, and L. S. Davis, "Background and foreground modeling using nonparametric kernel density estimation for visual surveillance," *Proceedings of the IEEE*, vol. 90, no. 7, pp. 1151–1163, 2002. [Online]. Available: http://dx.doi.org/10.1109/JPROC.2002.801448

[313] P. Fieguth and D. Terzopoulos, "Color-based tracking of heads and other mobile objects at video frame rates," in *CVPR '97: Proceedings of the 1997 IEEE Computer Society Conference on Computer Vision and Pattern Recognition (CVPR '97)*. Washington, DC, USA: IEEE Computer Society, 1997.

[314] G. J. Edwards, C. J. Taylor, and T. F. Cootes, "Interpreting face images using active appearance models," in *FG '98: Proceedings of the 3rd. International Conference on Face & Gesture Recognition*. Washington, DC, USA: IEEE Computer Society, 1998.

[315] B. Moghaddam and A. Pentland, "Probabilistic visual learning for object representation," *IEEE Trans. on Pattern Analysis and Machine Intelligence*, vol. 19, no. 7, pp. 696–710, 1997.

[316] M. J. Black and A. D. Jepson, "Eigentracking: Robust matching and tracking of articulated objects using a view-based representation," in *ECCV '96: Proceedings of the 4th European Conference on Computer Vision-Volume I*. London, UK: Springer-Verlag, 1996, pp. 329–342.

[317] V. Lepetit and P. Fua, "Monocular model-based 3d tracking of rigid objects: A survey," in *Foundations and Trends in Computer Graphics and Vision*, 2005, pp. 1–89.

[318] Y. Luo, F. J. Perales, and J. Villanueva, "An automatic rotoscopy system for human motion based on a biomechanic graphical model," *Computer Graphics*, vol. 16, pp. 355–362, 1992.

[319] Y. Guo, G. Xu, and S. Tsuji, "Tracking human body motion based on a stick figure model, visual communication and," *Image Representation*, vol. 5, pp. 1–9, 1994.

Ioanna-Ourania Stathopoulou and George A. Tsihrintzis

[320] A. Bharatkumar, K. Daigle, M. Pandy, and J. Aggarwal, "Lower limb kinematics of human walking with the medial axis tranfromation,," in *IEEE Workshop on Motion of Non-rigid and Articulated Objects*, 1994.

[321] D. Gavrila and L. Davis, "3-D model based tracking of humans in action: A multiview approach," *In: Proc. 1996 IEEE Computer Society Conference on Computer Vision and Pattern Recognition, San Francisco, CA, USA*, pp. 73–80, 1996.

[322] S. Iwasawa, K. Ebihara, J. Ohya, and S. Morishima, "Real-time estimation of human body posture from monocular thermal images," in *Proc. IEEE Computer Society Conference on Computer Vision and Pattern Recognition*, 1997, pp. 15–20.

[323] C. Yaniz, J. Rocha, and F. Perales, "3D region graph for reconstruction of human motion," in *Proc. of Workshop on Perception of Human Motion (ECCV)*, 1998.

[324] Y. Iwai, K. Ogaki, and M. Yachida, "Posture estimation using structure and motion models," *Proc. of International Conference on Computer Vision, Greece, September*, 1999.

[325] I. A. Karaulova, P. M. Hall, and A D. Marshall, "A hierarchical model of dynamics for tracking people with a single video camera," in *in: Proc. British Machine Vision Conference*, 2000, pp. 352–361.

[326] C. R. Wren, A. Azarbayejani, T. Darrell, and A. P. Pentland, "PFINDER: Real-time tracking of the human body," *IEEE Trans. on Pattern Analysis and Machine Intelligence*, vol. 19, pp. 780–785, 1997.

[327] C. R. Wren and A. P. Pentland, "Understanding purposeful human motion," in *MPEOPLE '99: Proceedings of the IEEE International Workshop on Modelling People*. Washington, DC, USA: IEEE Computer Society, 1999.

[328] Y. Kameda and M. Minoh, "A human motion estimation method using 3-successive video frames," in *Proceedings of International Conference on Virtual Systems and Multimedia*, September 1996, pp. 135–140.

[329] D. Morris and J. Rehg, "Singularity analysis for articulated object tracking," *Computer Vision and Pattern Recognition, IEEE Computer Society Conference on*, vol. 0, p. 289, 1998.

[330] G. Rogez, C. Orrite-Ururuela, and J. M. del Rincon, "A spatio-temporal 2d-models framework for human pose recovery in monocular sequences," *Pattern Recognition*, vol. 41, no. 9, pp. 2926 – 2944, 2008. [Online]. Available: http://www.sciencedirect.com/science/article/B6V14-4S0JMWY-2/2/0eca113ba69026b5d824587d91bb4af6

[331] H. Sidenbladh, M. J. Black, and L. Sigal, "Implicit probabilistic models of human motion for synthesis and tracking," in *In European Conference on Computer Vision*, 2002, pp. 784–800.

[332] S. A. Niyogi and E. H. Adelson, "Analyzing and recognizing walking figures in XYT," *in Proc. of IEEE Conf. on Computer Vision and Pattern Recognition*, pp. 469–474, 1994.

[333] M. K. Leung and Y. H. Yang, "First sight: a human-body outline labeling system," *IEEE Trans. on Pattern Analysis and Machine Intelligence*, vol. 17, pp. 359–377, 1995.

[334] I.-C. Chang and C.-L. Huang, "Ribbon-based motion analysis of human body movements," *in Proc. of International Conference on Pattern Recognition*, pp. 436–440, 1996.

[335] C. Hu, "Extraction of parametric human model for posture recognition using generic algorithm," *Proc. of the Fourth Intl. Conf. on Automatic Face and Gesture Recognition*, 2000.

[336] J. Pantrigo, A. Sanchez, K. Gianikellis, and A. Montemayor, "2d human tracking by efficient model fitting using a path relinking particle filter," 2004, pp. 202–213.

[337] J. Pantrigo, A. Sanchez, K. Gianikellis, and A. Montemayor, *Structural, Syntactic, and Statistical Pattern Recognition*, ser. LNCS: Lecture Notes in Computer Science. Springer Berlin / Heidelberg, October 2004, vol. 3138, ch. Path Relinking Particle Filter for Human Body Pose Estimation, pp. 653–661.

[338] K. Rohr, "Towards model-based recognition of human movements in image sequences," *CVGIP: Image Understanding (Computer Vision, Graphics and Image Process)*, vol. 59, no. 1, pp. 94–115, 1994.

[339] F. Perales and J. Torres, "A system for human motion matching between synthetic and real images based on a biomechanic graphical model," *in: Proc. IEEE Workshop on Motion of Non-Rigid and Articulated Objects*, pp. 83–88, 1994.

[340] N. Goddard, "Incremental model-based discrimination of articulated movement from motion features," *In: Proc. of IEEE Workshop on Motion of Non-Rigid and Articulated Objects*, pp. 89–94, 1994.

[341] L. Goncalves, E. D. Bernardo, E. Ursella, and P. Perona, "Monocular tracking of the human arm in 3d," *in IEEE International Conference on Computer Vision*, 1995.

[342] J. Rehg and T. Kanade, "Model-based tracking of self-occluding articulated objects," in *Proc. of ICCV: IEEE Int. Conf. on Computer Vision*, 1995, pp. 612–617.

[343] I. A. Kakadiaris and D. Metaxas, "Model-based estimation of 3D human motion with occlusion based on active multi-viewpoint selection," in *CVPR '96: Proceedings of the 1996 Conference on Computer Vision and Pattern Recognition (CVPR '96)*. Washington, DC, USA: IEEE Computer Society, 1996.

[344] C. Bregler, "Learning and recognizing human dynamics in video sequences," *In: Proc. of IEEE CS Conf. on Computer Vision and Pattern Recognition*, pp. 568–574, 1997.

[345] E. A. Hunter, P. H. Kelly, and R. C. Jain, "Estimation of articulated motion using kinematically constrained mixture densities," *in: Proc. IEEE Workshop on Motion of Non-Rigid and Articulated Objects*, pp. 10–17, 1997.

[346] O. Munkelt, "A model driven 3D image interpretation system applied to person detection in video images," *In: Proc. of International Conference on Pattern Recognition*, 1998.

[347] S. Wachter and H.-H. Nagel, "Tracking persons in monocular image sequences," *Computer Vision and Image Understanding*, vol. 74, pp. 174–192, 1999.

[348] Q. Delamarre and O. Faugeras, "3d articulated models and multi-view tracking with silhouettes," *In: Proc. of International Conference on Computer Vision*, 1999.

[349] J. Luck, D. Small, and C. Q. Little, "Real-time tracking of articulated human models using a 3d shape-from-silhouette method," in *RobVis '01: Proceedings of the International Workshop on Robot Vision*. London, UK: Springer-Verlag, 2001, pp. 19–26.

[350] T. Zhao and R. Nevatia, "Bayesian human segmentation in crowdedsituations," in *Proc. of 2003 IEEE Computer Society Conf. on Computer Vision and Pattern Recognition*, vol. 2, 2003, pp. 459–466.

[351] A. O. Balan, L. Sigal, and M. J. Black, "A quantitative evaluation of video-based 3D person tracking," in *ICCCN '05: Proceedings of the 14th International Conference on Computer Communications and Networks.* Washington, DC, USA: IEEE Computer Society, 2005, pp. 349–356.

[352] I. Haritaoglu, D. Harwood, and L. S. David, "W4: Real-time surveillance of people and their activities," *IEEE Trans. Pattern Analysis and Machine Intelligence*, vol. 22, pp. 809–830, 2000.

[353] R. Collins, A. Lipton, T. Kanade, H. Fujiyoshi, D. Duggins, Y. Tsin, D. Tolliver, N. Enomoto, and O. Hasegawa, "A system for video surveillance and monitoring," Robotics Institute, Carnegie Mellon University, Pittsburgh, PA, USA, Tech. Rep. CMU-RI-TR-00-12, May 2000.

[354] S. J. McKenna, S. Jabri, Z. Duric, A. Rosenfeld, and H. Wechsler, "Tracking groups of people," *Computer Vision and Image Understanding*, vol. 80, no. 1, pp. 42 – 56, 2000. [Online]. Available: http://www.sciencedirect.com/science/article/B6WCX-45FBSGJ-J/2/c250805dc8a42d25e4465bdc99d22bb5

[355] J. Martinez del Rincon, "Feature-based human tracking: from coarse to fine," Ph.D. dissertation, University of Zaragosa, 2008.

[356] J. E. Herrero-Jaraba, "Analisis visual del movimiento humano," Ph.D. dissertation, University of Zaragosa, 2005.

[357] P. L. Rosin and T. Ellis, "Image difference threshold strategies and shadow detection," in *BMVC '95: Proceedings of the 1995 British conference on Machine vision (Vol. 1).* Surrey, UK, UK: BMVA Press, 1995, pp. 347–356.

[358] A. Baumberg and D. Hogg, "Generating spatiotemporal models from examples," in *BMVC '95: Proceedings of the 6th British conference on Machine vision (Vol. 2).* Surrey, UK, UK: BMVA Press, 1995, pp. 413–422.

[359] A. M. Baumberg and D. C. Hogg, "An efficient method for contour tracking using active shape models," in *In Proceeding of the Workshop on Motion of Nonrigid and Articulated Objects. IEEE Computer Society*, 1994, pp. 194–199. [Online]. Available: http://citeseerx.ist.psu.edu/viewdoc/summary?doi=10.1.1.16.1396

[360] M. Isard and A. Blake, "Contour tracking by stochastic propagation of conditional density," in *ECCV '96: Proceedings of the 4th European Conference on Computer Vision-Volume I.* London, UK: Springer-Verlag, 1996, pp. 343–356.

[361] D. Meyer, J. Denzler, and H. Niemann, "Model based extraction of articulated objects in image sequences for gait analysis," *In: Proc. of IEEE Intl. Conference on Image Processing*, pp. 78–81, 1997.

[362] N. Peterfreund, "Robust tracking of position and velocity with kalman snakes," *IEEE Trans. on Pattern Analysis and Machine Intelligence*, vol. 21, no. 6, pp. 564–569, 1999.

[363] N. Paragios and R. Deriche, "Geodesic active contours and level sets for the detection and tracking of moving objects," *IEEE Trans. on Pattern Analysis and Machine Intelligence*, vol. 22, pp. 266–280, 2000.

[364] M. Bertalmío, G. Sapiro, and G. Randall, "Morphing active contours," *IEEE Trans. on Pattern Analysis and Machine Intelligence*, vol. 22, no. 7, pp. 733–737, 2000.

[365] Y. Zhong, A. K. Jain, and M.-P. Dubuisson-Jolly, "Object tracking using deformable templates," *IEEE Trans. on Pattern Analysis and Machine Intelligence*, vol. 22, no. 5, pp. 544–549, 2000.

[366] F. Buccolieri, C. Distante, and A. Leone, "Human posture recognition using active contours and radial basis function neural network," in *Advanced Video and Signal Based Surveillance, 2005. AVSS 2005. IEEE Conference on*, 15-16 2005, pp. 213 – 218.

[367] J. Segen and S. G. Pingali, "A camera-based system for tracking people in real time," in *ICPR '96: Proceedings of the International Conference on Pattern Recognition (ICPR '96) Volume III-Volume 7276*. Washington, DC, USA: IEEE Computer Society, 1996.

[368] D. Jang and H.-I. Choi, "Moving object tracking by optimizing active models," in *ICPR '98: Proceedings of the 14th International Conference on Pattern Recognition-Volume 1*. Washington, DC, USA: IEEE Computer Society, 1998.

[369] Q. Cai and J. K. Aggarwal, "Tracking human motion using multiple cameras," in *ICPR '96: Proceedings of the International Conference on Pattern Recognition (ICPR '96) Volume III-Volume 7276*. Washington, DC, USA: IEEE Computer Society, 1996.

[370] A. Utsumi, H. Mori, J. Ohya, and M. Yachida, "Multiple-view-based tracking of multiple humans," in *ICPR '98: Proceedings of the 14th International Conference on Pattern Recognition-Volume 1*. Washington, DC, USA: IEEE Computer Society, 1998.

[371] R. Rosales and S. Sclaroff, "3D trajectory recovery for tracking multiple objects and trajectory guided recognition of actions," Boston, MA, USA, Tech. Rep., 1998.

[372] L.-Q. Xu and D. C. Hogg, "Neural networks in human motion tracking – an experimental study," *Image and Vision Computing*, vol. 15, no. 8, pp. 607 – 615, 1997, british Machine Vision Conference. [Online]. Available: http://www.sciencedirect.com/science/article/B6V09-3SNVMWX-K/2/7ca504f2cd70d533cdf4702f38a012be

[373] R. Polana, R. Nelson, and A. Nelson, "Low level recognition of human motion (or how to get your man without finding his body parts)," in *In Proc. of IEEE Computer Society Workshop on Motion of Non-Rigid and Articulated Objects.* Press, 1994, pp. 77–82.

[374] D.-S. Jang and H.-I. Choi, "Active models for tracking moving objects," *Pattern Recognition*, vol. 33, pp. 1135–1146, 2000.

[375] H. Breit and G. Rigoll, "A flexible multimodal object tracking system," *In: Proc. of 2003 IEEE Internat. Conf. Image Process.*, vol. 133-136, pp. 133–136, 2003.

[376] J. K. Aggarwal and S. Park, "Human motion: modeling and recognition of actions and interactions," 2004, pp. 640–647. [Online]. Available: http://dx.doi.org/10.1109/TDPVT.2004.1335299

[377] B. Schiele, "Model-free tracking of cars and people based on color regions," *Image Vision Computing*, vol. 24, pp. 1172–1178, 2005.

[378] P. D. Varcheie and G.-A. Bilodeau, "Human tracking by ip ptz camera control in the context of video surveillance," in *ICIAR '09: Proceedings of the 6th International Conference on Image Analysis and Recognition.* Berlin, Heidelberg: Springer-Verlag, 2009, pp. 657–667.

[379] W. Stokoe, *Sign Language Structure: An outline of the visual communication systems of the American deaf.* University of Buffalo Press, 1960.

[380] A. Kendon, *Biological Foundations of Gesture Hillsdale.* New Jersey: Lawrence Erlbaum, Associates, 1986, ch. Current issues in the study of gesture, pp. 23–47.

[381] D. McNeill, *Hand and mind: what gestures reveal about thought.* Chicago, USA: University of chicago press, 1992.

[382] A. Kendon, *The relation of verbal and nonverbal communication.* The Hague, The Netherlands: Mouton, 1980, ch. Gesticulation and speech: two aspects of the process of utterance, pp. 207–228.

[383] J. Nespoulos and A. Roch Lecours, *The biological foundations of gestures: motor and semiotic aspects.* Hillsdale, New Jersey, USA: Lawrence Erlbaum Associates, 1986, ch. Gestures: nature and function, pp. 49–62.

[384] F. K. H. Quek, "Eyes in the interface," *Image and Vision Computing*, vol. 13, no. 6, pp. 511 – 525, 1995. [Online]. Available: http://www.sciencedirect.com/science/article/B6V09-3Y45100-V/2/c75e206210a2ecfb78b2e8736ddca2ab

[385] F. K. H. Quek, "Toward a vision-based hand gesture interface," in *VRST '94: Proceedings of the conference on Virtual reality software and technology.* River Edge, NJ, USA: World Scientific Publishing Co. Inc., 1994, pp. 17–31.

[386] R. Watson and T. College, "A survey of gesture recognition techniques," Department of Computer Science, Trinity College, Tech. Rep., 1993.

[387] Y. Cui, D. L. Swets, and J. J. Weng, "Learning-based hand sign recognition using SHOSLIF-M," in *Proc. of 5th Int Conf. on Computer Vision*, 1995, pp. 631–636.

[388] J. Triesch and C. von der Malsburg, "Robust classification of hand postures against complex backgrounds," in *FG '96: Proceedings of the 2nd International Conference on Automatic Face and Gesture Recognition (FG '96).* Washington, DC, USA: IEEE Computer Society, 1996, pp. 937–943.

[389] F. K. H. Quek and M. Zhao, "Inductive learning in hand pose recognition," in *FG '96: Proceedings of the 2nd International Conference on Automatic Face and Gesture Recognition (FG '96).* Washington, DC, USA: IEEE Computer Society, 1996.

[390] C. Nolker and H. Ritter, "Illumination independant recognition of deictic arm postures," in *Proc. 24th Annual Conference of the IEEE Industrial Electronic Society*, 1998, pp. 2006–2011.

[391] T. Starner and A. Pentland, "Visual recognition of american sign language using hidden markov models," in *Proc. of International Workshop on Automatic Face and Gesture Recognition*, 1995, pp. 189–194.

[392] V. Athitsos and S. Sclaroff, "Estimating 3d hand pose from a cluttered image," *Computer Vision and Pattern Recognition, IEEE Computer*

Society Conference on, vol. 2, pp. 432–439, 2003. [Online]. Available: http://dx.doi.org/10.1109/CVPR.2003.1211500

[393] J. J. Kuch and T. S. Huang, "Human computer interaction via the human hand: a hand model," in *Proc. of the Twenty-Eighth Asilomar Conference on Signals, Systems and Computers*, vol. 2, 1994, pp. 1252–1256. [Online]. Available: http://dx.doi.org/10.1109/ACSSC.1994.471659

[394] J. Lee and T. Kunii, "Constraint-based hand animation," *in: Models and Techniques in Computer Animation, Springer, Tokyo*, pp. 110–127, 1993.

[395] J. Lin, Y. Wu, and T. S. Huang, "Modeling the constraints of human hand motion," in *HUMO '00: Proceedings of the Workshop on Human Motion (HUMO'00)*. Washington, DC, USA: IEEE Computer Society, 2000.

[396] B. Stenger, A. Thayananthan, P. H. S. Torr, and R. Cipolla, "Filtering using a tree-based estimator," in *ICCV '03: Proceedings of the Ninth IEEE International Conference on Computer Vision*. Washington, DC, USA: IEEE Computer Society, 2003.

[397] H. Zhou and T. S. Huang, "Tracking articulated hand motion with eigen dynamics analysis," in *ICCV '03: Proceedings of the Ninth IEEE International Conference on Computer Vision*. Washington, DC, USA: IEEE Computer Society, 2003.

[398] A. Thayananthan, B. Stenger, P. Torr, and R. Cipolla, "Learning a kinematic prior for tree-based filtering," in *British Machine Vision Conference, BMVC 2003 Proceedings, Norwich, UK, 9-11 September 2003*, R. Harvey and A. Bangham, Eds. BMVA: British Machine Vision Association, September 2003, online (at 2.11.2007) at: http://www.bmva.ac.uk/bmvc/2003/index.html. [Online]. Available: http://publications.eng.cam.ac.uk/13302/

[399] B. Stenger, P. R. S. Mendonca, and R. Cipolla, "Model-based 3d tracking of an articulated hand," in *CVPR 2001: Proceedings of the 2001 IEEE Computer Society Conference on Computer Vision and Pattern Recognition (CVPR 2001)*, vol. 2, 2001, pp. 310–315. [Online]. Available: http://dx.doi.org/10.1109/CVPR.2001.990976

[400] Y. Wu, J. Y. Lin, and T. S. Huang, "Capturing natural hand articulation," in *In ICCV: Proceedings of the Eighth IEEE International Conference on Computer Vision*, 2001, pp. 426–432.

[401] S. Ahmad, "A usable real-time 3d hand tracker," in *In Proceedings 28th Asilomar Conference on Signals, Systems and Computers*. IEEE Computer Society Press, 1995, pp. 1257–1261.

[402] R. Kjeldsen, J. Kender, and "Visual hand gesture recognition for window system control," in *in Proc. of IWAFGR'95*, 1995.

[403] S. Malik and J. Laszlo, "Visual touchpad: a two-handed gestural input device," in *ICMI '04: Proceedings of the 6th international conference on Multimodal interfaces*. New York, NY, USA: ACM, 2004, pp. 289–296.

[404] Y. Kuno, M. Sakamoto, K. Sakata, and Y. Shirai, "Vision-based human interface with user-centered frame," in *Proceedings of the IEEE/RSJ/GI International Conference on Intelligent Robots and Systems '94,'Advanced Robotic Systems and the Real World' (IROS '94)*, vol. 3, sep 1994, pp. 2023–2029.

[405] J. Lee and T. L. Kunii, "Model-based analysis of hand posture," *IEEE Comput. Graph. Appl.*, vol. 15, no. 5, pp. 77–86, 1995.

[406] H. Koike, Y. Sato, and Y. Kobayashi, "Integrating paper and digital information on enhanceddesk: a method for realtime finger tracking on an augmented desk system," *ACM Trans. on Computer-Human Interactio*, vol. 8, no. 4, pp. 307–322, 2001.

[407] K. Oka, Y. Sato, and H. Koike, "Real-time tracking of multiple fingertips and gesture recognition for augmented desk interface systems," in *FGR '02: Proceedings of the Fifth IEEE International Conference on Automatic Face and Gesture Recognition*. Washington, DC, USA: IEEE Computer Society, 2002, pp. 429–434.

[408] J. MacCormick and M. Isard, "Partitioned sampling, articulated objects, and interface-quality hand tracking," in *ECCV '00: Proceedings of the 6th European Conference on Computer Vision-Part II*. London, UK: Springer-Verlag, 2000, pp. 3–19.

[409] Y. Kuno, K. Hayashi, K. Jo, and Y. Shirai, "Human-robot interface using uncalibrated stereo vision," *in Proc. of IEEE/RSJ: International Conference on Intelligent Robots and Systems*, vol. 1, 1995.

[410] M. Kolsch and M. Turk, "Robust hand detection," in *Proc. of International Conference on Automatic Face and Gesture Recognition, Seoul, Korea*, 2004, pp. 614–619.

Ioanna-Ourania Stathopoulou and George A. Tsihrintzis

[411] E.-J. Ong and R. Bowden, "A boosted classifier tree for hand shape detection," *in Proc of IEEE International Conference on Automatic Face and Gesture Recognition*, 2004.

[412] N. Shimada, Y. Shirai, Y. Kuno, and J. Miura, "Hand gesture estimation and model refinement using monocular camera - ambiguity limitation by inequality constraints," in *FG '98: Proceedings of the 3rd. International Conference on Face & Gesture Recognition*. Washington, DC, USA: IEEE Computer Society, 1998.

[413] Y. Wu and T. S. Huang, "Capturing articulated human hand motion: A divide-and-conquer approach," in *Proc. of 7th Int. Conf. on Computer Vision*, vol. 1, 1999, pp. 606–611.

[414] J. L. Crowley, F. Berard, and J. Coutaz, "Finger tracking as an input device for augmented reality," 1995, pp. 195–200.

[415] R. O'Hagan and A. Zelinsky, "Finger track - a robust and real-time gesture interface," in *Proc. of Australian Joint Conference on Artificial Intelligence*, 1997, pp. 475–484.

[416] J. Rehg and T. Kanade, "Visual tracking of self-occluding articulated objects," Computer Science Department, Pittsburgh, PA, Tech. Rep. CMU-CS-94-224, 1994.

[417] J. Segen and S. Kumar, "Gesture VR: vision-based 3D hand interace for spatial interaction," in *MULTIMEDIA '98: Proceedings of the sixth ACM international conference on Multimedia*. New York, NY, USA: ACM, 1998, pp. 455–464.

[418] R. O'Hagan and A. Zelinsky, "Visual gesture interfaces for virtual environments," in *AUIC '00: Proceedings of the First Australasian User Interface Conference*. Washington, DC, USA: IEEE Computer Society, 2000.

[419] J. Segen and S. Kumar, "Shadow gestures: 3D hand pose estimation using a single camera," in *Proc. of IEEE Conf. on Computer Vision and Pattern Recognition*, 1999, pp. 479–485.

[420] A. Thayananthan, B. Stenger, P. Torr, and R. Cipolla, "Shape context and chamfer matching in cluttered scenes," in *Proc of 2003 IEEE Computer Society Conference on Computer Vision and Pattern Recognition (CVPR '03)*, vol. 1, 2003, pp. 127–133.

[421] B. Stenger, A. Thayananthan, P. Torr, and R. Cipolla, "Hand pose estimation using hierarchical detection," in *Proc. of Intl. Workshop on Human-Computer Interaction*. Springer, 2004, pp. 102–112.

[422] J. J. Kuch and T. S. Huang, "Vision based hand modeling and tracking for virtual teleconferencing and telecollaboration," in *ICCV '95: Proceedings of the Fifth International Conference on Computer Vision*. Washington, DC, USA: IEEE Computer Society, 1995.

[423] J. Y. Lin and T. S. Huang, "3D model-based hand tracking using stochastic direct search method," in *Proc. of Sixth IEEE International Conference on Automatic Face and Gesture Recognition*, 2004.

[424] D. G. Lowe, "Fitting parameterized three-dimensional models to images," *IEEE Trans. on Pattern Analysis and Machine Intelligence*, vol. 13, no. 5, pp. 441–450, 1991.

[425] M. Bray, E. Koller-Meier, P. Muller, L. V. Gool, and N. N. Schraudolph, "3D hand tracking by rapid stochastic gradient descent using a skinning model," in *Proc. of 1st European Conference on Visual Media Production (CVMP*, 2004, pp. 59–68.

[426] H. Ouhaddi and P. Horain, "3D hand gesture tracking by model registration," in *Proceedings of International Workshop on Synthetic - Natural Hybrid Coding and Three Dimensional Imaging (IWSNHC3DI'99)*, 1999, pp. 70–73.

[427] K. Nirei, H. Saito, M. Mochimaru, and S. Ozawa, "Human hand tracking from binocular image sequences," *Proc. of 22th International Conference on Industrial Electronics, Control, and In*, pp. 297–302, 1996.

[428] Q. Delamarre and O. Faugeras, "3D articulated models and multiview tracking with physical forces," *Computer Vision Image Understanding*, vol. 81, no. 3, pp. 328–357, 2001.

[429] E. Ueda, Y. Matsumoto, M. Imai, and T. Ogasawara, "A hand-pose estimation for vision-based human interfaces," *IEEE Transactions on Industrial Electronics*, vol. 50, pp. 676–684.

[430] T. Heap and D. Hogg, "Towards 3d hand tracking using a deformable model," in *FG '96: Proceedings of the 2nd International Conference on Automatic Face and Gesture Recognition (FG '96)*. Washington, DC, USA: IEEE Computer Society, 1996.

[431] R. Rosales, V. Athitsos, L. Sigal, and S. Sclaroff, "3D hand pose reconstruction using specialized mappings," in *Proc. of ICCV'2001*, 2001, pp. 378–385.

[432] Y. Wu, T. S. Huang, and T. S. Huang, "View-independent recognition of hand postures," in *CVPR 2000: Proceedings of the 2000 IEEE Computer Society Conference on Computer Vision and Pattern Recognition (CVPR 2000)*, 2000, pp. 88–94.

[433] N. Bianchi-Berthouze and A. Kleinsmith, "A categorical approach to affective gesture recognition," *Connection Science*, vol. 15, no. 4, pp. 259–269, December 2003. [Online]. Available: http://eprints.ucl.ac.uk/3368/

[434] D. Bernhardt and P. Robinson, "Detecting emotions from everyday body movements," in *Presenccia PhD Symposium*, Barcelona, Spain, May 2007.

[435] A. Camurri and Lagerl "Recognizing emotion from dance movement: comparison of spectator recognition and automated techniques," *International Journal of Human-Computer Studies*, vol. 59, no. 1-2, pp. 213 – 225, 2003, applications of Affective Computing in Human-Computer Interaction. [Online]. Available: http://www.sciencedirect.com/science/article/B6WGR-48JCBRX-1/2/1b943bf020c4742bcfe85f83836992af

[436] A. Camurri, B. Mazzarino, M. Ricchetti, R. Timmers, and V. G., *LNAI 2915: Gesture-based Communication in Human-Computer Interaction*. Springer Verlag, 2004, ch. Multimodal analysis of expressive gesture in music and dance performances.

[437] G. Castellano, S. D. Villalba, and A. Camurri, "Recognising human emotions from body movement and gesture dynamics," in *ACII '07: Proceedings of the 2nd international conference on Affective Computing and Intelligent Interaction*. Berlin, Heidelberg: Springer-Verlag, 2007, pp. 71–82.

[438] J. K. Burgoon, J. M. L., T. O. Meservy, J. Kruse, and J. F. Nunamaker, "Augmenting human identification of emotional states in video," in *In: Proceedings of the International Conference on Intelligent Data Analysis*, 2005.

[439] A. Kapur, A. Kapur, N. Virji-Babul, G. Tzanetakis, and P. F. Driessen, "Gesture-based affective computing on motion capture data. in: Affective computing and intelligent interaction," in *in 1st Int. Conf. Affective Computing and Intelligent Interaction (ACII'2005)*, 2005, pp. 1–7.

[440] J. M. J. Murre, R. H. Phaf, and G. Wolters, "Original contribution: Calm: Categorizing and learning module," *Neural Netw.*, vol. 5, no. 1, pp. 55–82, 1992.

[441] F. E. Pollick, H. M. Paterson, A. Bruderlin, and A. J. Sanford, "Perceiving affect from arm movement," *Cognition*, vol. 82, no. 2, pp. 51–61, December 2001. [Online]. Available: http://eprints.gla.ac.uk/25001/

[442] A. Camurri, P. Coletta, A. Massari, B. Mazzarino, M. Peri, M. Ricchetti, A. Ricci, and V. G., "Toward real-time multimodal processing: Eyesweb 4.0," in *In: AISB 2004 Convention: Motion, Emotion and Cognition*, 2004.

[443] S. Lu, G. Tsechpenakis, and D. N. Metaxas, "Blob analysis of the head and hands: A method for deception detection," in *and Emotional State Identification," Hawaii International Conference on System Sciences, Big Island*, 2005.

[444] T. Balomenos, A. Raouzaiou, S. Ioannou, A. Drosopoulos, K. Karpouzis, and S. Kollias, *Emotion Analysis in Man-Machine Interaction Systems*, ser. Lecture Notes in Computer Science. Springer, 2005, vol. 3361.

[445] H. Gunes and M. Piccardi, "Bi-modal emotion recognition from expressive face and body gestures," *J. Netw. Comput. Appl.*, vol. 30, no. 4, pp. 1334–1345, 2007.

[446] H. Gunes and M. Piccardi, "A bimodal face and body gesture database for automatic analysis of human nonverbal affective behavior," in *ICPR '06: Proceedings of the 18th International Conference on Pattern Recognition*. Washington, DC, USA: IEEE Computer Society, 2006, pp. 1148–1153.

[447] R. E. Kaliouby and P. Robinson, "Generalization of a vision-based computational model of mind-reading," in *1 st Intl. Conf. on Affective Computing and Intelligent Interaction, LNCS 3784*. Springer, 2005, pp. 582–589.

[448] S. Baron-Cohen, O. Golan, S. Wheelwright, and J. J. Hill, *Mind Reading: The Interactive Guide to Emotions*. London: Jessica Kingsley Publishers, 2004.

[449] P. Ekman and W. Friesen, *Facial Action Coding System: A Technique for the Measurement of Facial Movement*. Consulting Psychologists Press, Palo Alto, 1978.

[450] I. Russel, "Emotion and Memory," *Behavioural Brain Research*, vol. 58, no. 1-2, p. R9, December 1993.

[451] H. Graf, E. Cosatto, V. Strom, and F. Huang, "Visual prosody: Facial movements accompanying speech," in *5th IEEE International Conference on Automatic Face and Gesture Recognition*, 2002, pp. 381–386.

Ioanna-Ourania Stathopoulou and George A. Tsihrintzis

[452] L. S. Chen, T. S. Huang, T. Miyasato, and R. Nakatsu, "Multimodal human emotion/expression recognition," in *Proc. Int'l Conf. Automatic Face and Gesture Recognition*, vol. pp, 1998, pp. 366–371.

[453] C. Busso, Z. Deng, S. Yildirim, M. Bulut, C. M. Lee, A. Kazemzadeh, S. Lee, U. Neumann, and S. Narayanan, "Analysis of emotion recognition using facial expressions, speech and multimodal information," in *ICMI '04: Proceedings of the 6th international conference on Multimodal interfaces*. New York, NY, USA: ACM, 2004, pp. 205–211.

[454] E. Alepis, M. Virvou, and K. Kabassi, "Affective student modeling based on microphone and keyboard user actions," in *ICALT '06: Proceedings of the Sixth IEEE International Conference on Advanced Learning Technologies*. Washington, DC, USA: IEEE Computer Society, 2006, pp. 139–141.

[455] M. Virvou, G. A. Tsihrintzis, E. Alepis, I. O. Stathopoulou, and K. Kabassi, "Combining empirical studies of audio-lingual and visual-facial modalities for emotion recognition," in *KES '07: Knowledge-Based Intelligent Information and Engineering Systems and the XVII Italian Workshop on Neural Networks on Proceedings of the 11th International Conference, LNAI: Vol. 4693*. Berlin, Heidelberg: Springer-Verlag, 2007, pp. 1130–1137.

[456] M. Virvou, G. A. Tsihrintzis, E. Alepis, I.-O. Stathopoulou, and K. Kabassi, "On combining audio-lingual and visual-facial modalities for emotion recognition: Empirical studies," in preparation.

[457] G. A. Tsihrintzis, M. Virvou, E. Alepis, and I.-O. Stathopoulou, "Towards improving visual-facial emotion recognition through use of complementary keyboard-stroke pattern information," in *ITNG '08: Proceedings of the Fifth International Conference on Information Technology: New Generations*. Washington, DC, USA: IEEE Computer Society, 2008, pp. 32–37.

[458] I. O. Stathopoulou, E. Alepis, G. A. Tsihrintzis, and M. Virvou, "On assisting a visual-facial affect recognition system with keyboard-stroke pattern information," *Know.-Based Syst.*, vol. 23, no. 4, pp. 350–356, 2010.

[459] M. Virvou, G. A. Tsihrintzis, E. Alepis, and I.-O. Stathopoulou, "Designing a multi-modal affective knowledge-based user interface: combining empirical studies," in *JCKBSE: 8th Joint Conference on Knowledge-Based Software Engineering*, 2008, pp. 250–259.

[460] G. A. Tsihrintzis, M. Virvou, I.-O. Stathopoulou, and E. Alepis, "On improving visual-facial emotion recognition with audio-lingual and keyboard stroke pattern information," in *WI-IAT '08: Proceedings of the 2008 IEEE/WIC/ACM International Conference on Web Intelligence and Intelligent Agent Technology.* Washington, DC, USA: IEEE Computer Society, 2008, pp. 810–816.